HOGARTH TO CRUIKSHANK: SOCIAL CHANGE IN GRAPHIC SATIRE

W. Hogarth invt et del.

A REAL SCENE in S.ᵗ PAULS CHURCH YARD, on a WINDY DAY.

Frontispiece A Real Scene in St Paul's Church Yard on a Windy Day, after Dighton

M. Dorothy George

HOGARTH TO CRUIKSHANK: SOCIAL CHANGE IN GRAPHIC SATIRE

Viking

VIKING

Penguin Books Ltd, 27 Wrights Lane, London w8 5tz (Publishing and Editorial)
and Harmondsworth, Middlesex, England (Distribution and Warehouse)
Viking Penguin Inc., 40 West 23rd Street, New York, New York 10010, USA
Penguin Books Australia Ltd, Ringwood, Victoria, Australia
Penguin Books Canada Ltd, 2801 John Street, Markham, Ontario, Canada l3r 1b4
Penguin Books (NZ) Ltd, 182–190 Wairau Road, Auckland 10, New Zealand

First published 1967
Reprinted 1968, 1987

Copyright © M. Dorothy George, 1967

Designed by Germano Facetti

Printed in Great Britain by Butler & Tanner Ltd, Frome and London

ISBN 0-670-821160-0

Library of Congress Catalog Card No.: 87-51090

Contents

List of Colour Plates

Acknowledgements

The author and publisher wish to acknowledge permission to print extracts from the following: *The Journals of Mrs Arbuthnot, 1820–1832*, edited by Francis Bamford and the Duke of Wellington, and *Wellington and his Friends, Letters of the First Duke Selected and Edited by the Second Duke of Wellington*, both published by Macmillan; *Dr Campbell's Diary of a Visit to England*, edited by J. L. Clifford, published by the Cambridge University Press; *Call the Doctor*, by E. S. Turner, published by Michael Joseph; *The Diary of Benjamin Robert Haydon*, edited by W. B. Pope, published by the Harvard University Press; *Thraliana*, edited by K. C. Balderston, *Hogarth: The Analysis of Beauty*, edited by J. Burke, and *Lichtenberg's Visits to England*, edited by W. M. Mare and W. H. Quarrell, all published by the Clarendon Press; *Life and Letters of Lady Sarah Lennox*, edited by Lady Ilchester and *Journals of a Somerset Rector*, by John Skinner, edited by H. Coombe and A. N. Bax, both published by John Murray; *Impressions of England*, by E. G. Geijer, published by Jonathan Cape; *A Regency Visitor, The English Tour of Prince Pückler-Muskau*, edited by E. M. Butler, published by Collins; *Taine's Notes on England*, translated by E. Hyams, published by Thames & Hudson; *Glenbervie Journals*, edited by W. Sichel, published by Constable; *Hogarth and His Place in European Art*, by F. Antal, published by Routledge & Kegan Paul; *Journeys to England and Ireland*, by A. de Tocqueville, edited by J. P. Mayer, published by Faber & Faber; *The Correspondence of George, Prince of Wales*, edited by A. Aspinall, published by Cassells; *Correspondence of Horace Walpole*, edited by W. S. Lewis, published by the Yale University Press; and James Laver's introduction to *The Regency Road*, by N. C. Selway, published by Faber & Faber.

Reference to prints sold to George IV is made by gracious permission of H.M. the Queen and thanks are due to the Librarian of the Royal Collection at Windsor.

List of Black and White Illustrations

Acknowledgements are made to the Metropolitan Museum, New York for no. 40; to the London Museum for nos. 48, 53, 57, 59, 156; to the Parker Gallery for nos. 51, 61, 63, 76; to Mrs Minto Wilson for no. 134; to the Mansell Collection for nos. 161, 167; to the Victoria and Albert Museum for no. 164. All other illustrations are by courtesy of the Trustees of the British Museum. Acknowledgement is made also to Mr and Mrs Paul Mellon, see p. 52.

Boswell: I mentioned that I was afraid I put into my journal too many little incidents.

Johnson: There is nothing sir too little for so little a creature as man.

14 July 1763

How Times and Fashions change! *Mrs Thrale, 1778*

Great changes have occurred in this country while deep below the surface the continuity has been maintained as a living thing. *H. Butterfield, 1944*

Introduction

The subject of this book is graphic social satire before the days of *Punch* and illustrated journalism, when prints were engraved and sold separately. In the eighteenth century there was a great vogue for satirical prints – political and social. This was the golden age of the English engraver. Despite the many 'straight' prints – topographical, naval, military, sporting – and the more important engravings after paintings, the caricature shops had a popularity of their own. Their prints were virtually the only pictorial rendering of the flow of events, moods and fashions. Especially, they reflect the social attitudes of the day. When in the 1750s the word 'caricatura' or 'caricature' came into use, the print shops applied it indiscriminately to any print with a comic or satirical intention. Very many of the illustrations in this book are caricatures, but some, and notably most of Hogarth's, are not. Pure comic art without an element of satire is outside its scope. Some prints that today seem charming period pieces were in fact satirical, for instance those castigating vulgarity of dress or gesture, now scarcely recognizable. Conversely, the grosser and harsher aspects of life, heavy eating and drinking, extreme poverty, sometimes make realism seem caricature. It is difficult now to realize the eighteenth-century coexistence of stylized formality and elegance with (tolerated) grossness and eccentricity.

'Satire', like 'caricature', is used loosely;* it covers Hogarth's moralizing, Gillray's irony, Rowlandson's comedy, Newton's burlesque. To find that the word derives from *satura*, 'a medley', gives it appropriateness. This book is a medley – an olio. Political satires preceded and usually outnumbered social ones. No clear line divides them; a classic example of this is Hogarth's *Election* series. In 1720–21 the South Sea Bubble evoked an unprecedented crop of satirical prints. Most were reissues or adaptations of Dutch ones, but some were English, including two by Hogarth while he was still a bookseller's hack. For our purpose social satire begins with Hogarth, though for a century there had been a sporadic output of political or 'emblematical' prints. The more genial social satire hardly begins before the 1720s, apart from prints of common life, London 'cries', tattling women, headings to broadside ballads. Very many of these, especially woodcuts, must have disappeared.

Satire was the language of the age – the age of Pope, Swift, Gay, Prior, Fielding, Churchill, leading on to Canning, Byron, Moore, not to speak of a mass of forgotten verse and prose. 'Squibs were on every table . . . satire was in the air.'[1] The Grub Street author, like the hack engraver, found his readiest market in satire. It was a malicious world. Wit and ridicule were admired and feared to a degree that now seems strange. Violent personal vendettas found expression both in print and in prints and counter-prints. And though satire reflected the (diminishing) scurrility of the day, it could be enjoyed because basically society was assured, stable and content. Uninhibited ridicule and/or castigation was tolerated – more or less – in the theatre. This was Foote's speciality, as playwright and actor, and he defended it as 'the correction of individuals and an example . . . to the whole community'.

The world was small. Notabilities were well known by sight, partly owing to the print shops, and they were of all classes. Another favourable condition for the satirical print as a picture of manners was intense interest in the visual aspect of daily life. The popularity of Gay's *Trivia; or, the Art of walking the Streets of London* and its many imitations speaks for itself. Hogarth's paintings and prints convey his fascinated interest in the contrasts of his world. The splendour and glitter of high life, the sordid squalor of low life, are the outstanding contrasts of the century. The large tract between these extremes was filled with the rising middle ranks, and in graphic satire these are represented by the professions and by 'cits' – City merchants and tradesmen. John Bull appeared after the mid-century.*

The rich variety of graphic satire resists classification. Subjects and periods overlap. There are the stereotypes that persist – illustrations of fixed ideas and prejudices, coloured by the conventions of caricature. There is the social scene from St James's to St Giles's, the coffee-houses, the taverns, the streets, the shops, the clubs (from White's to the ale-house meeting), sport (where high life and low life met). From first to last the theatre was a major preoccupation. Travel: the Frenchman in England, the Englishman in France, were perennial topics. The prints

---

*Since the nineteenth century the British Museum has used the term for its large collection of hieroglyphical and allegorical prints, caricatures, and comic art generally, calling them 'Political and Personal Satires'.

*The time-lag from the John Bull of John Arbuthnot's *Law is a Bottomless Pit* to his appearance in caricature is from 1712 to *c.* 1756, and John Bull depicted as a typical Englishman appears first in 1779.

reflect tradition and continuity in conflict with changes that were becoming revolutionary. The middle ranks were progressively gaining in numbers, wealth and status. The ascendancy of the aristocracy and the prestige of fashion were not challenged. Patronage – 'interest', with its complicated network of obligations – was an essential part of the social fabric, though a diminishing one. Connoisseurship and taste were obligatory for the fine gentleman, but progressively less so. The horror of vulgarity, the importance of catching the *ton* of high life, of having or acquiring elegant, genteel manners, pervade contemporary literature. Social climbing was a national foible. Fanny Burney's novels and diaries are documentary on these points. She herself, according to Mrs Thrale, was 'a graceful looking Girl, but 'tis the Grace of an Actress, not of a Woman of Fashion'.[2] Fanny was more severe on Lady Miller (of the Batheaston verse contests): 'while all her aim is to appear an elegant woman of fashion, all her success is to seem an ordinary woman in very common life, with fine clothes on; her habits are bustling, her air is self-important and her manner very inelegant'. But she soon discovered: 'notwithstanding Bath Easton is so much laughed at in London, nothing here [Bath] is more tonish than to visit Lady Miller'.[3]

The immense prestige of 'people of fashion' – 'people of fascination' as Fielding called them – is reflected in the language of the day: the *haut ton*, the *beau monde*, tonish, the Great, the Quality.

'Numberless are the devices made use of by the people of fashion of both sexes, to avoid the pursuit of the vulgar and to preserve the purity of the circle,' wrote Fielding. 'Sometimes the perriwig covers the whole beau; sometimes a large black bag . . . at other times a little lank silk appears like a blackbird on his neck . . . he will transform himself into the vilest animal to avoid the resemblance of his own species. Nor are the ladies less watchful of the enemy's motions. What hoods and hats and caps and coifs have fallen a sacrifice in this pursuit.'[4]

His 'Modern Glossary' is a penetrating satire. For instance, '"No Body" . . . "All the people in Great Britain except about 1200". "World" – "Your own Acquaintance".'[5]

England differed from other European countries in that the world of fashion depended neither on the Court nor on rank. With luck, wit and charm the preserve could be entered, and, as Fielding says, 'By whatever means you get into the polite circle, when once you are there it is sufficient merit that you are there.'[6] (And with money, invested in land and borough interest, rank could be achieved.) England differed also from continental countries (and from Scotland, Ireland and Wales) in the numbers and wealth of the middle ranks, professional and commercial. This led English travellers to conclude that there was no middle class in the countries they visited. When George III's unfortunate sister Matilda travelled through Germany in 1766 as the new Queen of Denmark, she wrote 'There is no such thing as a middle class living in affluence and independence.'[7] And Johnson in France in 1779, 'There is no happy middle state as in England.' 'As soon as Dover is left behind,' wrote Mrs Piozzi (formerly Thrale), 'every one seems to belong to some other man and no man to himself.'[8] Even Horace Walpole, returning from the Grand Tour: 'I had discovered that there was nowhere but in England the distinction of *middling people*. I perceive now that there is peculiar to us middling houses.'[9]

Robinson Crusoe's father (1719) is eloquent on 'the middle state, or what might be called the upper station of low life, which he had found by experience was the best state in the world'. But (as Smollett complained, p. 151) wars and conquests threw up profiteers and *nouveaux riches*, and these were men accustomed to power, by no means satisfied with the middle state.

Since the prints illustrate social stratification we may begin with Strype's categories in 1720.[10] He divided Londoners into five classes. 1. The Nobility and Gentry. 2. The Merchants and First Rate Tradesmen. 3. The Lawyers and Physicians. 4. The Inferior Tradesmen. 5. The Apprentices, Hackney Coachmen, Chairmen, Porters and Servants. Clearly this does not take us far. No firm line divided one category from the next; each had its subdivisions, each occupation its different grades. Where are the clergy, the authors, the artists? And he leaves out the numerous lowest class of street-sellers, vagrants and beggars. Johnson's dictionary definition of a gentleman has more significance. 'A man of birth though not noble – a man raised above the vulgar by his character or post.'*

---

*Cf. A. de Tocqueville (1833), '"gentleman" in England is applied to every well-educated man whatever his birth, while in France *gentilhomme* applies only to a gentleman by birth', *Journeys to England and Ireland*, ed. J. F. Mayer (London: Faber, 1958), p. 67. John Selden had noted a similar distinction between England and other countries.

Strype adds, 'As to the wives and daughters of the Principal Tradesman, they endeavour to imitate the Court Ladies, in their Dress, and follow much the same Diversions.' There was a distinction between the 'cits', who formed the Corporation from rich aldermen to small shopkeepers, and the rising class of bankers, East India directors and financiers who were bridging the gap between Cheapside and St James's.

That the difference between the manners of the City and St James's was wide, though decreasing, is undeniable. In Johnson's *Dictionary*, the 'cit' is 'a pert low alderman or pragmatical trader'. And he had a poor opinion of City women. 'Tradeswomen (I mean the wives of tradesmen in the City),' he maintained to Boswell (1772), 'are the worst creatures upon earth, grossly ignorant, and thinking viciousness fashionable, jealously malignant against women of quality.' This is certainly the character of his 'Madam Bombazine, the great silk-mercer's lady ... two yards round the waist and her voice at once loud and squeaking', who was vulgar, purse-proud, bad tempered, and rancorous against 'people that live at the other end of the town'.[11]

It has often been remarked that the clear-cut class distinctions of the eighteenth century (less clear in England than elsewhere) made intercourse between classes easy. But if clear-cut they were far from rigid. What astonished foreigners was the free and easy jostling of high and low in the parks and public places, regarded, by natives and foreigners, as a manifestation of English liberty, like the comparative absence of distinctions in dress. There was Voltaire on his first day in England (1728) taking the apprentices, servants and journeymen disporting themselves in Greenwich Park in their holiday best (as in *Greenwich Hill: or, Holyday Gambols* [1], c. 1750) for people of fashion.

With such exceptions as the Squire Westerns (old-fashioned in 1749, extinct after 1760) and the Madam Bombazines, class antagonism is not discoverable before the French Revolution. It developed after 1815 and in the later Regency made a belated impact on social satire. Caste arrogance there was, but it attracted disfavour, examples being that Duchess of Buckingham who held (c. 1740) that it was 'monstrous to be told that you have a heart as sinful as the common wretches that crawl on the earth', and (in fiction) Lady Catherine de Bourgh. Significantly, both seemed absurd. Walpole calls the Duchess 'more mad with

pride than any mercer's wife out of Bedlam'.[12] In 1785 Mrs Piozzi attributed the easy mixing of classes in Italy to the '*Certainty* of *Distance* between High and low ... Jealousy of Rank has no place here.'[13] But she soon discovered the other side of class rigidity. Apropos of Fanny Burney's Court appointment she wrote in 1786, 'What a glorious country is ours! Where Talent and Conduct are sufficient to draw mean Birth and original Poverty out of the Shadow of Life and set their Merit open to the Sun. No such Hopes, no such Possibilities in these wretched Nations, where Pride & Prejudice, chain up every liberal Idea and keep the Mind enslaved.'[14] Young George Lyttelton, on the Grand Tour in 1728, shocked at poverty in France, thought it due 'above all to the chimeric distinction between a gentleman and a merchant'.[15]

'Strolled into the Chapter Coffee House',* reported Dr Campbell in 1775, '... I subscribed a shilling for the right of a year's reading & found all the new publications I sought. ... Here I saw a specimen of English freedom *viz.*, a whitesmith in his apron & some of his saws under his arm, come in, sat down & called for his glass of punch, & the paper, both of which he used with as much freedom as a Lord. Such a man in Ireland (& I suppose France too or almost any other country) would not have shown himself with his hat on, nor any way unless sent for by some gentleman.'[16]

Paradoxically, or perhaps naturally, the retreat from such manifestations of English liberty came with the decline of 'subordination' and the stirrings of democracy. Half a century later such a coffee-house happening was treated as fantasy. Later still (1862) Taine, on a visit to England, after some searing comments on the London Sunday, goes on, 'Other indications point to a country dominated by an aristocracy. The gates of St James's Park bear the following notice. "The Park keepers have orders to refuse admittance ... to all beggars or any person in rags, or whose clothes are very dirty, or who are not of decent appearance and bearing." At every step one feels very remote from France.' And after a more intensive study of English ways, 'This fundamental difference is always cropping up: the difference which divides the land of hierarchy from the land of equality.'[17] 'In France,' wrote Bagehot – preferring the English principle of 'removable inequality', '*Égalité* is

---

*The meeting-place of bookseller-publishers in Paternoster Row.

a political first principle. The whole of Louis Napoleon's régime depends upon it.'[18]

This matter of the parks was always cropping up as a yardstick of national manners. To the Abbé Prévost who came to England in 1728 and put his experiences into his novel, *Les Aventures d'un homme de qualité*, St James's Park was 'the public walk of London', and 'open to all', where he was astonished to see 'the flower of the nobility and the fine ladies of the Court mingling in confusion with the vilest populace'. He records also a complete mixture of classes in the coffee-houses, 'the seats of English Liberty', lords and tradespeople at one table 'discussing familiarly the news of the Court and town'.

To return to the parks. Queen Caroline, Walpole noted, 'spoke of shutting up St James's Park and converting it into a noble garden. . . . She asked my father [Sir Robert] what it might cost, who replied "*only three Crowns*".'[19] Cole noted in 1765, certainly without disapproval, the posting of 'centinels' at the entrance to the Tuileries Gardens 'To keep out people who are ill-dressed or who are not proper to mix with the People who resort there.'[20] And some fifteen years after Taine's animadversions, Henry James described St James's Park as 'perhaps the most democratic corner of London. There are few hours of the day when a thousand smutty children are not spreading over it, and the unemployed lie thick upon the grass and cover the benches with a brotherhood of greasy corderoys. If the London parks are the drawing rooms of the poor . . . these particular grass plots and alleys may be said to constitute the very salon of the slums.'[21]

One suspects that the notice that shocked Taine was a vain attempt to stem the influx from the alleys of Westminster. A St James's Park notice excluding 'soldiers or servants in livery, beggars and dogs' was *removed* in the 1830s.* Less than five years after Taine's visit a Sunday scene supports the suspicion. *The Times* reported: 'The number of persons in St James's Park from 2 until 5 o'clock was very great, the keepers reporting that upwards of 50,000 people passed in at the various gates. . . . The great

proportion . . . were respectable tradesmen and mechanics with their families, but there was also an immense assemblage of "roughs". Not being able to go on the ice they found amusement in snowballing and bonnetting each other. When tired of their rough play . . . they turned their attention to any respectably dressed persons who came in their way, and maltreated them and insulted them in the most disgraceful manner. The foot-bridge over the ornamental water was the chief scene of their exploits. This bridge *on these occasions is always* [my italics] crowded. . . . Gangs of these roughs and thieves assembled to the number of several hundreds at each end . . ., and at a given signal . . . they rushed on pell-mell, hustling and bonnetting all who came in their way, watches, purses and pins changing owners with extraordinary rapidity. This disgraceful scene was repeated about every half hour until it grew dark. The park-keepers did all they could . . . but they were comparatively powerless . . . the roughs had possession of the park until all respectable people had been chased away . . .'[22] We shall find the changing customs and conventions of the parks reflecting the *mores* of the day and a favourite subject of graphic satire.

Besides the jostling in the parks there were analogous manifestations of English liberty (or barbarism, according to the viewpoint) that persisted into the next century. The supremacy of pit and gallery, especially gallery, in the theatre. The custom of street fights, or boxing matches, for which the spectators made a ring. 'Who would dream,' asks Prévost, 'that the most wretched porter would dispute the wall with a lord . . . and if both are obstinate . . . they will come publicly to fisticuffs, and fight till the stronger remains master of the pavement.' Henry Fielding called the London 'mob' the Fourth Estate. 'First, they assert an absolute right to the river of Thames. It is true that other estates do sometimes venture themselves upon the river, but this is only upon sufferance, for which they pay whatever that branch of the fourth estate called watermen are pleased to exact of them. . . . They grumble whenever they meet any person in a boat, whose dress declares them to be of a different order from themselves. Sometimes they . . . endeavour to run against the boat and overset it; but if they are too goodnatured to attempt this, they never fail to attack the passengers with all kinds of scurrilous abusive and indecent language.

'The second exclusive right that they insist on is to those

* *The Diary of Benjamin Robert Haydon*, ed. W. H. Pope (Cambridge, Mass.: Harvard University Press, 1963), vol. v, p. 374. Today: 'during the summer months millions of people found their way into St James's Park and often joined long queues to buy a scruffy sandwich served in unhygienic conditions and competed with some of the toughest pigeons in the world.' 'Parliament', *The Times*, 4 March 1967.

parts of the streets that are set apart for foot-passengers. In asserting this privilege they are extremely rigorous; insomuch that none of the other orders can walk the streets by day without being insulted, nor by night without being knocked down. . . .

'Here it was hoped their pretensions would have stopped; but it is difficult to set any bounds to ambition; for having sufficiently established this right, they now begin to assert their right to the whole street, and have lately made such a disposition with their waggons, carts and drays, that no coach can pass along without the utmost difficulty and danger.'[23]

Who bought these prints? The prices ranged from 6d. (many much cheaper ones must have disappeared) to 10s. 6d. plain, a guinea coloured, for the long strip design (Bunbury's). Hogarth's great sequences were sold by subscription. His separate prints cost from 6d. to 7s. 6d.: *The March to Finchley* was 10s. 6d. (Allowing for the fall in the value of money these sums are considerable.) Many were aimed at the collector. In the later part of the century satirical prints in portfolios or bound in vast volumes were part of the furniture of a gentleman's library. Prices rose in the second part of the century and fell in the early nineteenth – or rather, inferior prints were sold in larger impressions. After about 1820, with the adoption of lithography and the revival of wood-engraving, prices fell again. Prints were pasted on large folding screens (Byron had a famous one) and on the walls of fashionable houses (the Thrales' dining-room at Streatham was papered with Hogarth's prints). Others were pasted up at street-corners and in ale-houses and gin-shops. In illustrations of sordid poverty-stricken rooms there are almost always prints on the wall, as on 'the humid wall with paltry pictures spread' where Goldsmith's poor poet sheltered from bailiffs.[24] Print-shop windows were the picture galleries of the public. Later in the century folios of prints were hired out for an evening's entertainment 'in the manner of a circulating library'. An item in Humphrey's bill for prints sold to the Prince of Wales in 1803 is 'for the loan of a Folio of Prints, £1.1.0'.* Grantley Berkeley records that in his youth caricatures were an unfailing resource for difficult guests in large country-houses.[25]

*According to Fores's practice, this included a deposit for the return of the folio on the following day, 2s. 6d. being the charge for an evening (advertisement in the Royal Archives, Windsor Castle).

The long stretch from the 1720s to the 1830s demands subdivision. The first forty years or so clearly belong to Hogarth to a degree that gives them exceptional unity. For this and other reasons there is an unusually abrupt break from about the time of his death in 1764. The golden age of English caricature was to follow – though not at once – with the supremacy of Rowlandson and Gillray. When both Gillray and George III became hopelessly insane in 1810, and disappeared from the world, it was the end of an age. The Regency followed, and by common consent 'Regency' stands for a longer period than its actual nine years – to 1830, or to 1837. Here, it is taken as ending in the early thirties, with the Reform Bill and before the railway age. Our three divisions then are 'Hogarth', 'George III', and 'Regency'. No division can be free from anomalies. A minor one is that Hogarth's life covered the first four years of George III. But in our context the artist is more important than the monarch. Moreover, those years were thin in social satire – politics were all-absorbing.

Notes to the Introduction

1. W. Bagehot, *Lady Mary Wortley Montagu*, 1862.
2. *Thraliana*, ed. K.C. Balderston (Oxford: O.U.P., 1952), p. 368 (February 1779).
3. *Diary and Letters of Madame D'Arblay*, 1890, vol. 1, p. 175 (May–June 1780).
4. *Covent Garden Journal*, 9 May 1752. Cf. below, p. 163.
5. Ibid., 14 January 1752.
6. *Tom Jones*, 1749. Cf. below, p. 211.
7. Quoted, *The Times Literary Supplement*, 27 July 1963.
8. *Observations and Reflections on a Journey through France, Italy and Germany*, 1789, vol. II, p. 341.
9. To Sir Horace Mann, 13 September 1741, O.S.
10. John Strype, *Stow's Survey . . . brought down . . . to the present Time*, 1720.
11. *The Rambler*, 25 April 1750.
12. To Sir Horace Mann, 21 December 1741.
13. *Thraliana* (see note 2), p. 624.
14. Ibid., p. 662.
15. S.C. Roberts, *An Eighteenth Century Gentleman* (Cambridge: C.U.P., 1930), p. 6.
16. *Dr Campbell's Diary of a Visit to England in 1775*, ed. C.L. Clifford (Cambridge: C.U.P., 1947), p. 58.
17. *Taine's Notes on England*, translated E. Hyams (London: Thames & Hudson, 1957), pp. 18, 202.
18. 'Sterne and Thackeray', *National Review*, 1864.
19. *Walpoliana*, ed. J. Pinkerton, 1799, pp. 15–16.
20. W. Cole, *Paris Journal*, ed. F.G. Stokes (London: Constable, 1931), p. 115.
21. *English Hours*, ed. A.L. Lowe (London: Heinemann, 1960), pp. 15–16.
22. *The Times*, 13 January 1967.
23. *Covent Garden Journal*, No. 49, 1752.
24. *The Citizen of the World*, Letter xxx, 1762.
25. *My Life and Recollections*, 1866, vol. IV, p. 135.

Ye sweetscented Sirs who are sick of the Sport
And the stale languid Follies of Ballroom or Court,
For a Change leave the Mall & to Greenwich resort;

GREENWICH HILL
or Holyday Gambols.

There heighten'd with Raptures, which never can pall,
Youl own, the Delights of Assembly and Ball,
Are as dull as Yourselves, & just nothing at all.

I HOGARTH

Could new dumb Fauftus, to reform the Age,
Conjure up Shakefpear's or Ben Johnson's Ghost,
They'd blush for shame, to see the English Stage
Debauch'd by fool'ries, at so great a cost.

What would their Manes say? should they behold
Monfters and Mafquerades, where usefull Plays
Adorn'd the fruitfull Theatre of old,
And Rival Wits contended for the Bays.

Price 1 Shilling. 1724

2 *Masquerades and Operas, Hogarth*

3 *A Rake's Progress, Pl. II, Hogarth*

Prosperity (with Harlots smiles)
Most pleasing when the most beguiles,
How soon Sweet joy can all thy'd rain
Of false gay frantick loud & vain

Enter the unprovided Mind,
And Misery in fetters bind,
Load faith and Love with golden chain
And sprinkle Lethe o'er the Brain.

Pleasure on her silver Throne,
Smiling comes, nor comes alone;
Venus moves with her along;
And smooth tongues croud among.

And in their Train, to fill the Press,
Come apish Dance, and swoln Excefs,
Mechanic Honour, vicious Taste,
And fashion in her changing Vest.

1 - Hogarth's World

Hogarth's part in the development of graphic satire is fundamental. He has been called the father of English painting and the father of English caricature. He was undeniably the father, and the supreme practitioner, of graphic social satire in England, though of course he was much more than the satirist of contemporary life. We see the London of his age through his eyes. Besides his penetrating artist's vision two sides of his nature made him a superb recorder of – to use his own words – 'the customs, manners, fasheons, Characters, and humours' of his times. His John Bullishness and his personal grievances against the virtuosi colour his attacks on foreigners and fashionable follies, and thus he voices a mass of contemporary opinion. There was a gulf between those who accepted French taste as supreme and those who abhorred it; between the devotees and the disparagers of Italian opera. His compassionate side, his urge to protest against social injustice and cruelty, underlies and is sometimes apparent in the great dramatic sequences, and is the *raison d'être* of *Gin Lane* and *The Four Stages of Cruelty*. The pictorial dramas seem to have an obvious moral: the rake, the harlot, the unfortunate married pair, are faulty, blameworthy creatures, but above all they are victims of their environment, of the follies and cruelties of society; it is against these that Hogarth directs his satire, and his main didactic purpose is to make society aware of them.

Hogarth called his 'Way of Designing' the 'Comic and Moral'. 'My picture was my stage and men and women my actors who were by means of certain Actions and Expressions to Exhibit a dumb shew.' Not finding his conversation pieces sufficiently profitable for the needs of his household, he turned 'to still a more new way of proceeding *viz*. painting and Engraving modern moral Subject a Field unbroke up in any Country or any age'.* '. . . by small sums from many by means of Prints which I could Engrave from my Picture myself I could secure my Property to my self'.[1] 'I esteem the ingenious Mr Hogarth,' wrote Fielding, 'as one of the most useful satirists any age hath produced . . . I almost dare affirm that those two works of his, which he calls the Rake's and the Harlot's progress, are calculated more to serve the cause of Virtue, and the Preservation of Mankind, than all the Folios of morality which have ever been written.'[2]

The end of Hogarth's life coincided with the end of an age. The early Georgian period, before the impact of Wilkes and Liberty, before the shock of the loss of America, is accepted as placid, optimistic, complacent, unreforming.

To contemporaries – to Defoe for instance – it was a world of rapid change, admired or deplored. It was also an age which was constantly being informed that it was decadent, corrupt, mad for pleasure. 'The fury after licentious and luxurious pleasures,' said Fielding, 'is grown to so great a height, that it may be called the characteristic of the present age.'[3]

Hogarth was singularly aloof from the politics of the day. Illustrations of this are the *Election* series with its absence of party bias; and his unlucky political print, *The Times*, published in 1762 to promote 'peace and unanimity' – a protest against war-mongering and a defence of that *bête noire*, Lord Bute, which unsuccessfully challenged the public mood. The four *Election* prints are a protest against corruption, brutality and meaningless slogans by both sides. Their deliberate inconsequence is shown in *Chairing the Member*, published in 1758. The election is supposed to be the famous contest at Oxford in 1754, but a milestone records 'XIX Miles from London'. And the successful candidate is Bubb Dodington, who in 1754 had been electioneering in Somerset, unsuccessfully, despite three days 'spent in the infamous and disreputable compliance with the low habits of venal wretches'.[4] He may owe his place here (as he owed his peerage) to the fact that he was a notorious trafficker in boroughs.

The first print Hogarth published on his own account illuminates his preoccupation with 'taste' and his great interest in the theatre. It introduces two standard themes which long prevailed: neglect of the drama for spectacle; resentment at large sums paid to foreigners; it also illustrates a recent scandal in high life. It was at once pirated, which shows its popularity. *Masquerades and Operas* [2], of 1724, is a blend of realism, symbolism and personalities. It attacks both the taste of the fashionable world, perverted by foreigners, and that of the public, and also William Kent and his patron Lord Burlington. On one side is the Opera House, Vanbrugh's building in the Haymarket (burnt down in 1789). Heidegger, the Swiss organizer of masquerades, leans from a window to watch a hurrying crowd of masqueraders led by Folly – supposed to be the future George II, a masquerade addict. The cardinal is a young lady, the milkmaid a notorious rake. As a result of this masquerade the lady lost her reputation.[5] A show-cloth hangs out; on this three fashionables kneel abjectly to three foreign singers; one, Lord Peterborough, pours out guineas which Francesca Cuzzoni greedily rakes up. An even bigger crowd pours into the opposite building, the Lincoln's Inn Fields theatre, where Harlequin (John Rich) points to a show-cloth advertising his pantomime, 'Dr Faustus'. In

---

*The novelty was not literal: Hogarth's sources have been traced by Dr Antal, see note 2.

A. P.^ra Plasterer white washing & Bespattering
B. any Body that comes in his way
C. not a Dukes Coach as appears by y Crescent at one Corner
D. Taste
E. a standing Proof
F. a Labourer.
Price 6^d

4 The Man of Taste, Hogarth

the foreground a woman wheels off for waste paper the neglected works of Congreve, Otway, Dryden, Shakespeare. This print is believed to have been published to coincide with the first performance of Handel's opera, *Giulio Cesare*.[6]

In the eighteenth-century conflict between Shakespeare and pantomime, the enormous popularity of Dr Faustus (long the anti-hero of ballads, chap-books and puppet-shows, not to speak of Marlowe) was a landmark. First, *Harlequin Dr Faustus* was produced at Drury Lane (1723). Rich at once staged another Faustus, *Harlequin Necromancer*. Both took the town by storm, to the dismay of the up-holders of the drama. A pamphlet attacked both: 'to the immortal honour of this age be it recorded that . . . they meet with far greater applause than the politest and most elegant play that ever appeared upon the British theatre'.[7]

To return to Hogarth's print. In the background, but important, symbolizing the entrance to this display of bad taste, is Burlington Gate, designed by Lord Burlington (who stands beside it with his architect Colen Campbell) for his new Piccadilly house on a Palladian plan. On the pediment stands Kent – a good architect but a bad painter – attitudinizing as a Roman emperor, while Raphael and Michelangelo recline at his feet like degraded slaves.

Hogarth returned to Burlington Gate and his *bête noire*, Kent, in *The Man of Taste* [4], 1731. Kent still attitudinizes; Raphael and Michelangelo still recline, but there is a scaffolding on which Pope stands, vigorously 'white washing & Bespattering'. The whitewash is for Burlington, who is climbing up a ladder, the dirt is for the Duke of Chandos, whose coach is passing along Piccadilly. This is an attack on Pope for his *Epistle to Burlington* which condemned Timon for his bad taste – Timon being generally assumed to be Chandos, though Pope denied it.*

The taste of the town is again a theme in *A Rake's Progress* in 1733. Tom Rakewell, raw from Oxford, who has just inherited a sordid miser's wealth, is set on becoming a man of fashion, and therefore a man of taste. In the second plate of the series [3], *Surrounded by Artists and Professors* – toadies and parasites – he stands in nightcap and morning-gown between a French dancing-master and a jockey who kneels to show him a big silver bowl won at Epsom by 'Silly Tom'. There is a French fencing-master and his rival, Figg the prizefighter. A typical bully or bravo offers his services (the bully in Gay's *Trivia* 'cocks his broad hat, edg'd round with tarnish'd lace'). A landscape gardener (Bridgman) holds out a plan. There is a poet seeking a patron; the title-page of his poem is on the floor dedicated to 'Tom Rakewell Esq.'; the subject is homage to Farinelli,† who (on the title-page) is on a pedestal adored by ladies offering burning hearts and exclaiming 'One God, one Farinelli'. A huntsman blows his horn regardless of the foreign player at the harpsichord from whose chair hangs a long scroll (not in the painting): 'A List of the Rich Presents Signor Farinelli condescended to accept of the British Nobility & Gentry for one night's Performance in the Opera.' The last item is 'A Gold snuff Box chas'd with the Story of Orpheus charming ye Brutes by T. Rakewell Esq.' Through the archway we see trades-people bringing their wares.

The levee of the Countess in Hogarth's masterpiece, *Marriage à la Mode* [5], 1745, also satirizes taste as the obsession of a decadent society. The scene is her bedroom. While her hair is being dressed by a French *frizeur* she listens to Counsellor Silvertongue who gives her a mas-querade ticket, pointing to a masquerade depicted on a screen. It is a masquerade that precipitates the tragic ending of this drama of mercenary marriage. She pays no attention to Carestini, the famous castrato whom she has engaged to sing. His voice enraptures the listening lady, recognized at the time as Mrs Fox Lane who had cried out in the Opera House, 'One God, one Farinelli'. The pictures, the objects of virtu on the floor (recently bought) are charged with significance. 'The very furniture of his rooms', said Horace Walpole, 'describes the character of the persons to whom they belong.' And, 'It was reserved to Hogarth to write a scene of furniture. The Rake's Levee room . . . the apart-ments of the husband and wife in *Marriage à la Mode*, the

*The print was used as frontispiece to a pirated edition, titled *Of Taste*, cf. p. 208, below.

†The castrato singer who was soon to leave England with a fortune (as he said) 'from England's folly'.

Poet's bedchamber, and many others, are the history of the manners of the age.'[8]

Condemnation of masquerades was part of the moral climate of the day; Fielding wrote 'The Masquerade', a poem, in 1728 and their ill effects appear in *Tom Jones* and *Amelia*. Hogarth did an emblematical *Masquerade Ticket* in 1727, inscribed 'A Sacrifice to Priapus'. A big clock shows that there is 'nonsense every second, impertinence every minute, wit only once an hour'. The royal arms are displayed with the lion and unicorn in ungainly attitudes as a rebuke to George II for his love of masquerades. There is a more dramatic verdict in his unfinished painting of 1740–45:[9] a husband returns to find his wife and sister in masquerade dress, takes the sister for a lover and kills them both.

After Covent Garden was opened by Rich, the rivalry between the two patent theatres was a persistent theme.

Rich's Glory or the Triumphant Entry into Covent Garden, a long processional design, attributed to Hogarth, illustrates the removal from Lincoln's Inn Fields in December 1732, a triumph also for Gay whose *Beggar's Opera* had made 'Rich gay, and Gay rich.' The crowd storms the new theatre; Gay is on a porter's back, Rich drives the car in which are Columbine and a famous pantomime dog; players and authors follow the procession. This landmark in theatrical history was followed by another, the appearance of Garrick. *The Theatrical Steel-Yards of 1750* might be called Garrick's Glory. Since 1747 he had been Manager, patentee and chief actor at Drury Lane. The steelyard, or balance, hangs from a satyr's mouth; Garrick alone outweighs the stars of Covent Garden – Mrs Woffington, Barry, Quin (Falstaff), Mrs Cibber. Woodward (Harlequin), who had been Rich's junior Harlequin, is about to hoist Queen Mab beside Garrick. Rich lies despairingly on

5 Marriage à la Mode, Pl. IV, Hogarth/S. Ravenat

Marriage-A-la-Mode, (Plate IV)

Invented Painted & Published by W.m Hogarth —   According to Act of Parliament. April 1.st 1745.   Engraved by S. Ravenet

6 *The Laughing Audience*, Hogarth

7 *Strolling Actresses dressing in a Barn*, Hogarth

the ground, a coat covering his harlequin suit: as actor and as Manager he is defeated. Garrick's famous prologue was for this occasion:

> Sacred to Shakespeare *was this spot design'd*
> *To please the heart and humanize the mind;*
> *But if an empty House, the Actor's curse,*
> *Shows us our Lears, and Hamlets, lose their force,*
> *Unwilling, we must change the nobler scene*
> *And, in our turn, present you Harlequin* . . .

Garrick disliked pantomime, but,

> *The Drama's laws the Drama's patrons give*
> *And we, who live to please, must please to live.*[10]

The pantomime of *Queen Mab* rivalled *Faustus*, and was performed, it is said, every winter for nearly thirty years. Burney composed the music, and this, according to his daughter Fanny, was 'taught to all young ladies, set to all barrel organs, and played at all familiar music parties'.[11] Henceforth pantomime at the rival houses stimulated elaborate scenic effects. Pantomime was unremittingly attacked by the satirists, including Pope and Fielding. Garrick and Colman (Rich's successor at Covent Garden) were denounced in prints and pamphlets for neglect of the serious drama. But the English passion for Shakespeare was a matter of repeated comment by foreign visitors.

In *The Laughing Audience* [6], 1733, Hogarth gives a close-up view of a theatre interior: the dejected boredom of the orchestra, the delight of the people in the pit, the orange girls flirting with the elderly beaux in the boxes who are totally uninterested in the play. This was something of a convention. When Roderick Random poses as a beau in his fine French clothes, he envies 'the happy indifference' of his 'fellow-beaux': 'I could not help weeping with the heroine on the stage, though I practised a great many shifts to conceal this piece of impolite weakness.'[12] Goldsmith's Chinese philosopher discovered that the fine folk in the boxes 'appeared in the most unhappy situation of all. The rest of the audience came merely for their own amusement. . . . Gentlemen and ladies ogled each other through spectacles, for, my companion observed, that blindness was of late become indispensable.' He noticed also that 'the order of precedence was inverted'. The gallery 'who were undermost all the day, now enjoyed a temporary eminence, and became masters of the ceremonies. It was they who called for the music, indulging every noisy freedom, and testifying all the insolence of beggary and exaltation.'[13]

This dictatorship of the gallery Grosley, a French visitor, called (in 1765) 'a branch of British Liberty'. He was recording a cliché.

The gallery could, and often did, damn a play on the first night and drive it from the stage. They expressed displeasure not only by missiles and cat-calls but by tearing up the benches. Disorder was endemic, it soon turned to riot, culminating in the riot of riots, the O.P. (Old Price) riot of 1809. When Garrick tried to stop the practice of half-price admissions after the third act for a special performance of Arne's *Artaxerxes* there were disturbances at both theatres – at Covent Garden a serious O.P. riot (24 February 1763) – all the benches, glasses and chandeliers were broken and an attempt to cut the wooden pillars supporting the gallery failed only because there was a core of iron. A broadside engraving shows the riot, and also the arrangement of the theatre with the 'rings' or chandeliers which lit the stage till Garrick introduced the French system of lighting from behind the scenery,[14] a vast improvement.

Strolling players, and the country theatre, shed or barn, played an important part in social life. No satire or burlesque could exaggerate the expedients, hardships, sordid surroundings, of these tragedy queens and kings, players of gods and goddesses, farce and pantomime. The gradation was extreme from the (genuine) London players on tour during the summer to the destitute troupers reinforced by runaway apprentices and stage-struck artisans. Mrs Charke (Colley Cibber's daughter) complained bitterly that 'the rights' of those bred to the profession were 'horribly invaded by barbers, printers, taylors and journeymen weavers'.[15] Hogarth's *Strolling Actresses dressing in a Barn* [7] is realistic in its details – for instance the ring of tallow candles stuck in clay – and the swirling grandeur and fantasy of the design is symbolic of the contrasts in the life of a poor player. Two play-bills (as in 1791) are on the London pattern; they show that the piece is *The Devil to pay in Heaven*, to be performed at the George Inn. The parts are Jupiter, Diana, Flora, Juno, Night, Siren, Aurora, Eagle, Cupid. All are 'M^{rs}' except Cupid who is 'M^r' also, 'Two Devils, Ghost & Attendance. To which will be added rope dancing and tumbling. Vivat Rex.'

Notes to Chapter I

1. Autobiographical notes quoted J. Burke, *Hogarth, The Analysis of Beauty* (Oxford: O.U.P., 1955), pp. 206, 209, 216.
2. *The Champion*, quoted F. Antal, *Hogarth and His Place in European Art* (London: Routledge & Kegan Paul, 1962), p. 8.
3. *Charge to the Grand Jury of Middlesex*, 1749.
4. *Diary of the late Bubb Dodington*, 1784, pp. 285–6.
5. Information from Mr Harry R. Beard.
6. H. H. Beard, *Burlington Magazine*, 1950, p. 266.
7. Quoted, T. Niklaus, *Harlequin Phoenix* (London: John Lane, 1956), pp. 150–2.
8. *Anecdotes of Painting*, 1849, vol. III, p. 727.
9. Ashmolean Museum; F. Antal (see note 2), pl. 73, pp. 28, 75, etc.
10. Johnson's prologue spoken by Garrick at the Drury Lane opening in 1747.
11. *Memoirs of Dr Burney*, 1832, p. 20.
12. Tobias Smollett, *Roderick Random*, 1748, Chapter 45.
13. *The Citizen of the World*, Letter XXI, 1762.
14. *Annual Register*, 1765, p. 130.
15. *Narrative of the Life of Mrs Charke*, 1755, p. 188.

8 *Burlesque sur le Burlesque*, P. Sandby

2 - Art and Letters

Hogarth on art is inseparable from Hogarth on taste: a protest against the connoisseurs and the picture jobbers who trafficked in old masters – bad or spurious – and promoted the fashionable belief that pictures by living English artists were inferior to the importations of the Grand Tour. He put all this into the frontispiece and tail-piece [9] of his *Catalogue of Pictures exhibited in Spring Gardens* in 1761 (sold as a ticket of admission for the benefit of distressed artists). In one, Britannia under the patronage of George III waters three small but promising plants – 'Painting', 'Sculpture' and 'Architecture'. In the other an ape-connoisseur waters three dead stumps: 'Exoticks'. Hogarth returned next year to the black and dead masters

– so ugly and so satisfied! The Athenian head [a barber's block] was intended for Stuart; but was so like, that Hogarth was forced to cut off the nose.' Compasses and scale, with the 'Advertisement', point the jest: 'In about seventeen years will be compleated in Six Volumes folio Price Fifteen Guineas. . . .' The parvenu peer, Bubb Dodington, now Lord Melcombe, is there, one of the 'Old Peerian or Aldermanic Order, corresponding to the Doric'. Stuart had the print pasted on a fire-screen in his parlour and used to point it out to visitors.[1]

Before this, Hogarth had been the target of one of those pictorial onslaughts so characteristic of the period, and in this the great question of taste and connoisseurship was

9 Tailpiece of Catalogue of Pictures exhibited in Spring Gardens in 1761, Hogarth

in *Time Smoking a Picture* [10], 1762, originally a subscription ticket for his *Sigismunda*. Besides the tone imparted by Time's tobacco-smoke, there is a big jar of varnish as used by dealers to give antiquity and enhance gloom.

When, in 1761, 'Athenian' Stuart and Nicholas Revett announced the publication of their great work, *The Antiquities of Athens Measured and Delineated*, Hogarth ridiculed it in his *Five Orders of Perriwigs as they were seen at the late Coronation measured Architecturally* [11]. Walpole sent a print to Montagu (7 November 1761):* 'The enclosed print will divert you, especially the baroness in the right-hand corner

involved. His opposition to the project of an academy had provoked the rancorous jealousy of Paul Sandby and others, and his attacks on the *cognoscenti* were an aggravating factor. The first opportunity came with the publication of *The Analysis of Beauty* in 1753, well received by literary critics. The second followed his unlucky venture into politics in 1762, with a print defending Lord Bute. Politicians (including members of the royal family) excepted, no Englishman was so ruthlessly and repeatedly attacked by caricaturists as Hogarth.

Sandby's *Burlesque sur le Burlesque* (*The Burlesquer burlesqued*) [8] in 1753 must serve as an example of many others on similar lines, deriding Hogarth as man, as artist and as author. It is one of those complicated satires dependent on inscriptions to stress the insults. There are echoes

*Vol. 1 of *Antiquities* appeared in 1762, but 'Stuart had expatiated fully upon its merits, and those of the artists concerned', *History of the Dillettante Society*, quoted H.B.Wheatley, *Hogarth's London*, 1909, p. 12.

10 *Time Smoking a Picture*, Hogarth

11 *Five Orders of Perriwigs as they were seen at the late Coronation measured Architecturally*, Hogarth

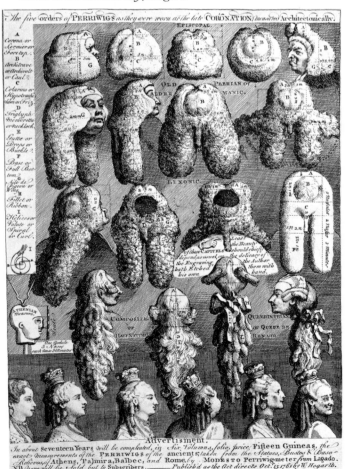

of his self-portrait, now in the Tate: the dog Trump, the detail of the artist's favourite books (Shakespeare, Milton, Swift) and the Line of Beauty (the theme of the *Analysis*), which is transferred from the palette to the bone in the dog's mouth. Hogarth was nicknamed Pugg, and he is depicted as half a pug-dog. On his shoulder is 'an insect [with butterfly-wings]* Inspiring ye Painter with Vanity'. He is working at 'A History Piece suitable to ye Painter's Capacity, from a Dutch Manus^t': Abraham (a butcher) shoots at Isaac who is saved by an angel. Stuck on his canvas are 'Old-prints from whence he steals Figures for his Design', with more in the big portfolio beside him. The window on the left is screened by 'Lives of all the best Painters torn in pieces'. The hinged shutters blocking the window on the right are 'a Variety of Lights . . . to produce ye Effect of all ye great Painters. Shewing how far in his Opinion he has excell'd them all in Design Colouring and Taste.' They are Raphael, Rubens, Titian, Lebrun, Rembrandt. Two men, one scrawling on a shutter, the other grinding colours, are his assistants. Above the easel is a little figure of Hogarth acting as a magic lantern, throwing on to a screen his burlesque (which he called 'Designed in the Rediculous Manner of Rembrandt') of his own Raphaelesque painting for Lincoln's Inn of *Paul before Felix*. Next this is a little travesty of *Calais Gate*: 'Roast Beef'. Beside him are a dustman and a hurdy-gurdy player – low-life figures. Other objects in the room are a stick-like layfigure, and books, 'admired authors', to indicate bad taste, literary and aesthetic: Vanbrugh's *Designs*, Joe Miller's *Jests*, Brook Taylor's *Perspective*, Sir Richard Blackmore's *King Arthur*, one of the worst poems of the most derided poetaster of the day. The only figure not explained by inscriptions is the man with the Dutch manuscript; he corresponds to Rowlandson's *Historian animating the Mind of a Young Painter* [112].

Below the title is a row of tiny low-life figures who are disposing of unsold sheets of the *Analysis*: a man wheels them off to the cook-shop, a chimney-sweep reads them, a trunk-maker buys them by weight, an old woman sells them from a stall, a hawker carries them dangling from a pole.

The other anti-Hogarth, anti-*Analysis* prints were also barbed. There were one or two counter-prints, for instance *Collection of Connoisseurs* who reverently study *Burlesque sur le Burlesque* and trample not only on the *Analysis* but on 'Milton' and 'Shakespeare'. Hogarth was silent. On the later and more distressing occasion he retaliated with vigour on Wilkes and Churchill.

Since the palmy days of Queen Anne 'authors by profession' had become so numerous, the shifts and importunities of Grub Street so endless, that they came to rely on the bookseller-publisher and ultimately on the rapidly growing public. 'The present age may be styled with great propriety the "*Age of Authors*"', for perhaps there never was a time in which men of all degrees of ability, of every kind of

---

*The butterfly is repeatedly a symbol of vanity and frivolity (in contrast with early Christian iconography), cf. below, p. 164.

THE DISTREST POET.

12 The Distrest Poet, Hogarth

His
HOLINESS
and his
PRIME MINISTER.

THE DUNCIAD with NOTES VARIORUM

A Letter to the Publishers *Art of politicks*

The PHIZ and CHARACTER of an ALEXANDRINE Hyper-critick & Comentator.

Nature her self shrunk back when thou wert born, | And half o'ercome with Beast, stood doubting long,
And cry'd the Works not mine ——— | Whose right in Thee were more:
The Midwife stood agast; and when she saw | —— thou art all one Error; Soul and Body:
Thy Mountain back, and thy distorted legs, | The first young tryal of some unskill'd Power,
Thy face half minted with the stamp of Man, | Rude in the making Art; an Ape of Jove.

Aw'd by no Shame, by no Respect controul'd, | Spleen to Mankind his envious Heart possest,
In Scandal busy in Reproaches bold. | And much he hated All, but most the Best.

Pope's character of Thersites:

See Granger for attributes. Front to Pope Alexanders Supremacy & infallibility examined 1729. price 6.d

13 *His Holiness and his Prime Minister*, anon.

education . . . every profession and employment were posting with ardour so general to the press.'[2]

The classic representation of the poet's lot – the lot of any Grub Street garretteer – is Hogarth's *Distrest Poet* [12], 1736. It was repeatedly reprinted, echoed and imitated. His was genteel poverty; the sword on the floor is the badge of gentility. Hogarth's poet is supposed to be Theobald, Pope's victim, and on the wall is a print of Pope thrashing Curll (altered in the second state to a map, 'A View of the Gold Mines of Peru'). It is Michaelmas quarter-day; the indignant milkmaid has climbed to the attic and holds out a heavy score. Goldsmith's poet was solitary, but there are similarities:

> The *morn was cold, he views with keen desire,*
> *The rusty grate, unconscious of a fire;*
> *With beer and milk arrears the frieze is scor'd*
> *And five crack'd tea-cups dress'd the chimney board;*
> *A night-cap deck'd his brows instead of bay,*
> *A cap by night – a stocking all the day.*[3]

Johnson's lines, written while he was still a bookseller's hack, are better known:

> *Deign on the passing world to turn your eyes,*
> *And pause a while from letters to be wise;*
> *There mark what ills the scholar's life assail,*
> *Toil, envy, want, the patron* and the jail,*
> *See nations slowly wise, and meanly just,*
> *To buried talent raise the tardy bust.*[4]

Authors in the public eye (not the Grub Street ones) were subjects of satire; inevitably Pope was the chief target of his day. We have seen him whitewashing Burlington Gate; he appears in *Rich's Glory* and many other prints. A characteristic attack is *His Holiness and his Prime Minister*† [13] with a venomous quotation from his own character of Thersites and the motto *Nosce Te Ipsum*.

In the sixties Sterne, who died in 1768, was the outstanding figure. *Sterne and Death* [14], etched in Florence by Thomas Patch, illustrates the passage from *Tristram Shandy* beginning 'and when Death himself knocked at my door ye bade him come again. . . .' This is quoted, with an Italian translation, and there are satirical allusions to his works, including a postillion's boot for La Fleur of *The Sentimental Journey*.

*'Patron' was substituted for 'garret' in the first edition after the famous letter to Lord Chesterfield, 1755.

†It was the frontispiece to *Pope Alexandee's Supremacy . . .*, 1729, and also issued separately.

Notes to Chapter II
1. J. T. Smith, *Nollekens and his Times* (Oxford: O.U.P., 1929), p. 27.
2. Johnson (?), *The Adventurer*, 1752–4, No. 115.
3. *The Citizen of the World*, Letter XXX, 1762.
4. *The Vanity of Human Wishes*, 1749.

;and when Death himself knocked at my door
;ye bad him come again; and in so gay a tone
;of careless indifference, did ye do it, that he
;doubted of his Commission. There must cert:
; ainly be some Mistake in this Matter; quoth he

E quando la Morte istessa mi picchio alla
porta, voi Spiriti miei le diceste che tornasse, e lo
faceste con si buon viso, e con tanta indifferen
za, che ella dubito d'avere sbagliato, e disse fra
se; ci avrebbe a essere di certo qualche sbaglio

Price half-Crown

T.S.

Patch Pinx et Sculp ther. et

14 *Sterne and Death, Thomas Patch*

CREDULITY, SUPERSTITION, and FANATICISM.
A MEDLEY.

Believe not every Spirit, but try the Spirits whether they are of God: because many false Prophets are gone out into the World.

1 John. Ch 4. V.1.

Design'd and Engrav'd by Wm Hogarth.   Publish'd as the Act directs March yⁱ 15ᵗʰ 1762.

15 *Credulity, Superstition, and Fanaticism. A Medley, Hogarth*

3 - The Professions

The Church and the Universities

Of the three learned professions the clergy were the most subject to caricature, though not (till 1819 and after) the most harshly treated. There were so many varieties and in their black gowns (not worn off duty in the later part of the century) they were so conspicuous. The basic fact about the clerical calling was its entire dependence on patronage. The chief fields of attack were those ancient evils, pluralism, and the gulf between the higher and the inferior clergy. These were developed later, but the demerits of pluralists and bishops were not neglected. The personification of sour uncharitableness (p. 41) is a pluralist.

An Ass loaded with (Church) *Preferments* [17], 1737, attacks pluralism and nepotism. Wake, the Archbishop, drives the ass, who is the Dean of Canterbury and his son-in-law; the beast turns its (human) head from a miserably poor parson who kneels at its feet. Besides much else, the Dean is Master of 'the two Hospitals in Canterbury' and also of St Cross, Winchester, recalling the very different fate of Trollope's Warden in Barchester, with only one of these preferments. Verses include the lines:

> *Ten thousand Souls in one Squab Doctor's care,*
> *Give him no Pain, Since Curates are not dear.*

An over-rich bishop was an outrage: 'When Bishop Chandler [Durham] died [1750], scandalously rich for a bishop, the Nation was stunned by it', the Reverend William Cole recorded in his diary.[1]

Another aspect of patronage and the Church is touched on in Robert Dodsley's lines, 1738:

> *When Dukes or noble Lords a Chaplain hire,*
> *They first of his Capacities enquire,*
> *If stoutly qualified to drink and smoke,*
> *If not too nice to bear an impious joke,*
> *Or tame enough to be the common Jest,*
> *This is a Chaplain to his Lordship's Taste.*

In Hogarth's conversation piece of Lord Hervey and his friends, also in 1738, the jest is against the chaplain, who, disregarded by the others, stands on a chair to gaze through a telescope at his preferment, a church in the distance, so absorbed that he does not notice that his chair is tilting. In this commissioned work the jest must be his lordship's, but Hogarth's clergy are depicted without sympathy. In *The Sleeping Congregation*, 1736, he satirizes the somnolent early Georgian Church. The painting (1728) differs in spirit and detail from the print. The first preacher is a personification of languid fashionable vacuity; the second is older and reads his sermon through a glass. In *A Christening* the parson holds the infant, but is absorbed in an attractive woman beside him. Then there are the toping parson of Plate 23, the Ordinary of Newgate (p. 45) and the guzzling parson in *The Election Entertainment.*

The parson who is to conduct the funeral in the sixth plate of *A Harlot's Progress*, where he is 'toying with a harlot', is a 'Fleet Chaplain'. Fleet parsons were a class of clergy, peculiar to the years from about 1666 to 1754, that reached the lowest depth of degradation. Two things made this possible. One, the fact that marriages without banns or licence, performed anywhere, at any time, were valid, though against the canons. In 1666 the Ecclesiastical Commissioners took steps to prevent the controllable and removable clergy from performing such marriages. But among the debtors in the Fleet Prison and its Rules (extending nearly a mile outside it), there were many derelict and dissolute parsons who saw their opportunity. First, in the prison chapel and then outside; in taverns or gin-shops or anywhere, in a room fitted up for the purpose, they performed these marriages, competitively employing touts called 'plyers'. Fees of course were the sole object. The result was the encouragement of every abuse connected with marriage – seduction, marriage as a drunken frolic, pretended marriages. Entries in the Fleet Registers could – at a price – be antedated, inserted or removed. Women were decoyed, stripped of their fortune and deserted. Men also could be ruined, as we shall see. These Fleet marriages were mostly of the humbler classes, but some were not. The most celebrated ever recorded in the Registers is that of Charles Fox's parents (but they were married in Sir Charles Hanbury Williams's house).

Writing of Fleet Street in his youth, Pennant says, 'I have often been tempted by the question, "Sir, will not you be pleased to walk in and be married?" Along this most lawless space was hung up the frequent sign of a male and female conjoined, with *Marriages performed within*, written beneath. A dirty fellow invited you in. The parson was seen walking before his shop, a squalid profligate fellow, clad in a tattered plaid nightgown, with a fiery face. . . .'[2] Some of the notes in the (extant) Registers are revealing. 'August 5, 1736, Give to every man his due and learn ye way of truth. This advice cannot be taken by those that are concerned in ye Fleet Marriages . . . unless he designe to starve, for by Lying, Bullying and Swearing to extort money from ye silly and unwary people, you advance your business, and gets your pelf which always melts like snow on a Sun Shiney Day.' And the same man, whose Fleet ministry lasted from 1713 to 1750, recorded, 'If a Clark or a Plyer tells a Lye you must vouch it to be as true as ye Gospel, and if disputed you must affirm with an Oath to ye truth of a downright Damnable Falsehood. Virtus Laudatur et Alhet.'[3]

A Fleet Wedding – Between a brisk young Sailor & his Landlady's Daughter at Rederiff [Rotherhithe] [16], 1747, is a scene in Fleet Market. The groom, fashionably dressed for the occasion, and the bride, a prostitute, have just left their coach to be met by two eager rival parsons. Another sailor helps the bride's mother, a bawd, out of the coach. According to the engraved verses there are also plyers who advocate rival marriage shops, the 'Pen in Hand' and the 'True and Ancient Register'. The sequel is related in a companion plate, *The Sailor's Fleet Wedding Entertainment*, a rollicking feast at which 'Jack rich in Prizes, now the Knot is ty'd,/ Sits pleas'd by her he thinks his maiden Bride.' Sailors and women make merry, parson and bawd are tipsily amorous. The door opens, a creditor and two bailiffs enter to arrest the bridegroom for his wife's debts, '70 Pound for Cloaths and Board' (to her mother). This cautionary tale might be from life, such tricks were notorious, and sailors were fleeced by their 'landladies'. Lord Hardwicke's Act (1753) put an end to the sordid traffic in Fleet Street and some other places, which had struck at the root of family security. It was violently attacked on grounds of liberty, morality, humanity and population. One of the slogans of Plate I of Hogarth's *Election* series is against the Act: 'Marry and Multiply in spite of the Devil and the—— [Court]'.

But at this time 'enthusiasm' was more under attack than the shortcomings of the Church, and the assault was generally aimed at Whitefield. Hogarth's *Credulity, Superstition, and Fanaticism. A Medley* [15] is in spirit and composition *The Sleeping Congregation* (painting) in reverse, and crowded with symbolical detail. In the first state, *Enthusiasm Delineated*, dedicated to the Archbishop of Canterbury, it was an attack on Popery and on pictures and images in churches. Before publication Hogarth altered it and made his chief target the Methodists and the preaching of Hell and Damnation, and tales of witches and demons. The woman in the foreground is Mary Tofts (p. 37) an exploiter of credulity, altered from Mother Douglas, a notorious bawd who was a sanctimonious church-goer. The winged cherubs beside the clerk recall a passage in *The Analysis of Beauty* on 'admired and ornamental monsters': 'the most extraordinary of all . . . an infant's head of about two years old, with a pair of duck's wings placed under its chin, supposed always to be flying about and singing psalms. A painter's representations of Heaven would be nothing

16 A Fleet Wedding – Between a brisk young Sailor & and his Landlady's Daughter at Rederiff, anon.

A FLEET WEDDING.

Between a brisk young Sailor & his Landlady's Daughter at Rederiff.

without swarms of these little inconsistent objects, flying about or perching on the clouds, and yet there is something so agreeable in their form, that the eye is reconciled, and overlooks the absurdity, and we find them in the carving and painting of almost every church. St Paul's is full of them.'

By this time (1762) attacks on Methodists had died down. It was the open-air preaching in the thirties that attracted satire, for instance *Enthusiasm Display'd; or, the Moor Fields Congregation*, 1739, where Whitefield preaches, supported by two women, 'Hypocrisy' and 'Deceit', while Folly listens, and 'Enthusiasm revives her old Pretence' – as in the days of Puritan zealots and sectaries.

The Church and the universities are overlapping topics. Hogarth makes the audience in *Scholars at a Lecture* [18], 1737, specimens of stupidity and empty-headedness. The lecturer is Mr Fisher of Jesus, Oxford, Registrar of the University, who had given Hogarth leave to draw him.[4] The Fellows wear square caps, the undergraduates (only three) round ones. It was not till 1769 that the round caps or hoods were abolished in favour of squares: '. . . for all our Scholars square the circle now'.[5]

The Dublin Orator at Oxford, c. 1760, shows Thomas Sheridan (father of R.B.S.) lecturing on elocution to Oxford doctors, including the Vice Chancellor. Most of them have the horn-books from which children learnt the alphabet, and their remarks reveal them as Jacobite Tories. The Savilian Professor of Astronomy (Dr James Bradley) is dressed up as some sort of astrologer. He was in fact a most distinguished man, Astronomer Royal since 1742, remarkable not only for his discoveries, but for giving seventy-nine courses of lectures between 1729 and 1760 – remarkable indeed in those days. It was later in the century that the universities made their impact on the print shops, but contemporary comment invites quotation. That college Fellows were commonly topers and guzzlers was a common theme of satire – not of course baseless. One remembers that Gibbon's months at Magdalen (1752–3) were the most idle and unprofitable of his life, and that the Fellows were 'decent easy men' whose 'dull and long potations excused the brisk intemperance of youth'. Chesterfield's character of a don, 'Doctor Carbuncle' (a scholar and a gentleman), is less well known. 'As he had resided long in college he had contracted all the habits and prejudices, the lazyness, the soaking, the pride and pedantry of the cloisters. . . . He considered the critical knowledge of Greek and Latin words as the utmost effort of human understanding, and a glass of good wine in good company as the highest part of human existence.'[6]

Tom Warton's lines on the life of an Oxford Fellow were written in 1746 when he was an undergraduate:

> *Too fond of Liberty and Ease*
> *A Patron's Vanity to please,*
> *Long Time he watches, and by Stealth,*
> *Each frail Incumbent's doubtful Health,*
> *At length – and in his fortieth Year*
> *A Living drops – two Hundred clear.*[7]

AnASS loaded w.th PREFERMENTS.

17 *An Ass loaded with Preferments*, anon.
18 *Scholars at a Lecture*, Hogarth

Medicine

The doctor is an ancient cock-shy. A Greek epigram (first century A.D.) anticipates many later gibes: 'Yesterday Dr Marius touched the statue of Zeus. Though it is stone, and Zeus too, the funeral's today.' And Molière: '*Presque tous les hommes meurent de leurs remèdes et non de leurs maladies.*' And Wellington: 'All Doctors are more or less *Quacks*!'[8] Emblems of death surround Hogarth's print, *A Consultation of Physicians* [19], 1737, and the sub-title is *Company of Undertakers*. It was advertised as 'Quacks in Consultation' and though the three notorious quacks are separated from the more orthodox, these, by implication, are also charlatans. The three are Mrs Mapp, the famous bone-setter, between 'Chevalier' John Taylor, the oculist (a skilled operator but a bombastic advertiser; Johnson called him 'an instance how far impudence could carry ignorance'), on her right, Joshua – 'Spot' – Ward, famous for his pill, who appears in the death scene in *The Harlot's Progress* and was patronized by George II.*

'The physicians in Hogarth's prints are not caricatures,' wrote Sir John Hawkins, 'the full dress with the sword and great tye-wig, and the hat under the arm, and the doctors in consultation, each smelling to a gold-headed cane . . . are pictures of real life in his time' [Johnson's early days in London].[9]

In the eighteenth century as in the seventeenth there were in England physicians – Fellows of the Royal College with degrees from Oxford or Cambridge, few and dignified; Licentiates of the College with degrees from Scottish or continental universities; surgeons who, till 1745, belonged to the Company of Barber-Surgeons. Lowest in the hierarchy were the apothecaries, who sold medicines, sometimes kept shops and like the surgeons had served an apprenticeship and belonged to a City company: they were an inferior – but often more knowledgeable – kind of doctor. Throughout the century the surgeons and apothecaries were improving their training and prestige; the physicians, *as a body*, were an oligarchy, concerned mainly with their own dignity and their control over the lower 'orders' of the profession. They claimed to be gentlemen with a classical education, while the Licentiates had (socially) inferior degrees or diplomas. It was against the Licentiates that Dr William Browne, in 1753, asserted a rule of the College 'calling for those only to be Fellows, who by being graduates of Oxford and Cambridge, besides approved learning and morals, have also agreeable and sociable dispositions'.[10] The fact was that the Oxbridge medical education was markedly inferior to that of the other universities – except that a degree could be purchased from St Andrews, which had no medical school. The College was engaged in re-elaborating the system of Galen (second century A.D.): 'diagnosis became more and more dogmatic, authoritarian and erratic, and treatment more and more violent, authoritarian and dangerous'.[11]

Feuds and jealousies and demarcation disputes raged in the Press and the law courts, with crises that the print shops treated as 'battles'. In theory, the physician never used his hands – except, I suppose, for pulse-feeling; the surgeon treated his patients by the hands only: he operated and applied blisters and salves, etc. – external and internal treatment were separate provinces. The distinction became increasingly difficult to maintain in practice. We see this aspect of the profession in *Passages from the Diary of a late Physician.** The young doctor (Cambridge degree), who had starved for four years of London practice, is watching the mêlée of carriages leaving the Opera House. There is a call for a doctor – a young lady's shoulder dislocated, arm lacerated. He gets into the family coach, sends a servant for a famous surgeon (Cline), watches him dress the arm, etc. 'I then prescribed what medicines were necessary – received a cheque of ten guineas from the Earl', and was asked to call next morning. His fortune was made.

The apothecaries' feud with the College was of long standing. They won a decisive victory after a protracted lawsuit (1701–4) by a decision in the Lords, on the ground of public interest, that they might prescribe as well as dispense (they had long been doing so). Increasingly, they turned to medical practice and away from the shop which the chemists and druggists – strongly resisted by the apothecaries – were taking over. They were now launched on the course that was to make them general practitioners,† while the physicians would evolve into consultants, though the term dates from the later nineteenth century.

As a matter of prestige as well as ethics it was a tradition of the College that high fees should be taken from the rich, none from the poor. The standard fee was a guinea, but much more was expected from 'the Great'. Dr Richard Bathurst (d. 1762), unsuccessful in London, confessed to his friend Johnson that in ten years' practice 'he had never closed his hand on more than a guinea'. There was also, in the earlier part of the century, a custom introduced by Dr Mead (who made a fortune by it) of giving half-guinea consultations to apothecaries in a coffee-house without seeing the patient. Batson's, in Cornhill, was the house of call for doctors, 'who flock together like birds of prey, waiting for carcasses at Batson's'.[12]

Then as now the doctor was debarred from advertisement, the province of the quack, and could publicize himself only by his coach and the semblance at least of prosperity. Many physicians made large fortunes. So did quacks. The physicians' business, according to Hawkins, 'was to be indiscriminately courteous and obsequious to all men, and to appear much abroad and in public places, to increase his acquaintance, and form good connexions, in the doing whereof, a wife . . . that could visit, play at cards and tattle was often times very serviceable.' These are an old man's memories in the 1780s. In 1777 Mrs Thrale recorded: 'One Dr Argent was the last Physician that called on Patients on horseback, and took fees; he was nearly at

---

*He was exempted by special Act of Parliament from the Act of 1748 against the compounding of medicines by the unqualified.

*By Samuel Warren, F.R.S., barrister and best-seller novelist (1830). He had been a medical student in Edinburgh 1826–7.

†The term was first used in the *Medical and Physical Journal* for January 1813, but was not in general use till the mid-century.

the head of his profession; those below him used to walk the town in spatterdashes to look as if they rode sometimes; since then for the last fifty years, no Doctor dreamed of being seen in the streets without his Chariot, but now again my Friend Jebb, though I think he has no less than three Equipages . . . rides very often to look like the gay Fellows about Town. How Times and Fashions change!'[13]

Though medicine was not, like the Church, controlled by patronage, no physician could establish himself without the patronage of well-placed patients. A paper in *The World*[14] relates the sad fate of an able and diligent pupil of the great Boerhaave at Leyden University. Without private means he returned to London to starve, while 'fellow-students who were esteemed very dull fellows' were 'lolling at their ease in warm chariots upon springs'. 'It is much more to the purpose of a physician to have the countenance of a man or woman of quality, than the sagacity even of a Boerhaave. . . .'

The profession acquired deserved discredit over the case of Mrs Tofts (1724–6). This illiterate 'rabbit woman' pretended to give birth to seventeen rabbits and was believed by leading surgeons and physicians. Whiston, Newton's successor as Lucasian Professor at Cambridge, proved in a pamphlet that the 'miracle' fulfilled a prophecy in *Esdras*. Pope wrote to a friend 'I want to know what faith you have in Guildford. All London is divided in factions about it.' Of course there were prints, scornful ones, but not till after her exposure. In Hogarth's *Cunicularii or the Wise men of Godliman* [Godalming] *in Consultation* [20] three credulous surgeons are pilloried. The deception was possible because, for propriety's sake, the accoucheur operated under a covering.

19 A Consultation of Physicians, Hogarth

20 Cunicularii or the Wise men of Godliman in Consultation, Hogarth

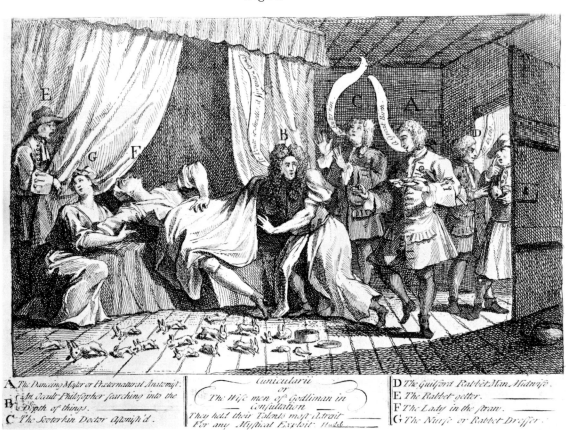

The Law

The lawyer – barrister (counsellor) or attorney – is inevitably a shark and a rogue who strips his clients of their property. In Johnson's *London* it is 'the fell attorney' who 'prowls for prey'. In *The Bench* in 1758 [21], Hogarth pillories, not the dishonesty of lawyers, but the harsh insensitiveness of the law. These are 'character' portraits, contrasted with the caricature heads added in a later state. Like Daumier's *Gens de Justice* they symbolize injustice, negligence and stupidity. The Chief Justice, Willes, holds the pen; on his left sleeps Bathurst, Lord Chancellor (in 1771 as Lord Apsley), and generally regarded as the least efficient Chancellor of the century.

Another aspect of the law, the specious, insinuating orator, is reflected in Counsellor Silvertongue, the evil genius of the Countess in *Marriage à la Mode*. Four barristers, by their callous stinginess, cause the catastrophe in Plate II of Hogarth's *Four Stages of Cruelty* (1751). They have clubbed their threepences for the longest shilling fare in London – from Thavies Inn to Westminster Hall. The over-weighted hackney coach collapses, the wretched horse is moribund but is mercilessly thrashed by Tom Nero, ex-charity-school boy of St Giles's. Representatives of the three learned professions are among the topers in *Midnight Modern Conversation* (p. 42).

As we shall find later, this distrust of lawyers has nothing to do with the severity of the criminal law. These men practise in the civil courts at Westminster Hall, not at the Old Bailey. The attack is on legal chicanery, writs, endless suits leading to the ruin of both parties, debt and imprisonment. In fact, 'Liberty and Property' were invaded. The traditional theme is that of 'a suit of law' by which one litigant gains his suit but loses his country seat, and both are reduced to rags, while the lawyer gets a fortune. This is the subject of a print of 1749 and of a complicated design in 1828 (p. 195) in which the cautionary verses of the early plate are repeated.

Hogarth was fascinated by *The Beggar's Opera*. He painted it (six times) – variants of the prison scene, Macheath between Polly and Lucy – burlesqued it in a print. Ironic contempt for the legal profession is manifest in this 'Newgate pastoral', where the moral code of thieves and highwaymen is identified with that of the governing classes. The professions as well as Ministers are aimed at, especially the law:

> *The gamesters and lawyers are jugglers alike,*
> *If they meddle your all is in danger,*
> *Like gipsies, if once they can finger a souse,*
> *Your pockets they pick, and they pilfer your house,*
> *And give your estate to a stranger.*

When Hannah More saw the play in 1778 she wrote, 'but the best of all was Sir William Ashurst who sat in a side box and was perhaps one of the first judges who ever figured away at the *Beggar's Opera*, that strong and bitter satire against the professions, and especially his.'

Notes to Chapter III

1. *Blecheley Diary* (1765), ed. F.G. Stokes (London: Constable, 1931), p. 53.
2. Thomas Pennant, *London*, 1790, pp. 208–9.
3. J. S. Burn, *History of Fleet Marriages*, 1833; W.C. Sydney, *England and the English in the Eighteenth Century*, 1891, vol. II, Chapter 20.
4. C. Wordsworth, *Social Life at the Universities*, 1874, p. 510.
5. *Cambridge Chronicle*, 1 July 1769, quoted C.H. Cooper, *Annals of Cambridge*, vol. IV, p. 35.
6. *The World*, 19 September 1754.
7. Quoted, C. Wordsworth (see note 4), p. 158.
8. To Mrs Arbuthnot (1822), *Wellington and His Friends*, ed. seventh Duke of Wellington (London: Macmillan, 1965), p. 37.
9. *Life of Johnson*, 1787, p. 238 n.
10. Quoted, E.S. Turner, *Call the Doctor* (London: Michael Joseph, 1958), p. 121.
11. *The Evolution of Medical Practice in Britain*, ed. F.N.L. Poynter (London: Pitman, 1961), p. 29.
12. *Connoisseur*, 31 January 1754.
13. *Thraliana*, ed. K.C. Balderston (Oxford: O.U.P., 1952), p. 35.
14. *The World*, 1 May 1755.

Design'd & Engrav'd by W. Hogarth. The BENCH. Publish'd as the Act directs 4 Sep. 1758.

Of the different meaning of the Words Character, Caracatura and Outrè in Painting and Drawing.
Address'd to the Honble Coll.^s T........d.

21 *The Bench, Hogarth*

39

22 The March to Finchley, Hogarth

4 - Sailors and Soldiers

The jovial devil-may-care sailor on shore belongs chiefly to our second period. He is foreshadowed in Hogarth's sailor on the roof of the coach (p. 52) and we have seen him as the victim of harpies. It is sometimes said that interest in the sailor's life began, in 1748, with Smollett's *Roderick Random*, but both these sailors appeared in 1747. The plight of the discharged soldier or sailor is a recurrent theme. They are usually maimed beggars with at least one peg-leg. The satire is for the hard-hearted public, often represented by a parson, as in *The Pluralist and Old Soldier* by Tim Bobbin (John Collier). This Lancashire production (1762) was published in London and advertised in the London papers in March 1763, when peace with France was at last proclaimed. The thin, ragged, sadly maimed old soldier begs from a fat, arrogant parson, who holds a glass of ale and a pipe. 'Soldier: At Guadeloupe my leg and thigh I lost;/No pension have I, tho' its right I boast;/Your Revce some Charity bestow. Heav'n will pay you double; when you're there you know.'

Unjust promotion in the Navy is attacked in *The Naval Nurse, or Modern Commander* in 1750. An insolent 'Boy Captain' sits in his cabin, giving orders to his 'Nurse', an experienced elderly officer, for the flogging of a sailor.

> *From Mid to Lieutenant Bluff quickly doth rise;*
> *Then next gets command by the aid of a Prize.*
> *By brave Warren* and such our Foes were Opprest*
> *But not by Boy Captains*
> *Just wean'd from the breast.*

Did *Roderick Random*† beget this onslaught? With exceptionally powerful interest boys of eighteen or so sometimes became captains. Hogarth's strange and attractive portrait group of Lord George Graham in his cabin, a breakfast scene with a Negro beating a drum, might pass as a satire on naval officers if we did not know it is nothing of the kind, and was probably painted to commemorate a naval action at Ostend in 1745.‡

The classic satire on the soldiers of George II is Hogarth's *March to Finchley* [22] in 1745. The scene is the north end of Tottenham Court Road, then in the country, between two famous inns that were holiday resorts for Londoners. The turmoil and confusion in which these men begin their march against the invading Scots is a quality of London life immortalized by Hogarth. But, like some other Hogarth prints, it is open to different interpretations. The tradi-

tional one, that it attacks a scene of military indiscipline, depends largely on the doubtful story of George II's indignation at a burlesque of his Guards, the occasion (according to John Ireland) of his pronouncement, 'I hate Boetry and Bainting'. The disorder (in 1745) was more the natural result of such an occasion, in such a place, than it can have seemed to later commentators.* And there is nothing unnatural in the dedication to the King of Prussia: in 1750 Frederick had a European reputation as 'An Encourager of Arts and Sciences'.

This is a patriotic print, against Popery and French spies and Jacobites – there are analogies with *Calais Gate* (1749) and *The Invasion*, Plate II (1756), a care-free recruiting scene where the young fifer reclining against a drum, plays 'God save Great George our King'. The tall Grenadier is beset by contrasted women; one is young, loyal and weeping, she sells patriotic papers, a portrait of Cumberland and 'God save our Noble King' – then, literally, A New Song. The other is a virago and a Papist, a hawker of seditious or disloyal papers. This centre group is said to be a parody of *Hercules between Vice and Virtue* by Rubens – from one of the 'Old-prints from whence he steals Figures for his Design', as his enemies alleged (p. 28).

The men who have passed the turnpike barrier are marching steadily enough towards the first camp on the road to the north. The Foot Guards, some of them, had recently returned from France. When in London they were billetted in public houses, barracks being regarded as tending to military despotism. Discipline was both harsh and lax. The men could add to their pay by civilian jobs – for instance, when there was a glut of coal ships in the Thames they acted as coal-heavers. The drummer and the boy-fifer *may* be merely adding to the noise or drowning the din, but as I see them, they express martial ardour or regimental duty resisting the pull of civil life. Behind the drummer a Frenchman is secretly conveying a paper to a frenchified Scot. It may be significant that the hopelessly drunken soldier and the young man caressing the milk-girl are both officers, as their laced hats show.

The setting is a mixture of realism and fantasy. In front of the Adam and Eve is a platform on which a boxing match is being watched by a crowd, among them the blind Lord Albemarle Bertie. There was such a platform, and, till recently, Broughton had displayed himself there as 'Public Bruiser'. Hogarth has transformed the King's Head into a brothel to which Mother Douglas has transferred her Covent Garden establishment. She leans from the nearest ground-floor window, her girls fill the other windows, making a most effective pattern. The sign, the head of Charles II, is doubly appropriate; Tottenham Manor (the whole district) had descended from Barbara Villiers to the Fitzroy family – hence the future Fitzroy Square. Details of this large print (17 × 22 ins.) are inevitably lost in reproduction. The country village of Highgate is on the sky-line.

---

*Sir Peter Warren (1703–52) naval commander at the taking of Louisbourg in 1745.

†Captain Whipple in *Roderick Random* is supposed to be Lord Henry Paulet (sixth Duke of Bolton).

‡In the Maritime Museum, Greenwich.

---

* John Ireland, *Hogarth Illustrated*, 1791. John Nichols, *Biographical Anecdotes of William Hogarth and a Catalogue of his Works* (by Nichols, George Steevens and others), 1781.

23 *A Midnight Modern Conversation, Hogarth*

24 *A Rake's Progress, Pl. VI, Hogarth*

All the plates of the *Four Times of the Day* in 1738 are vivid renderings of the London scene, the people, the atmosphere, the incidents, from morning to night. *Evening* [25], not the best of the series, was the begetter of a succession of illustrations of that most characteristic feature of London life, especially on Sunday, the resort of Londoners – 'cits' – to the inns, ale-houses, taverns and tea-gardens of the suburbs to enjoy country air, a topic that belongs pictorially – this print excepted – to the later part of the century, when there are variations on the theme of an overbearing wife, a henpecked husband who carries or drags a child, all exhausted by their outing. Here, the scene is Islington by the New River (where Londoners optimistically fished) and the Sir Hugh Middleton tavern, where the usual smoking and drinking at close quarters is going on. A cow is being milked and her horns are placed to convey the traditional gibe that cits were cuckolds.

In any view of eighteenth-century London there should be a tavern scene and a gaming house. For the first there is Hogarth's *A Midnight Modern Conversation* [23], 1733. In England it was pirated and copied. It decorated punch-bowls and tea-cups and elicited a lengthy description in verse. It was the origin of a play at Covent Garden 'taken from Hogarth's celebrated print'. There were copies in France and Germany, where travelling showmen exhibited (1786) wax figures of the characters. The verses on one of the French copies make it an illustration of national character: '*Chaque peuple a son goût*' – the Frenchman sings, the Italian has his concert, the German the pleasures of the table, for the Englishman '*sa Ponche et la Pipe*'. The vivid characterization fascinated, and though Hogarth asserted 'think not to find one meant resemblance here', it does contain portraits.

One only of the topers is completely master of himself, and that is the parson with a brimming punch-bowl, Cornelius Ford, whom no amount of liquor could disturb. He is remarkable as a first cousin (and early friend) of Johnson and also a friend of Lord Chesterfield.[1] The story of his ghost appearing in the Hummums (a bagnio), Covent Garden (where he died) was told by Johnson to Boswell. Standing beside him is a tipsy tobacconist whose singing of bacchanalian songs admitted him to tavern society. On his left is a feeble beau – beaux (in satire) were commonly rakish and derelict. A barrister, noted for a satanic smile and a diabolical squint, sits on Ford's right. A military officer falls prone, while a physician tipsily pours liquor over him. The scene is a well-furnished club room at a tavern. Taverns were divided between those that admitted women – when they verged on brothels – and those that

did not. It is in a room in the famous Rose tavern next Drury Lane theatre (respectable enough in the day-time) that Tom Rakewell revels with harlots after a street brawl in which he has captured a watchman's lantern and staff (*Rake's Progress*, III, 1735).

The gaming-house scene [24] is the sixth plate of that series. Tom stakes and loses the fortune he got with his elderly wife. The place is White's Chocolate House, not yet a club, and (till 1736) open to all who could pay. Swift called it 'the common rendezvous of infamous sharpers and noble cullies'. There is a noble cully in the foreground, borrowing from a Jew. A highwayman broods over the fire. The gamesters are so absorbed that they have not noticed that the room is ablaze, near the ceiling, and a watchman rushes in to give the alarm. This is the fire that broke out at four a.m. (28 April 1733) and destroyed the building and two other houses. It started in a room called Hell, which is clearly the one depicted.

After the fire, Arthur, the proprietor, advertised that he had moved to another house in St James's Street. There, as White's (or Arthur's) the place flourished (and flourishes) as a club, at first for fashionable gamesters – one blackball to exclude. In 1756, Horace Walpole and his friends designed a satirical coat of arms for the club with emblems of gaming: card-table, hazard-table, dice, with a white ball (argent) for election; it was engraved by Grignon [27], copied and widely circulated. The supporters are an old knave of clubs (dexter) and a young one, for the Old and Young Clubs. The punning Latin motto implies play with cogged dice. Lord Chesterfield, who lived at White's, 'gaming and pronouncing witticisms among the boys of quality',[2] told his son, 'a member of a gaming club should be a cheat or he will soon be a beggar'.

Another gaming scene was the cockfight which long survived other forms of brutal sport (survives to this day, or till recently, in Cumberland), and was a favourite diversion of all classes in town and country. In *The Cockpit* [26], 1759, Hogarth records the tense and wild excitement that prevailed. The place is the Old Cockpit in Birdcage Walk, St James's Park. The characters are from high life and low life – aristocrats, jockeys, butchers, thieves, a chimney sweep. A Frenchman, wearing the Order of St Louis, watches with contemptuous interest. The air is filled with the clamour of shouted bets. 'The noise is terrible', wrote a French visitor in 1724, 'and it is impossible to hear yourself speak unless you shout.' The central figure with a pile of bank-notes is Lord Albemarle Bertie, though blind, an addict of cockfights and prize-fights (he appears in *The March to Finchley*). The shadow on the little arena is from

This Proof was Delivered by Mr. Baron to Mr. Hogarth, & it being told him, this boy has no Apparent Cause to Wimper, he put in his Sister, threatning him to deliver his Gingerbread Sling, now he put in Tears. The Character Hogarth, altered where he is, Crying

Engraved by Mr. Baron price 2 shillings.

25 *Evening* (*The Four Times of the Day, Pl. III*), Hogarth

44

26 The Cockpit, Hogarth

27 Cog it Amor Nummi, C. Grignon

a man who has been hoisted in a basket for not paying his debts; he tries to pawn his watch.

A most characteristic manifestation of London turbulence was Tyburn Fair, which came eight times a year. It was in fact treated as a public holiday. Tradesmen reminded their customers 'that will be a hanging-day, my men will not be at work'.[3] In pl. XI to *Industry and Idleness* [28], 1747, the idle 'prentice is hanged at Tyburn. The macabre procession has reached its destination by the north-east corner of Hyde Park. This is a documentary print, charged with realism and social comment. The permanent 'triple tree' (soon to be removed) and the stand for spectators are in the background of this scene of low life. The ballad-singer with a swaddled infant bawls a 'last dying Speech' (p. 73). The Ordinary of Newgate looks from his coach, portly and indifferent; Tom Idle is exhorted and comforted by 'the

The IDLE 'PRENTICE Executed at Tyburn.

Proverbs CHAP: I. Verf: 27.28.
When fear cometh as desolation, and their
destruction cometh as a Whirlwind; when
distress cometh upon them, then they shall
call upon God, but he will not answer.

Design'd & Engrav'd by W.m Hogarth.   Plate II   Publish'd according to Act of Parliam.t 30. 1747.

28 The Idle 'Prentice executed at Tyburn (Industry and Idleness, Pl. XI). Hogarth

Prisoners' Chaplain', who was Silas Told, a Methodist. Though obstructed by the Ordinary, he ministered selflessly to the prisoners in Newgate and elsewhere. Wesley records in his *Journal* (1778): 'I buried what was mortal of honest Silas Told. For many years he attended the malefactors in Newgate without fee or reward; and I suppose no man for this hundred years has been so successful in this melancholy office. God had given him peculiar gifts for it; and he had amazing success therein.'[4]

In the print the man holding a dog by the tail is about to hurl it at Told. In his autobiography Told mentions a fight between the 'surgeons' mob' (p. 95) and a party of sailors, and adds, 'There was a very crowded concourse, among them were numberless gin and gingerbread sellers, accompanied by pickpockets . . .'. Here, the chief gingerbread vendor is the famous Tiddy Doll. Gillray was to caricature Napoleon in 1806 as Tiddy Doll, baking gingerbread kings and queens, while Talleyrand, the baker's man, mixed the dough.

Hogarth's plate was a protest, one of many, against this saturnalia, an education in brutality and an encouragement to crime. It was not stopped till 1783 and then only because it had become intolerable to the new houses near by. This series is the most didactic of Hogarth's prints. Like Lillo's play, *Barnwell*, on which it was partly based, it was a warning against an ever-present danger. Apprentices *were* seduced by prostitutes, *did* rob their masters, *did* come to bad ends. Francis Place (b. 1771), a model of industry, belonged to a club of Fleet Street apprentices. He records that out of twenty-one, only himself and one other (who married his master's daughter, turned Methodist, and became a street preacher) made their way in the world respectably. One was transported for a robbery, another hanged for a murder he did not commit: as he was engaged in the then equally capital crime of burglary he could not prove an alibi.[5]

Those who died at Tyburn usually said (or the Ordinary of Newgate said for them) that they began their downfall by breaking the Sabbath. Tom Idle does this in a blatant way by gambling on a tombstone outside a church while the congregation enters, with youths whom the moralizing Trusler calls 'the off-scourings of the people, these meanest of the human species, shoe-blacks, chimney sweepers, &c'.[6] This [29] is a typical low-life scene. It is interesting to compare the miserable shoe-black with his successor in

1824 (p. 200), not to speak of the few survivors in this London occupation.

The promenade in St James's Park was one of the sights of the town. It was a ritual that took place in the morning, that is, before dinner, the dinner-hour advancing during the century from two or three to five or six or later, lateness being always a mark of superior fashion and status.* '*Ce qui en gate beaucoup le promenade,*' wrote Baron Pollnitz in the thirties, '*est que le monde y est fort mêlée, le livrée* [servants] *et le plus vil peuple s'y promène, de même que les gens de condition.*' We have seen that the unrestrained mixture of classes and the later attempts at restraint, appeared to have deep social significance. Park scenes were a favourite subject for the caricaturist.

The London streets live in Hogarth's prints. Less well known is this scene at Charing Cross [30], 1750, allegedly 'from fact': *Stand Coachman, or the Haughty Lady well fitted.* The tale is told in verse. A lady's coach outside a 'Toy Shop' obstructed the footway. A passer-by asked the coachman to move on; being 'rudely denied', he opened the carriage door and 'very genteely went through'. 'The Mobb', much amused, and bespattered and dirty, began to march through. This was too much for the lady and she ordered the coachman to drive on: ''Tis hoped the fair Ladies from hence will beware,/How they stop a Free Passage with such Haughty Air.' Typical street characters are here; the chimney sweep, a French *frizeur* with a wig-box, a porter with his load, a Savoyard girl with her hurdy-gurdy on her back.

*Madam Bombazine (p. 15) dined aggressively at one. Boswell in 1775 met a London mercer in Durham who said '"to a man accustomed to dine between two and three, it seemed strange to dine at one, as they do in this country." . . . He looked big as one accustomed to dine between two and three. . . . How *poor* would he seem to a fashionable man in London who dines between four and five', Boswell, *The Ominous Years*, ed. C. Ryskamp and F. A. Pottle (London: Heinemann, 1963), p. 79. The dandies (p. 164) affected very late hours.

Notes to Chapter V

1. J. L. Clifford, *Young Samuel Johnson* (London: Heinemann, 1955), pp. 76ff., etc.
2. H. Walpole, *Memoirs of the Reign of George II*, 1847, vol. I, p. 51.
3. Henry Angelo, *Reminiscences*, 1904, vol. I, p. 367.
4. Quoted, A. Dobson, *Eighteenth Century Vignettes* (Oxford: O.U.P., 2nd Series), 1923, p. 176.
5. Francis Place, Autobiography, British Museum Add. MSS. 35142.
6. J. Trusler, *Hogarth Moralised*, 1768.

29 The Idle 'Prentice at Play in the Church Yard during Divine Service (Industry and Idleness, Pl. III), Hogarth

LONDON.Printed for BOWLES & CARVER.   No.69 ST.PAUL'S CHURCH YARD,2 Oct.

AN ORDINARY ON SUNDAY'S AT TWO O'CLOCK.

I *An Ordinary on Sundays at Two O'Clock, after Dighton*

II *John Gilpin's return from Ware, after Dighton*

JOHN GILPIN's return from WARE.

III *A Rich Privateer brought safe into Port, by Two First Rates, after Dighton*

A RICH PRIVATEER brought safe into PORT, by TWO FIRST RATES.

STAND COACHMAN, OR THE HAUGHTY LADY WELL FITTED.

30 Stand Coachman, or the Haughty Lady well fitted, anon.

31 A Harlot's Progress, Pl. I, Hogarth

6 - Travel

To contemporaries the speed and amenities of travel were the yardstick of social progress. Improvement was progressive, but partial and local – more turnpikes, lighter coaches. Hogarth has immortalized the arrival of the country wagon at its London headquarters and the departure of the stage-coach from a country inn. In Plate I of *A Harlot's Progress* [31], 1732, the York wagon has just arrived at the Bell Inn in Wood Street. Some girls are still inside, still holding on to a rope or bar which was a defence against murderous jolts. The wagon was the slowest and cheapest form of travel, where passengers sat or lay among the goods and the wagoner rode or walked beside his team of six or eight (in single file till the roads were improved). If these girls have come the whole distance they have been many days on the road, at a cost of about a shilling a day, which meant a halfpenny a mile,* the fare sometimes more, occasionally less. Their nights have been spent in the wagon or in an out-house or barn: the humblest class of traveller was seldom admitted to the inns where the wagon put up, and could seldom afford the cost. This first scene in the downfall of Moll Hackabout was one often acted in real life. Mistresses in want of servants met the wagons in search of country girls, bawds took advantage of the custom. Here

---

*To multiply this sum in terms of current values would be fallacious. See E.V. Morgan, *The Study of Prices and the Value of Money*, Historical Association, 1952. But for most of the century the agricultural labourer earned 1s. a day or less, the London artisan considerably more. The weekly rent of a miserable London attic, 'ready furnished', 1s. 6d. The cheapest theatre seat (top gallery) 1s. Against this the physician's guinea (and a guinea a mile for travelling outside his radius) seems enormous.

32 *The Stage Coach or Country Inn Yard*, Hogarth

Price one Shilling.   Design'd and Engrav'd by W. Hogarth. ——— Publish'd According to Act of Parliament. 1747.

the bawd addressing Moll is the notorious Mother Needham; her employer, Colonel Charteris, watches from the doorway (both were recently dead). It was also the practice of women who had lost their character in London to make a short trip into town in a wagon, and so pass as a country girl. Miss Williams, the essentially virtuous courtesan in *Roderick Random*, practises what Smollett calls this 'honest deceit' with complete success.

In *The Stage Coach or Country Inn Yard* [32] in 1747 Hogarth depicts a galleried courtyard much like those of the Southwark inns that were the headquarters of traffic to the southern counties. The heavy coach of the period is about to leave the Angel (undisturbed by an election procession). It is hung on leather straps (steel springs for stages were a novelty in 1754). The dark interior will hold five, perhaps six. The little hunch-backed postillion will ride the off-leader. Those travelling on the outside could choose between the dangers and discomforts of the roof and of the basket. A cheerful sailor who has been round the world with Anson – his bundle is labelled 'of the Centurion' – is on the roof (only a sailor could feel safe there), with a morose French footman. An old woman smokes a pipe in the basket. As late as 1782 Parson Moritz found the roof a terrifying experience, but the basket even worse from the battering of trunks and packages. Tate Wilkinson the actor relates that in 1758 he failed to get a place in a coach, the insides being obstinate against his being 'squeezed in'. He tried the box; the coachman saved him from disaster, and he was 'chucked into the basket ... it was most truly dreadful, and made me suffer almost equal to the sea-sickness'.[1]

The pace of the heavy coach was little better than that of the wagon – twenty-eight or twenty-nine miles a day; the fare something like twopence a mile (later in the century it was more, but faster travel reduced costs), half-price for outsides, who were usually admitted only to the kitchens of the coaching inns. The wagon might well be more comfortable, passengers lying in the straw and looking out under the tilt (as Gainsborough did with satisfaction on one occasion). But the choice was governed by the social hierarchy. The insides would refuse entrance to an outside on grounds of class; Joseph in *Joseph Andrews* was so excluded, in savage weather, because he was a footman. The gentry, if possible, avoided the stage-coach and travelled expensively by post-chaise or in their own carriages.

Pennant, in 1782, described the ordeal of a journey in March 1739 from Chester to London – the main route from Ireland – in a stage, 'then no despicable vehicle for country gentlemen. The first day, with much labour ... we got to Whitchurch, twenty miles; the next day, to the Welsh Harp; the third, to Coventry; the fourth, to Northampton;

the fifth, to Dunstable, and as a wonderful effort, on the last to London before the commencement of night. The strain of six good horses, sometimes eight, drew us through the marshes. ... We were commonly out before day, and late at night; and in the depth of winter proportionately later. The single gentlemen rode post through thick and thin ... their enervated posterity sleep away their rapid passage in easy chaises fitted for the conveyance of the soft inhabitants of Sybaris.'

The fashionable coaches of 1750 and the outstanding sensation of the day are illustrated in a satirical print on the London earthquake. A slight shock was followed, exactly four weeks later, by a second shock, rather less slight – crockery was broken. Earthquake literature was poured out, sermons were preached about divine vengeance on a corrupt city; masquerades were denounced. Whiston, undeterred by the failure of the comet of 1712 to destroy the globe as he had foretold, again produced a prophecy, this time from *Revelation*: there would be a third shock of great violence and destructiveness – place not named, but clearly London. Then, when nerves were on edge, an insane Life Guardsman broadcast a prophecy that at a further four weeks' interval (on 4 April) London would be destroyed. Panic followed with a stampede from the town. Walpole wrote (2 April) 'that within three days seven hundred and thirty coaches have been counted passing Hyde Park Corner'. It was said that 'perhaps 100,000 people left their homes to take refuge in Hyde Park'.[2] Lodgings became unobtainable in places of refuge. All the boats on the river were hired, women ordered 'earthquake gowns'. What would the panic have been like if the scare had happened *after* the Lisbon earthquake of 1755? The panic-stricken, with their 'guilty consciences', were harshly treated (after the event) by the Press. They were ridiculed in *The Military Prophet or a Flight from Providence* ... advertised as showing 'Several of the Principal Characters drawn from the Life' [33]. The stream of coaches passing along Piccadilly at the top of St James's Street is going in the wrong direction – the engraver has not reversed the drawing.* The Guardsman is on horseback (on 3 April he had been sent to Bedlam); and a fat old woman is selling broadsides, 'The Guardsman's Prophecy'.

*The drawing, by J.P.Boitard, is in the collection of Mr and Mrs Paul Mellon, to whom I am indebted for a photograph, not reproduced; the carriages drive westwards, but the architectural background is omitted.

Notes to Chapter VI
1. T.Wilkinson, *Memoirs*, 1790, pp. 125–7.
2. *General Evening Post*, 17–19 April, quoted T.Kendrick, *The Lisbon Earthquake* (London: Methuen, 1956), pp. 13–14.

33 The Military Prophet or a Flight from Providence, L. P. Boitard

II GEORGE III

7 · After Hogarth

In the 1760s there was an unusually abrupt shift in the pattern of graphic satire, though Hogarth's prints continued to be sold, reissued, copied, imitated and commented on. The sixties are an accepted watershed in English life; for the satirical print the change was from the Hogarthian engraving to the light etching sold plain or coloured. Caricature had become a fashionable hobby and the influence of the amateur made for the acceptance of incorrect but expressive drawing (Max Beerbohm was to be the classic example). Mat Darly, drawing-master, print-seller, designer of *chinoiseries* and caricaturist, dominated the transition from Hogarth to Gillray and Rowlandson. After 1766 he abandoned political prints and concentrated on social subjects, chiefly after amateurs, his pupils and others. He etched and published their designs, first separately, then in series or 'volumes' which he called 'Macaronies, Characters and Caricatures' and prefaced as 'Comic Humour, Caricatures, &c. in a series of Drol Prints, consisting of Heads, Figures, Conversations, and Satires upon the Follies of the Age Design'd by several Ladies, Gentlemen, and the most Humourous Artists, &c.'. His shop, 39 Strand (formerly the Acorn), appeared in the series as *The Macaroni Print Shop* in 1772. About 1773 he held an exhibition of the drawings for these prints, and the catalogue records 233 exhibits; 106 are by 'Gentlemen', 74 by 'Ladies', 27 by 'Artists', 26 unspecified. All are anonymous.

The prestige of the amateur, in art as in letters, was excessive, as Walpole's letters often reveal, and still more his *Anecdotes of Painting* where he calls Bunbury* (a man of fashion) 'the second Hogarth, and first imitator who ever fully equalled his original'. From this time until the age of illustrated journalism, amateurs provided the print shops with sketches, descriptions and 'hints'. Gillray has a claim to be the first English professional caricaturist. Many painters, engravers, illustrators, watercolourists, topographers, drawing-masters, produced caricatures (even Reynolds, though not for the print shops).

* His reputation is illustrated by the advertisement (1788) of a Plymouth bookseller, of engravings from 'great masters': Guido, Rembrandt, L. de Vinci, Raphael, S. Rosa, Claude, Sir J. Reynolds, Bunbury, Cipriani, Gainsborough, Cosway, &c.' E. George, *Life and Death of Benjamin Robert Haydon* (Oxford: O.U.P., 1967), p. 12.

The transition from Hogarth to Rowlandson and Gillray was bridged also by the humorous mezzotint, advertised as '. . . (commonly called Postures) one shilling plain, two shillings coloured'. From the later sixties to about 1795* they were issued in a numbered series by the ancient Bowles 'Map & Print Warehouse' in St Paul's Churchyard. At first many were after paintings by Collett, a follower of Hogarth who died in 1780. From then or earlier Robert Dighton was the (unacknowledged) artist; he provided watercolours closely followed by the engraver. His 'posture', *A Real Scene in St Paul's Church Yard, on a Windy Day* in 1783 [frontispiece], shows the window exactly as in a mezzotint of ten years earlier, though displaying different prints. Another Bowles shop, John's in Cornhill, shared in the enterprise and is the subject of a posture. Other City shops published, less consistently, similar but inferior mezzotints. All differed from the prints of Darly and his successors in the more fashionable part of the town in being seldom personal and wholly professional.

The dwindling importance of Darly's prints after 1778 and their disappearance in 1781 coincide with the early work of Rowlandson and Gillray and the golden age of English caricature, at its peak in the last two decades of the century and slow to decline. After Darly gave up, the leaders were Fores in Piccadilly, Holland, first in Drury Lane and then in Oxford Street, and Hannah Humphrey, though she did not rival the others till her exclusive relation with Gillray about 1791, or surpass them till she moved in 1797 from Bond Street to the famous shop in St James's Street. These shops were 'lounges', their owners were characters. The morning routine of a man of fashion, according to a German visitor in 1803, included a visit to Tattersall's and to the caricature shops to see the latest caricatures. From about 1784 to 1794 the first two held caricature exhibitions, entrance a shilling. Young Richard Newton did a large watercolour of Holland's show, with a self-portrait, his own designs prominently displayed, and the Duchess of Devonshire and her sister in the foreground. In prints, these ladies personify high life at its most attractive.

*They were often reissued with obliterated or altered dates.

The Conftant Couple

34 *The Constant Couple, anon.*

35 *A Milliner's Shop, (?) Kingsbury*

A MILLINER's SHOP.

8 - High Life and Low Life

London's extremes of wealth and poverty, the glitter and the squalor, were reflected in prints of high and low life. The former usually connotes the fashionable world, to which George III and his family – with the important exception of the Prince – did not belong. Indeed, it was his unfashionable domesticity that exposed him to the wits and the print shops, though it endeared him (from 1783) to most of his subjects. Peter Pindar (John Wolcot), in a flow of verse satires for a decade from 1785, was the chief inspiration to caricaturists of the Court. These were highly disrespectful and extremely popular. Easy money was his object; the King, he said, had been a good subject to him, and he a bad one to the King. The exposure of the royal family to ribald comment was one of the ways in which England was unique – it was of course a manifestation of Liberty. 'The misfortune is,' George III wrote to his eldest son for his eighteenth birthday, 'that in other countries national pride makes the inhabitants wish to paint their Prince in the most favourable light, and consequently be silent upon any indiscretion; but here most persons, if not concerned in laying ungrounded blame, are ready to trumpet any speck they can find.'[1] The Prince's attachment to Fox, his Opposition politics, the dissipations and debts which estranged him from his father, were important both socially and politically, with Devonshire House as the centre of a brilliant Whig society.

George III's domestic parsimony and his admirable farming activities in Windsor Great Park, overlapping topics, together with his manner of speech and love of asking questions ('What! What!'), were favourite themes. The first of many plates of the royal pair as a farmer and his wife was *The Constant Couple* [34], 1786, the title taken from Farquhar's play. *A Milliner's Shop* [35], 1787, is based on Peter Pindar's *Ode upon Ode* (satirizing the Laureate's annual Birthday production). In this Windsor scene the Queen is cheapening tape, with one of the princesses and the King. The excellent view of a shop interior also ridicules the eccentricities of fashion in 1785–6.

Gillray made some noted contributions to the theme of royal parsimony. The move to boycott sugar as a protest against the slave trade was the opportunity for this tea-table scene in 1792, *Anti-Saccharites – or – John Bull and his Family leaving off the use of Sugar* [36], an excuse to the Queen for petty savings. The six princesses are there, sulky and resentful, ages from eight to fifteen. 'O my dear Creatures do but Taste it! You can't think how nice it is without Sugar: – and then, consider how much Work you'll save the poor Blackeemoors . . . and above all, remember how much expence it will save your poor Papa! . . .'

From the domesticities of Kew and Windsor to the hectic world of St James's is to return to the Macaronies who dominated the print shops and the magazines from about 1770 to 1773. In the prints they are of all ranks, the notorieties of the day. There were *The Turf Macaroni* (the Duke of Grafton) and *The Grub Street Macaroni* (p. 126). Banks (the future Sir Joseph, President of the Royal Society), was in the public eye in 1772 and appears twice. He is *The Botanic Macaroni* and *The Fly Catching Macaroni* [37]: striding from Pole to Pole, he pursues a butterfly, symbol of idle frivolity, and is given ass's ears and a Macaroni hair-do. He had been with Cook to the South Seas (1768–70) and had recently returned from his expedition to Iceland with a valuable collection of plants and insects. The real Macaronies were travelled, Italianate young men who by 1764 had formed a 'Subscription Table' at Almack's: 'the younger and gayer sort of our nobility and gentry, who at the same time that they gave into the business of eating went equally into the extravagance of dress; the word Macaroni then changed its meaning to that of a person who exceeded the ordinary bounds of fashion and is now . . . a term of reproach to all ranks of people who fall into absurdity.'[2] It was claimed in 1773 that they had been laughed out of existence by pen and pencil.[3] At all events, after 1774 the vogue had passed. 'They have lost all their money and credit and ruin nobody but their tailors', Walpole wrote on 14 February 1774. The word survived for an effeminate fop. 'You are a Macaroni, you cannot ride', Boswell told Johnson to prod him into activity on their Highland journey.

Macaroni dress was a last flare-up of extravagant male attire before the soberer fashions of the 1780s. Its chief features were a huge queue of powdered (false) hair; gay, embroidered silks, short coat, tight sleeves and a nosegay [38]. There are obvious analogies and striking contrasts with the dandies of the Regency. Unlike their successors, the Macaronies claimed to be *cognoscenti* and arbiters of taste in 'polite learning and genteel sciences'. They had returned from the Grand Tour: a few of the dandies from the Peninsula and Waterloo. But the chief Macaroni activity was gaming for high stakes. Charles Fox, in his blue hair powder and red-heeled shoes was the Macaroni *par excellence* after his return from Italy in 1768 (in a print he is *The Original Macaroni*). He and his elder brother Stephen are almost certainly prominent in *The Macaroni Cauldron* [39], 1772, and the scene is clearly at Almack's. The evolution of the club has made them more of a piece than the gamesters at White's in 1733 (p. 43). All are young men of fashion. 'The gaming at Almack's which has taken the *pas* of

36 *Anti-Saccharites – or – John Bull and his Family leaving off the use of Sugar, Gillray*

White's,' Walpole wrote in 1770, 'is worthy the decline of the empire, or commonwealth, which you please.' They are dressed for all-night play, wearing greatcoats (they turned these inside out for luck), conical caps to shade their eyes and cover their toupées. When Sir Matthew Mite,* Foote's *Nabob* (Haymarket, 29 February 1772), returned from India with a vast ill-gotten fortune to buy himself into English society, he acquired a Macaroni coat for the hazard table and hired a waiter from Almack's to teach him to throw dice in a dashing fashionable manner. Almack's was taken over by Brooks, wine-merchant and money-lender, in 1778 and removed from Pall Mall to St James's Street, where, like White's, it still flourishes. The club element gained at the expense of its casino character, but (as in other clubs) play remained very high.

All classes gamed, especially the high and the low: 'my lord and the chairman are upon a level in their amusements, except that his lordship is losing his estate with great temper and good-breeding at White's, and the chairman beggaring his family with oaths and curses in a night-cellar'.[4] Women were inveterate card-players and many played deep. 'Conversation among people of fashion,' wrote Cowper, 'is almost annihilated by universal card-playing, insomuch that I have heard it given as a reason, why it is impossible for our present writers to succeed in the dialogue of genteel comedy, that the people of quality scarce ever meet but to game.'[5]

The enormous gaming debts of the Duchess of Devonshire brought her endless misery and anxiety. Rowlandson's watercolour purports to represent a faro table at Devonshire House [40]. Other women of fashion kept faro tables as a source of income (the holder of the bank was bound to win). 'Faro goes on as briskly as ever,' Storer wrote: 'those who have not fortune enough of their own . . . have recourse to this profitable game. The ladies are all embarked in banks . . . Lady Archer, Mrs Hobart . . . are avowed bankers; others, I suppose, are secretly concerned.'[6] *Modern Hospitality, – or – A Friendly Party in High Life*, 1792, is Gillray's rendering of a faro table where the chief ladies are this notorious pair, and the players include Fox and the Prince. Lady Archer, the dealer, is the dominant figure, triumphant and rapacious; the fat Mrs Hobart is angry and defeated. Gillray apostrophizes the gaming ladies: '. . . O Woman! Woman! everlasting is your power over us, for in youth you charm our hearts, and in after years you charm away our purse.' Ageing harpies in fact. Mrs Hobart (Lady Buckinghamshire from 1793) was accused of fleecing 'the unfledged ensigns of the Guards and those emigrés from France whose slender hoards are not utterly exhausted'.[7]

Gillray's *Exaltation of Faro's Daughters* in 1796 shows Lady Archer and Lady Buckinghamshire weeping angrily in the pillory. Lord Kenyon, in a civil case between two publicans over a gaming debt, had just deplored the prevalence of gaming and wished for 'the punishment of the

---

*Probably (though Foote denied it) General Richard Smith, whose father reputedly kept a little cheesemonger's shop in Jermyn Street. Blackballed for Almack's, member of Brooks's in 1779.

The FLY CATCHING MACARONI 1772
I rove from Pole to Pole, you ask me why,
I tell you Truth, to catch a _____ Fly.
Sir Jos. Banks.

37 *The Fly Catching Macaroni (Joseph Banks), M. Darly*

38 *The Lilly Macaroni (the Earl of Ancrum, afterwards fifth Marquis of Lothian), M. Darly*

THE *LILLY MACARONI.*
Pub.'accor.' to Act of Parl.' by M. Darly 39 Strand Nov.' 13 1771.

Some muffled, like the witches in Macbeth,
Brood o'er the magic circle, pale as death!
Others, the Cauldron go about — about —
And ruin enters as the fates run out!

THE MACARONI
CAULDRON.

Bubble, bubble,
Toil and trouble,
Passions burn,
And bets are doubled!
Double, double,
Toil and trouble,
Passions burn,
And all is bubble!

Britons were ne'er enslaved by evil pow'rs;
To peace, and wooded love, they gave their midnight hours;
From Slumbers pure, no rattling dice can wake 'em;
Who make the laws were never known to Break 'em.

39 *The Macaroni Cauldron*, M. Darly

highest ranks of society'. 'If any prosecutions are fairly brought before me, and the parties are justly convicted, though they should be the first ladies in the land, they shall certainly exhibit themselves in the pillory.' What he meant is unclear: the pillory was not a penalty for gaming. Soon after this, a faro bank of five hundred guineas was stolen from Lord Buckinghamshire's house; two footmen, discharged on suspicion, informed against four ladies for playing at faro, doubtless hoping for punishment *à la* Kenyon. Fines were imposed at a police court, despite protests against 'a new mode of peculation'. The usual crop of prints followed, and in Gillray's *Discipline à la Kenyon* [41], 1797, the judge is flogging Lady Bucks at the cart's tail (flogging for women had been abolished in 1791), while two others stand in a pillory assailed by a mob. Gillray's lash is for Kenyon as well as for his victims.

Isaac Cruikshank's contribution was *Dividing the Spoil!!* [42]: two scenes, one in 'St James's', the other in 'St Giles's'. Four women, dominated by Ladies Archer and Buckinghamshire, divide their faro bank winnings (the sword must mean the ruin of an 'unfledged ensign'); four prostitutes, younger than the fashionables, divide *their* night's plunder – watches, seals, etc. St James and St Giles

stood for high and low life, contrasted or sardonically equated as in a nineteenth-century street ballad, *St James and St Giles*: 'Two places there are where the poor and the rich/Live so like each other there's no knowing which.' The chorus ends 'In the former they live on the National Debt/In the latter they live on what they can get.'[8]

Lady Archer and Lady Buckinghamshire were social notorieties and print-shop targets, personifications of the *beau monde* at its least attractive. As Mrs Hobart, Lady Buckinghamshire had been the chief canvassing lady for the anti-Foxites at the famous Westminster Election of 1784, and thus the opposite number to the Duchess of Devonshire – opposite in every way. She was a very lively lady with a passion for youthful leads in amateur theatricals, another opening for ridicule. Lady Archer was a widow, an ex-beauty who painted her face, a noted whip, and reputedly a tyrant to her daughters, whose marriages she tried to prevent for financial reasons. Such things were godsends to the caricaturists.

Gillray's prints express a distaste for the *beau monde* and for elderly women of fashion that went deeper than personalities and scandal. *La Belle Assemblée* [43], 1787, where age apes youth, is a sort of manifesto against this aspect of

40 *The Gaming Table at Devonshire House* (drawing), *Rowlandson*

41 *Discipline à la Kenyon, Gillray*

Discipline à la Kenyon.

"*Vice, when it can not be Abash'd,*
"*Must be, or Ridicul'd, or Lash'd.*

42 *Dividing the Spoil!!, I. Cruikshank*

high life. Five women attend an altar of love: Mrs Hobart studies a role – *Ninon* (de l'Enclos); Lady Archer has a lamb and a whip; Lady Cecilia Johnstone, with a lyre, typifies aged and repulsive coquetry: she was noted for her bitter tongue and known ironically as 'the divine', or 'St Cecilia'; Walpole wrote (1799) of 'her narrow mind that never attracted any seed but that of wormwood'.

Social striving, intensified as the middle ranks gained ground, was an irresistible theme. 'The present rage of imitating high life hath spread itself so far among the gentlefolks of low life, that in a few years we shall probably have no common people at all' pronounced the *British Magazine* in 1763. With less extravagance, *The World* devoted a paper to 'The Genteel Mania': 'The mere word *genteel* seems to have had so singular an efficacy in the very sound of it, as to have done more to the confounding all distinctions, and promoting a levelling principle, than the philosophical reflections of the most profound teacher of republican maxims. . . . The imitating of every station above our own seems to be the first principle of the *Genteel Mania*, and operates with equal efficacy upon the tenth cousin of a woman of quality, and her acquaintance who retails *Gentility* among her neighbours in the Borough [Southwark].'[9]

The struggle upwards – usually seen as a feminine activity – is symbolized (in its higher ranges) in *The Quality Ladder* in 1793. A staircase spirals into space round a pole topped by a ducal coronet. Ladies climb up it, a duchess at the top, a baronet's wife at the bottom; she has managed to dislodge a citizen's lady, who has fallen heavily, saying, 'Whenever I try's to climb I always miss's my step'.

Given the contacts and contrasts between the City and St James's, the glamour, the remoteness, yet accessibility, of the *beau monde*, the striving was natural in this aristocratic, stratified, and expanding society. As Fielding had said, people of fashion were 'people of fascination'. 'Oh how I long to be transported to the dear regions of Grosvenor Square – far – far – from the dull districts of Aldersgate, Cheap, Candelwick, and Farringdon Without and Within', exclaimed the rich merchant's daughter in *The Clandestine Marriage** who was to marry – as she thought – a baronet whose contemptuous indifference troubled her not at all. 'My heart goes pit-a-pat at the very idea of being introduced at Court . . . Lady Melvil! My ears twingle at the sound – And then at dinner, instead of my father perpetually asking "any news upon change" – to say "well Sir John, any thing new from Arthur's? . . ." or to say to some other woman of quality – "was your ladyship at the Duchess of Ribbins last night? – Shall I see you at Carlisle House next Thursday?" Oh the dear Beau Monde! I was born to move in the sphere of the great world.' A

---

*This very popular comedy by Colman the elder and Garrick (Drury Lane, February 1766) long held the stage. There is a similar situation in *Eastward Hoe* by Jonson, Chapman and Marston, printed 1605, with contrasted daughters. Gertrude marries the worthless Sir Petronel Flash: 'Oh Sister Mill, though my father be a low tradesman, yet I must be a lady and my mother must call me Madam.' Touchstone, a goldsmith, is the first sympathetic picture of a tradesman.

The Cow-Pock — or — the Wonderful Effects of the New Inoculation! — Vide. — the Publications of y Anti-Vaccine Society.

V The Cow-Pock — or — the Wonderful Effects of the New Inoculation, Gillray

43 La Belle Assemblée, Gillray

visit to Carlisle House in Soho Square, where Mrs Cornelys had a brilliant but chequered reign from 1760 (when she bought the house) to 1778, giving concerts, balls, and masquerades, was part of the crowded day of a marriage-able daughter (not from the City):

> *In one continual hurry rolled her days*
> *At routs, assemblies, crushes, op'ras, plays,*
> *Subscription balls and visits without end,*
> *And poor Cornelys had no greater friend.*
> *From loo she rises with the rising sun,*
> *And Christies sees her aching head at one.*[10]

Subscription balls at Almack's come into the limelight in the Regency. They began in 1765 and lasted for almost a century. 'There is now opened at Almack's,' Williams wrote to Selwyn, 'in three very elegant new built rooms, and ten guineas subscription, for which you have a ball and a supper once a week for twelve weeks. You may imagine by the sum the company is chosen; though refined as it is, it will be scarce able to put old Soho out of countenance. . . .'[11]

The peak of gaiety and fashionable amusement was from the opening of the Pantheon in January 1772 till it was burnt down in 1790. The period opens with the Macaronies and the impact of the nabobs, and covers the years of war and national danger (1775–83), as well as of rapid post-war recovery. Mrs Cornelys ('old Soho') managed to found a 'society' of ladies of fashion with a duchess for a patroness, and flourished exceedingly. She told Casanova (who says he was the father of her children) that she gave twelve balls a year at two guineas a head and twelve for 'the middle classes'. She housed the Bach–Abel concerts, but her musical entertainments roused the jealousy of the Opera House, and despite the efforts of her duchess she was fined at Bow Street (1771) for performing an opera without licence. This and the Pantheon ruined her, though there were 'promenades' at Carlisle House in 1780.

Wyatt's Pantheon was the climax of splendour. 'A new winter Ranelagh in Oxford Road', a manifesto of 'luxury and expence' Walpole wrote to the French Ambassador when it was nearly finished. 'It amazed me myself. Imagine Balbec in all its glory . . . a dome like the Pantheon glazed.' And he afterwards called it 'the most elegant edifice in England'. Gibbon's verdict: 'In point of ennui and magnificence, the Pantheon is the wonder of the eighteenth century and of the British Empire.'[12] Attempts were made to exclude undesirables – 'gay ladies' – in the interests of 'elegance and propriety'. They failed. Subscribers, male and female, had to be recommended by a peeress, but once accepted they could introduce their friends. At the opening, according to the *Annual Register*, 'the company were an olio of all sorts, peers, peeresses, honourables and right honourables, Jew brokers, demi-reps, lottery insurers and quack doctors'. 'Most of the gay ladies in town, and ladies of the best rank and character', wrote Mrs Harris.[13]

Assemblies, balls, concerts, masquerades at the Pantheon were magnificent. Gibbon describes the masquerade given by Boodles Club in 1774. 'The most splendid and elegant Fête that was perhaps ever given in a seat of the Arts and Opulence. It would be as difficult to describe the magnificence of the Scene, as it would be easy to record the Humour of the Night. The one was above, the other below, all relation.'[14] A favourite character at this masquerade was the Macaroni [44], sometimes adopted also by women.

The rotunda, with the promenading company drowning music by conversation (Fanny Burney describes it in *Cecilia*), is the setting for a satire on the extravagant hairdressing of 1776 [45]. The ladies' feathers, rather less rampant, must have added to the brilliance of the scene. In this year, Boswell, at the trial in the Lords of the (so-called) Duchess of Kingston for bigamy, 'was enchanted at the beautiful exhibition of Ladies . . . I thought the mode of dressing with a deal of hair and feathers and flowers of various colours, more beautiful than what I had ever seen before'.[15]

In this same year another new fashion hit the print shops, adventurous driving for both sexes in light spidery carriages with very high box-seats. These, and monstrous hair-dressing, are caricatured together in, for instance, *The New Fashioned Phaeton – Sic Itur ad Astra* [46]. The driving mania was the subject of Colman's prologue to *The Suicide* in 1778:

> *'Tis now the reigning taste with Belle and Beau,*
> *Their art and skill in horsemanship to shew;*
> *A female Phaeton all danger scorns,*
> *Half coat, half petticoat, she mounts the box.*

The last line reflects a striking innovation, not confined to sporting ladies. J. T. Smith records for 1778 (his sole comment on costume) 'Ladies appeared for the first time in riding habits of men's cloth, only descending to the feet; they also walked with whips like small canes with thongs at the end.'[16] Men of fashion had begun to imitate the dress of the professional coachman. Colman's prologue continues:

> *Nobles contend who throws a whip the best,*
> *From head to foot like hackney coachman dress'd.*

The driving fashion (for men) had begun earlier. *The Present Age 1767* is a complicated attack on modish follies, and is addressed to 'Professors of Driving, Dancing, Ogling . . . &c. &c. &c.': a young man in a high gig is called 'a Feather of the Turf'. Before 1770 Smollett's Jack Holder, 'intended for a parson', but suddenly rich through the death of a brother, was 'at the Bath, driving about in a phaeton and four, with French horns'.[17] And about the same time, Martin Rishton, who married Fanny Burney's step-sister, was an Oxford undergraduate, driving a phaeton with four bays.[18]

The new fashion inevitably attracted satire on social striving. Courtesans were often noted horsewomen. There was Agnes ('Vis-à-vis') Townshend who drove her phaeton and four across country. In a print of 1781 (title missing)

PANTHEON MACARONI.

44 *Pantheon Macaroni* (*proof*) (*The Macaroni. A Real Character at the Late Masquerade*), P. Dawe

45 *A Hint to the Ladies to take Care of their Heads*, P. Dawe

46 *The New Fashioned Phaeton – Sic Itur ad Astra*, (?) P. Dawe

A Hint to the Ladies to take Care of their HEADS.

London, Printed for R. Sayer & J. Bennett N.º 53 Fleet Street, as the Act directs 16 March 1776.

The NEW FASHIONED PHAETON.
Sic Itur ad Astra.
London, Printed for R. Sayer & J. Bennett N.º 53 Fleet Street, as the Act directs 15 Feb.y 1776.

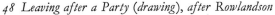

47 *Sir Gregory Gigg*, Bunbury

48 *Leaving after a Party (drawing), after Rowlandson*

she drives standing, to the terror of her companion: '. . . I can swear Sir, & What's more drive four Horses in Hand'. In *Two Impures of the Ton, Driving to the Gig Shop, Hammersmith* (1781), by Dighton, one impure in a habit of masculine cut, drives a pair of ponies, standing. The other sits demurely beside her. They are passing St George's Hospital and Tattersall's. In *A Lesson Westward* a young miss is being taught to drive, in a cart, placarded 'Tom Long Trot's Academy for Young Ladies; Driving taught to an inch. Ladies completely finish'd in a Fortnight, for Gig, Whiskey or Phaeton. Single Lessons Half-a-crown, Five for half a Guinea.' The scene is the Hammersmith Road, outside the Bell & Anchor, still there, but engulfed and rebuilt. In *Sir Gregory Gigg* [47], 1781, Bunbury returns to his favourite theme of bad and vulgar horsemanship. Today this is apparent from the title only: 'Sir Gregory Gigg, the City Beau', is a song from O'Keefe's *Son-inLaw* (1779). He is more explicit in *Richmond Hill** [49], a mixture of people of fashion and would-be fashion and weary plebeian pedestrians on a Sunday outing. The two miserable hacks harnessed to the high phaeton refuse to move.

Four-in-hand driving as a fashionable craze persisted. Aged nineteen, the Prince boasted in a letter (1781) to his brother that he had driven a phaeton and four 'twenty-two miles in ye two hours at a trot, wh. is reckoned pretty good driving'.[19] Later on, one of the sights of Brighton was the Prince driving his barouche and four or sometimes six, under the tuition of Sir John Lade, as in *Birds of a Feather* in 1802, where the passengers are Mrs Fitz and a Miss Snow. 'Ah the old times was the rackety times', an ancient hackney coachman told Mayhew. He had been called to the British Coffee House and ordered to get inside: 'the Prince is going to drive himself'. Before he could do so, the Prince had hurled him into the coach: 'he wasn't so very drunk neither . . ., he drove very well for a Prince . . . he hadn't no pride for such as me'.[20]

What can little T.O. do? . . . Why drive a Phaeton and Two!! – Can little T.O. do more – Yes drive a Phaeton and Four!!!! was Gillray's contribution to the driving saga in 1801. Tom Onslow, with his team of four, is dressed as a stage coachman even to the straw twisted round his legs. The crest on the carriage is a man in a fool's cap riding a rocking horse. The craze was manifested in two driving clubs, both aristocratic. The Bensington† from 1807, limited to twenty-five, and the overflow, founded next year, the Four Horse, often called the Four-in-hand, the Whip, or the Barouche.[21] Like the earlier craze (which had never subsided) it coincided with war and national danger. In the eighteenth century, Gillray excepted, satire was chiefly for those who imitated fashionable follies, now it has a harsher note. The club was ridiculed in *Hit or Miss* (1810), a musical farce in which Mathews, as Cypher, impersonated a member and the use of coaching slang was ridiculed. In *Sketches of Fairy-Land* . . . in 1810 'Cypher' is one of the examples of English

---

*The drawing was exhibited at the Royal Academy in 1781 and given to Walpole, who praised it ecstatically, cf. above, p. 57.

†Members were required to drive twice a year to Bensington in Oxfordshire, fifty-seven miles from London.

49 *Richmond Hill, Bunbury*

50 *An Admiral's Porter, after Woodward*

decadence with the legend 'There a young man of Fashion apes the slang and manners of a Stage Coachman, so unlike the natural refinement of our own Country'. In other prints these young aristocrats, with their extravagant teams, barouches and uniforms, refuse to pay the bills of angry tradesmen, or drive furiously 'with hostility to every thing that comes in their way', and a club dinner at Salt Hill (near Slough) is depicted as a drunken orgy. The most serious protest was in some execrable verse in the *Annual Register*:

> *Two varying races are in Britain born,*
> *One courts a nation's praises, one her scorn;*
> *Those pant her sons o'er tented field to guide,*
> *Or steer her thunders thro' the foaming tide;*
> *Whilst these, disgraceful born in luckless hour,*
> *Burn but to guide with skill a coach and four. . . .*
> *These are the coachmen's sons, and those my Lord's. . . .*
> *Give them their due, not let occasion slip;*
> *On those thy laurels lay, on these thy whip!*[22]

Domestic servants, a hierarchy within a hierarchy, are a link between high life and low life. They were under a strain in a shifting social stratification, with some relics of their earlier position in noble households, when these were run on the lines of a Court, but a few were moving upwards – the steward evolving into the land agent, the valet (the gentleman's gentleman) into the secretary, while my lady's own woman was poised between the companion and the lady's maid. Their numbers give them social importance, and the parts they play in fiction and the theatre speak for themselves. Service to the Great could be an avenue to posts in the Customs, Excise or Stamp Office – to tavern-keeping, even to the Church or to commissions in the Army. Such service was a resort for children of the impoverished clergy and gentry.* Footmen, their number, liveries and physique, were status symbols. In Georgian England gentility demanded footmen as personal attendants to women. Prints illustrating tales of the Lady Booby–Joseph Andrews sort abound. Swift expects a lady 'to cast an eye upon a handsome footman'. The elegance and assurance of the footman in *Leaving after a Party* [48], after Rowlandson, has some such implication. Roderick Random gained his future wife's affection while serving as her footman. A typical *mésalliance*, according to Foote, was 'a lady of fortune setting out for Edinburgh in a post-chaise with her footman'.† Footmen walked beside their mistress's sedan chair, and behind her to church carrying her prayer-book, like the shivering little foot-boy in Hogarth's *Morning*. Miss Reynolds's distress at not having a man to send with a note to Mrs Montagu, her scheme to send it by a chairman who might be taken for her servant, her dismay when it was delivered by the greengrocer's errand girl, are amusingly related by Fanny Burney.

Except for Swift's *Directions to Servants* (his footman is the subject of a horrifying plate by Rowlandson) the leading satire on the eighteenth-century servant is Garrick's popular play, *High Life below Stairs* (Drury Lane, October 1759). The themes are wholesale and brazen plunder, and the imitation of their employers' affectations and language (in no spirit of mockery). Not only do the servants take precedence according to their employers' rank, but they assume their titles. 'The Duke', 'Sir Harry' and the lady's-maids, 'Lady Babs' and 'Lady Charlotte', are invited by other servants to a party in the supposed absence of their master, a rich young man, who is disguised as a raw country lad, anxious to be trained for service. In a print after Collett, *c.* 1770, his hair is being dressed by Mrs Kitty (Mrs Clive) to prepare him to wait on 'the gentlefolks' – the other servants. The curtain falls on blame for 'persons of rank' whose ridiculous affectations make imitation easy. On the first and following nights the footmen in the gallery rioted against the wounding picture.

In this age of patronage the great man's porter was a person of importance; he controlled access to his master, and was naturally satirized as Cerberus who must be appeased by a sop (for instance by Fielding and Foote). George Primrose encountered a literary impostor who lived by importuning the wealthy for subscriptions to a non-existent work. But, 'I am too well known, I should be glad to borrow your face for a bit, my face is too familiar to his porter . . . and we divide the spoil'.[23] *The Inflexible Porter, a Tragedy* [51], 1783, is Bunbury's rendering of some such situation. There is more of tragedy in *An Admiral's Porter* [50], 1790, where Cerberus confronts two maimed sailors: for a place at Greenwich Hospital a recommendation from an influential naval officer was indispensable.[24] Boswell gives us a glimpse of the porter in action. After failing once or twice to find the Duke of Queensberry at home, he was advised to use 'the silver key'. 'I therefore called today, and chatting with the surly dog, "Mr Quant", said I, "I give you a great deal of trouble", bowed and smiled and put half a crown into his hand. He told me the duke would be pleased to see me next morning at nine.' This was no levée; the duke was alone.[25]

The woman servant's lot was far more precarious, though it had its prizes: for instance, Pamela in fiction – founded on fact – Emma Hamilton in life. *The Modern Harlot's Progress, or Adventures of Harriet Heedless*, 1780, illustrates social change since 1731 (the date on Moll Hackabout's coffin). The story is essentially Hogarth's, but the protector is not a Jew, and the lover is a footman, not a fencing-master. The first scene is not an inn yard but a Statute Hall [52], where masters and mistresses went to engage servants for a small fee; they were so called

---

* In *Tom Jones*, both Mrs Honour and Black George's wife had 'sprung from the clergy'. Fielding (who married his first wife's maid) adds a footnote: 'it is to be hoped that such instances will in future ages, when some provision is made for the families of the inferior clergy, appear stranger than can be thought at present', Book IV, Chapter 14.

† *The Devil upon Two Sticks*, 1772. Lady Harriet Wentworth, Lord Rockingham's sister, made a sensation in 1764 by marrying her footman (after settling her fortune on their children and her own family, with only an annuity of £100 for her husband). John Macdonald, according to his own not incredible account, was irresistible. *Travels . . .* (1790), ed. J. Beresford as *Memoirs of an Eighteenth Century Footman* (London: G. Routledge, 1927).

THE INFLEXIBLE PORTER.
a Tragedy.

Design'd by H.W. Bunbury Esq.

London Publish'd Mar. 24, 1780 by I.R. Smith N.63 opposite y.e Pantheon Oxford Street

51 *The Inflexible Porter, a Tragedy, Bunbury*

52 *The Modern Harlot's Progress, Pl. I, anon.*

BOOK 25   The Modern HARLOT's PROGRESS, or Adventures of HARRIET HEEDLESS.   1

Harriet Heedless, applying to a Statue Hall for a Place; is seen by a Rake, and decoy'd by a Bawd. An Old Fellow chucks a Girls chin,
and other Characters are looking for Servants, or Services.

Printed for & Sold by CARINGTON BOWLES, at his Map & Print Warehouse, N.o 69 in S.t Pauls Church Yard, LONDON. Published as the Act directs, 15 May 1780.   97

Within the image: SILK STREET · PANTHEON CONCERT · Theatre Royal Drury Lane · LOYAL CREW · MAY.DAY · PETER.PI... PEWTERER · SHAVE for a Penny · Original Shaving SHOP A Room for Ladies

Collings del. — Blake sculp.

MAY-DAY IN LONDON.

53 May-Day in London, S. Collings/Blake

from the statute fairs or mops for hiring country servants. The Register Office, drawn by Rowlandson, was a similar place with a different name. Both were denounced as bare-faced cheats.[26] (Mrs Cole, the wicked sanctimonious bawd in Foote's *The Minor*, advertises in the Register Office for servants under seventeen.) Harriet is seen by a rake and decoyed by a bawd. The most significant changes from Hogarth's series are that there is nothing corresponding to the Bridewell scene, and Harriet dies in a workhouse, attended by a doctor and nurse, in marked contrast with the sordid squalor in Hogarth's fifth plate.

Low life usually connotes the disreputable, and was traditionally a subject for ridicule, not compassion. Typical low-life figures were the ballad-singer, the chimney sweep and the dustman. The first bawled the songs she sold, which were generally lewd; on execution days she sold 'Dying Speeches':

> Let not the ballad-singer's thrilling strain
> Amid the swarm thy list'ning ear detain,
> Guard well thy pocket, for these syrens stand
> To aid the labours of the diving hand:
> Confed'rate in the cheat, they draw the throng;
> And cambrick handkerchiefs reward the song.[27]

Gay's warning was often repeated from Bow Street by Sir John Fielding. Rowlandson's drawing, *Last Dying Speech and Confession* [54], with a pocket being picked in the background, belongs to a set of *Cries of London* satirizing the sentimentality of Wheatley's *Cries*, where its opposite number is a pretty girl with 'A New Love Song'.

The chimney sweep or climbing boy is a usual street-scene figure. May Day was his festival. Decked out in wigs and gilt paper they danced with the milk-maids and their 'garlands', pyramids of hired plate trimmed with greenery and ribbons. In *May-Day in London* [53], 1784, the garlands are poor, to suit the neighbourhood with its penny barber's sign. Among many prints of sweeps this is the only one I know of the infantine climbing boy, sold by his parents, or kidnapped, at the age of four or five.* About the turn of the century the milkmaids' garlands disappeared and the sweeps went round with a Jack in the Green.

Also at the bottom of the social ladder were the rag-pickers or cinder-sifters and the dustmen. We have seen the last as a low-life symbol: he was to become much more of one. In Rowlandson's *Love and Dust* [55], 1788, they are at work on one of the huge laystalls that disgraced the fringes of London. Though burlesqued (but certainly less so than they now seem) they are probably from life. Mayhew has a great deal to say about the dustmen and cinder-sifters of his day: the occupation was hereditary, dustmen married (i.e. lived with) cinder-sifters; their children worked in the dust-yards which had replaced laystalls. A man he interviewed was the son and grandson of dustmen

54 *Last Dying Speech and Confession, Rowlandson*

55 *Love and Dust, Rowlandson*

LOVE AND DUST.

---

*It was engraved by William Blake after Collings, and though it was hack work, it is impossible not to associate it with the little chimney sweepers in *The Age of Innocence* and *The Age of Experience* (1789, 1794).

– and Rowlandson's pair could have been parents or grandparents of those in a mid-nineteenth-century wood engraving, *View of a Dust Yard** which anticipates the setting immortalized in *Our Mutual Friend*.

A feature of disreputable (but not poverty-stricken) low life was the Cock and Hen Club, where youths and prostitutes (teenagers) met to drink and sing songs. Francis Place (b. 1771) describes those he frequented as an apprentice, especially a famous one in the Savoy. Upon one end of a long table was 'a chair filled by a youth, upon the other end a chair filled by a girl. The amusements were drinking and singing flash songs.'[28] The only improbable part of Newton's *Row at a Cock and Hen Club* [57], 1798, is the valour of the ancient watchmen: Bow Street would surely have tackled such an assembly. A similar club was so dealt with in 1774, when Lichtenberg recorded 'a club which used to meet on Tuesdays in Wych Street was dissolved. It consisted of servants, journeymen and apprentices. On these evenings every member laid down fourpence, for which he had music and a female gratis, anything else to be paid for separately. Twenty of the girls were brought before Sir John Fielding; the beauty of some of them roused general admiration.'[29]

From Hogarth to Cruikshank, and after, gin is a lamentable feature of low life. In *Gin Lane* (in 1751, when it was sold anywhere and everywhere) the poison is being sold from a shed. Rather later, the gin shop, or dram shop, was on its way to becoming the Victorian gin palace. Here is Rowlandson's drawing of a gin shop about 1810 [56].

Not much compassion for poverty and hunger *as such* is discoverable in the prints, with the exception of maimed soldiers and sailors who provide an opportunity for rebuking the uncharitable. Not much existed, though there was much humanitarianism. Dr Johnson was an exception.

Mrs Thrale recorded (1777) that he 'has more Tenderness for Poverty than any other Man I ever knew, and less for other Calamities. . . . The want of Food and Raiment is so common in London said Johnson that one who lives there has no Compassion to spare for the Wounds given only to Vanity or Softness.'[30]

*Mayhew, *London Labour and the London Poor*, 1851, vol. II, p. 208. The trade was more organized and extensive than in the eighteenth century, the 'dust' less valuable, though contractors still paid for removing it. The sifted breeze was used for making inferior bricks.

Notes to Chapter VIII
1. *Correspondence, George Prince of Wales*, ed. A. Aspinall (London: Cassells, 1963), vol. I, p. 35.
2. *Macaroni and Theatrical Magazine*, October 1772.
3. *Town and Country Magazine*, December 1773.
4. *The World*, No. 69, 25 April 1754.
5. *Connoisseur*, 6 September 1756.
6. *Journal and Correspondence of Lord Auckland*, 1861, vol. II, p. 384 (1 February 1792).
7. *The Whig Club*, 1794, pp. 90–91.
8. J. Ashton, *Modern Street Ballads*, 1888, pp. 399–402.
9. *The World*, No. 199, 21 October 1756.
10. C. Jenner, *London Eclogues*, 1772.
11. G. Williams to George Selwyn, 22 February 1765. *George Selwyn and his Contemporaries*, ed. J. H. Jesse, 1843–4.
12. *Miscellaneous Works*, 1814, vol. II, p. 74.
13. *Letters of the Earl of Malmesbury*, ed. his grandson the Earl of Malmesbury, 1870, vol. I, p. 247.
14. *Private Letters*, ed. R. E. Prothero, 1896, vol. I, p. 215.
15. Boswell, *The Ominous Years*, ed. C. Ryskamp and F. A. Pottle (London: Heinemann, 1963), p. 339.
16. *A Book for a Rainy Day*, 1845 (posthumous).
17. *Humphrey Clinker*, 1771 (but Smollett left England in 1769).
18. *The Early Diary of Fanny Burney*, ed. A. R. Ellis, 1907, vol. II.
19. *Correspondence, George Prince of Wales* (see note 1), p. 62.
20. H. Mayhew, *London Labour and the London Poor*, 1851, vol. III, p. 350.
21. Duke of Beaufort, *Driving*, Badminton Library, 1889, pp. 250–6; J. Ashton, *The Dawn of the Eighteenth Century in England*, 1906, pp. 189–94.
22. Vol. 59, p. 663, quoted J. Ashton (see note 21).
23. O. Goldsmith, *Vicar of Wakefield*, 1766, Chapter 20.
24. M. Lewis, *A Social History of the Navy 1793–1815* (London: Allen & Unwin, 1960), p. 45.
25. *Boswell's London Journal*, ed. F. A. Pottle (London: Heinemann, 1950), p. 59 (1 December 1762).
26. M. D. George, 'The early history of Registry Offices', *Economic Journal*, supplement, January 1929.
27. John Gay, *Trivia; or, the Art of walking the Streets of London*, 1716.
28. Francis Place, Autobiography, British Museum Add. MSS. 35142, ff 140, 140 b.
29. *Lichtenberg's Visits to England*, translated and annotated by W. M. Mare and W. H. Quarrell (Oxford: O.U.P., 1936), p. 118.
30. *Thraliana*, ed. K. C. Balderston (Oxford: O.U.P., 1952), p. 184.

56 A Gin Shop (drawing), Rowlandson

57 A Row at a Cock and Hen Club, R. Newton

DRAWN & ETCH'D BY R. NEWTON 1798

A ROW AT A COCK AND HEN CLUB

BAGNIGGE WELLS.

58 Bagnigge Wells, J. Sanders/J.R.Smith,

59 Taking Tea at the White Conduit House (drawing), Rowlandson

9 - The London Citizen

The 'cit' was a standing object of ridicule, and favourite topics were his Sunday outing, guzzling at City feasts or a Sunday ordinary, his 'country box', his soldiering (as a volunteer), his shooting, fishing, riding, and his seaside holiday.

The ring of pleasure gardens round London was an important feature of everyday life. There were places whose chief custom was on Sunday, when music and entertainment were forbidden, but many were places of evening amusement on other days. Vauxhall and Ranelagh of course were places apart, opened in spring and closed in August after the quality had left town. These were places where cits could rub shoulders with the Great. Their relative status is amusingly indicated by the lady's maids in *High Life below Stairs* (p. 70):

LADY C.'S: *Well I say it again, I love Vauxhall!*
LADY B.'S: *Oh, my stars! Why there is nobody there but filthy citizens* - Runelow *for my money.*

Everyone went to Vauxhall. There were 'dark walks', 'affrays', and music (as Boswell says) 'not too refined for the general ear'. Amelia, Evelina, Cecilia, had their misadventures there. To satirists it was peculiarly a place where cits went to stare at the *beau monde* and complain of the dearness of the food and the paper-thinness of the ham. Two famous supper parties stand out, that of Beau Tibbs and his friends who failed to get a genteel box since the keepers of the boxes 'chose to reserve genteel boxes for what they judged more genteel company'.[1] And Horace Walpole's, when Lady Caroline Petersham, 'gloriously jolly and handsome', minced seven chickens in a china dish and the party took up 'the whole attentions of the garden, so much so that from eleven till half an hour after one we had the whole concourse round our booth....'[2] Gradually, the genteel company dwindled, and by the end of the century Vauxhall was more or less taken over by the less genteel. Frere describes 'fair Vauxhallia',

Where each spruce nymph from city compters free,
Sips the froth'd syllabub or fragrant tea;
While with sliced ham, scraped beef, and burnt champagne,
Her 'prentice lover soothes his amorous pain.[3]

The classic picture of Vauxhall is Rowlandson's famous print from a watercolour exhibited at the Royal Academy in 1784, a social panorama, faintly tinged with satire [IV]. Mrs Weichsel sings, the *beau monde* are in the centre foreground. The Prince whispers to Perdita Robinson (their

liaison had ended), who is arm-in-arm with her dwarfish husband. The Duchess of Devonshire and her sister are there, and the ultra-fashionable Major Topham stares through a monocle. In the supper-box on the left are Dr Johnson, Boswell, Goldsmith (d. 1774), and reputedly Mrs Thrale. On the right two cits entertain courtesans at a table under trees.

The other gardens, with the partial exception of Marylebone, sacrificed to the builders in 1776, were 'frequented only by the middle and common class, people of distinction come rarely, ladies of quality never'.[4]

The chief outlet from the City was to Islington and Primrose Hill, and the two classic tea-gardens were Bagnigge Wells and White Conduit House.

Ah I loves life and all the joy it yields,
Says Madam Fussock, warm from Spittle Fields,
Bon ton's the space twixt Saturday and Munday,
And riding in a one-horse chair o'Sunday:
'Tis drinking tea on Summer's afternoons
At Bagnigge Wells with china and gilt spoons.[5]

Besides the grounds (sixpence entrance) with their arbours for tea-drinking, there was also, at places of any size, a Long Room for balls and concerts and Sunday tea-drinking. *Bagnigge Wells* [58], 1772, today seems a charming period piece, but it is a satire on apprentices, courtesans, and City fops at 'that rendezvous of thoughtless young men, and worthless young women, Bagnigge Wells'.[6] The elegant charm of Rowlandson's watercolour, *Taking Tea at the White Conduit House* [59] obscures similar implications. But both places and very many others, were also the resort of family parties like that of Zachary Treacle, whose wife dragged him on Sundays 'to Georgia, or Hornsea Wood, or the White Conduit House' where he grudged the cost of 'tea, and hot rolls, and sillabubs for the boy'.[7] Such a family is leaving Bagnigge Wells in *Mr Deputy Dumpling and Family enjoying a Summer Afternoon* [60], 1781, clearly deriving from Hogarth's *Evening* (p. 44). In *Melting Moments*, 1795, the overburdened cit is the traditional cuckold; his pretty young wife makes an assignation with Sir John: 'No more to Primrose Hill she'll go/But dash away to Brighton ho.' *Pastimes of Primrose Hill* [61] is a typical Sunday scene.

Besides the tea-gardens, almost every tavern and alehouse round London turned itself into a Sunday resort by providing a Sunday ordinary, to which cits trudged or drove to dine at prices ranging from 9d. to 8s. The savage competitive gormandizing was a stock subject of satire, written and pictorial. 'As Mr Quin has observed, it is not safe to eat at them without a basket-hilted knife and fork.'[8] *An Ordinary on Sundays at Two O'Clock* [I], 1792, is Dighton's rendering of a familiar scene; the pleasant room looks onto a lawn surrounded by arbours.

The country box was the target of witticisms in prose and verse. Both *The Connoisseur* and *The World*[9] had made it their own. For instance, on Sunday, 'the substantial citizen is wheeled down to his snug box, which has nothing rural about it except the ivy that over-runs the front, and is placed as near the road as possible'.[10] And Lord Cork's

> *A little country box you boast,*
> *So neat, 'tis cover'd all with dust*
> *And nought about it to be seen,*
> *Except a nettle-bed that's green . . .*
> *'Tis not the country you must own,*
> *'Tis only London out of town.*[11]

Then Cowper on suburbia,

> *Suburban villas, highway-side retreats,*
> *That dread th' encroachment of our growing streets,*
> *Tight boxes, neatly sashed and in a blaze*
> *With all a July sun's collected rays,*
> *Delight the citizen, who, gasping there,*
> *Breathes clouds of dust and calls it country air.*[12]

The implied contrast of course is with the patrician villas at Chiswick or Richmond, and the country houses of the gentry. (But Cole, in 1765, compared 'the elegant neat Boxes . . . beautiful and pleasant Gardens . . . in every Outlet for Miles from London', with the wretched buildings on the roads from Paris.)[13] Bunbury burlesques pretentious absurdity in *The Delights of Islington* in 1772. The cit stands in his garden under a placard denouncing depredations on his property; the 'New Pagoda' and 'the two new dolphins from the gazebo' as well as 'a great deal of timber that was planted last spring' have been 'clandestinely carried off'. The gazebo (summer house) is on a pole to overlook the garden wall. Bunbury's *Bethnal Green* [62], 1792, ridicules both the city sportsman in the suburbs and his country box, which has a fantastic gazebo with Chinese excrescences, a survival from the *chinoiserie* of the fifties. The horrors of a rich citizen's country place – 'quite another guess sort of a place than when I first took it my lord', – are a feature of *The Clandestine Marriage*:[14] 'the canal', 'the cascade', 'the four seasons in lead, the flying Mercury and the basin with Neptune in the middle . . . you have here as many rich figures as the man at Hyde Park Corner'. (These leaden garden figures were social and aesthetic equivalents of today's plastic garden gnomes.) Other features are an octagon summer house on a ship's mast 'that overlooks the whole road', a Chinese bridge, a Gothic dairy, a maze of zigzag paths 'turning and twisting like a worm'.

The humours of walking in St James's Park, riding and driving in Hyde Park, were popular subjects because of the attractiveness of the scene and the mixture of classes

60 *Mr Deputy Dumpling and Family, after Dighton*

Drawn by Cruikshanks   Published as the Act directs by W. Locke Sept. 1. 1791   Etch'd by Barlow.

PASTIMES OF PRIMROSE HILL.

61 Pastimes of Primrose Hill, after I. Cruikshank

62 Bethnal Green, after Bunbury

BETHNAL GREEN. Hie away Juno!

LONDON, Publish'd June 11 1793, by W. DICKINSON, N.º 158, Old Bond Street.

(which brings us back to high life). It was only on Sunday that citizens and apprentices could join the fashionable throng, though the rabble could annoy at any time.

> *On that dull day, which, ev'ry week affords*
> *A glut of 'prentices, in bags and swords;*
> *When sober families resort to pray'r*
> *And cits take in their weekly meal of air;*
> *Whilst, eastwards of St Pauls, the well-dressed spark,*
> *Runs two long miles to saunter in the Park.*[15]

One print (I know of only one), derides this conventional attitude to the cit and to the plebeian who apes the manners of the gentry, Gillray's *Hyde Park – Sunday – or – Both Hemispheres of the World in a Sweat* [63], 1789. One of its targets is Bunbury, but it is primarily aimed at the ultra-fashionable Major Topham, and the jargon of his daily paper, *The World or Fashionable Advertiser* (sub-title afterwards dropped), in which he stigmatized other papers as 'the low prints'. The two hemispheres are the worlds of Cheapside and St James's, and also the spherical persons (much exaggerated) of Topham and 'Becky' – Mrs Wells, the actress, Topham's mistress and a co-editor of *The World* – who are riding together, followed by 'Old Quiz' (the Duke of Queensberry). Here (abridged) is Gillray's parody of Topham's staccato journalese: 'The World – and all the Great "which it inherit" were there – Equestrian motion, universal – we saw all . . . down to the intelligencers of the Low-Prints . . . ; all was splendid – who (& what dignity not contained in that monosyllable?) not present? – Becky – was there!! – attraction spontaneous! – Old Quiz . . . but – Bunbury – where was Harry Bunbury? – we return'd – as (craving appetites of Cheapside satisfied) [the City dines early] cent pr cent Citz – Mans-mercers & womens mercers were arriving, to inhale the crouded Air – Heat – Ibid – Ibidem.'

The usual attitude to Hyde Park on Sunday is that of *Sunday Equestrians or Hyde Park Candidates for Admiration* [64], *c.* 1795. All are on hired horses except the undertaker (on the right) and the brewer, who mounts one of his dray-horses, because (he says) his 'blood-mare' is lame.

The enormous popularity of Cowper's *John Gilpin* illustrates the irresistible attraction – in the City as elsewhere – of the cit on horseback; Gilpin became a folk-character, almost a minor John Bull. The poem came out in the *Public Advertiser* in 1782; chap-book versions, usually illustrated, followed, then three well-known actors recited it, including Henderson (considered second only to Garrick). It was printed on broadsides with engravings of the headlong gallop. *John Gilpin's return from Ware* [II]

63 Hyde Park – Sunday – or – Both Hemispheres of the World in a Sweat, Gillray

HYDE-PARK ;— Sunday, — or - both Hemifpheres of the World in a Sweat ;

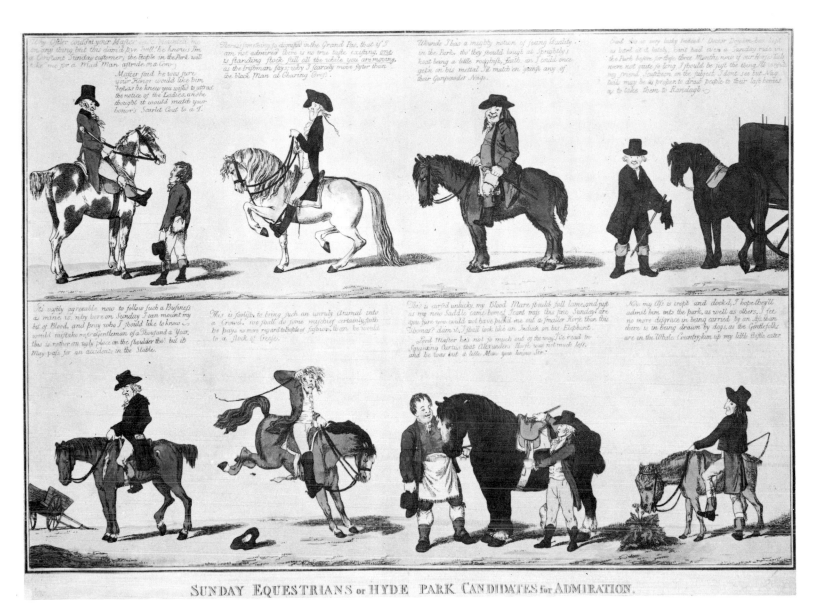

SUNDAY EQUESTRIANS or HYDE PARK CANDIDATES for ADMIRATION.

64 *Sunday Equestrians or Hyde Park Candidates for Admiration, after G. M. Woodward*

has a good view of the Bell Inn and is after Dighton. The poem has continued to fascinate the artist; for instance, George Cruikshank, Caldecott, Ronald Searle.

Before leaving the citizen, the shop demands attention, though, strictly speaking, only shopmen east of Temple Bar are within the category. Foreigners register astonished admiration at the window displays, the plate-glass, the lights, the luxury, the complaisance of the shopman: 'The richest merchant never shows ill-humour even if asked to unfold more than a hundred pieces of stuff.'[16] The milliner's shop has an interest of its own. Apprenticeship to a milliner was an alternative to domestic service for daughters of the impoverished gentry. It had also especial dangers: these girls were considered fair game by rakish 'men of pleasure' (as indeed were all women they regarded as below their own class). The milliner catered for men as well as women, and in guides to the trades of London there are emphatic warnings on the dangers of the occupation. Moreover, prostitutes adopted the character of a milliner, tripping along with her little box: 'With empty band-box she delights to range/And feigns a distant errand from the "Change"' (Trivia). The Rival Milliners [65], after Collett, tells its story, and is an interesting view of a shop-interior c. 1770.

Shops for women were usually served by men, a common subject of complaint – effeminacy, and waste of manpower. Southey's Spaniard was surprised to find (1807) 'that the finest gentlemen to be found in the streets of London are the men who serve at the linen-drapers and mercers', and asked for an explanation. He was told that the usual morning employment of ladies of fashion was to 'go a'shopping', not to buy, but to amuse themselves.

'Women have not enough patience for this idle and fastidious curiosity'; 'young men were more assiduous, more engaging'.[17] Mrs Circuit, a brazen social striver, wife of the knavish barrister in Foote's The Lame Lover (1770) deplored 'the most horrible chasm' 'from 12, the hour of one's rising, to dinner . . . for though teasing the mercers and milliners, by tumbling their wares, is now and then an entertaining amusement, yet upon repetition it palls'. In all seriousness, the qualifications for a London shop-keeper were said to be 'To speak fluently, to entertain the ladies, and to be the master of a handsome bow and cringe: he should be able to hand a lady to and from her coach politely, without being seized with a palpitation of the heart at the touch of a delicate hand, the sight of a much expos'd limb, or a handsome face. . . .'[18]

Notes to Chapter IX
1. O. Goldsmith, The Citizen of the World, Letter LXXI, 1762.
2. To G. Montagu, 23 June 1750.
3. 'The Loves of the Triangles', Anti-Jacobin, 1798.
4. J. W. von Archenholtz, Tableau d'Angleterre, 1788.
5. Colman's prologue to Garrick's Bon Ton, 1775 (which satirizes high life).
6. Memoirs of Angelo, 1828, vol. I, p. 284.
7. Samuel Johnson, The Idler, 22 July 1758.
8. St James's Chronicle, 2 May 1761.
9. Weekly essays, 1753–6.
10. Connoisseur, 26 July 1754.
11. Ibid., 12 September 1754.
12. Retirement, 1782.
13. W. Cole, Paris Journal, ed. F. G. Stokes (London: Constable, 1931), pp. 44–45.
14. By Garrick and Colman, 1766.
15. C. Jenner, London Eclogues, 1773.
16. J. G. A. Forster, Voyage en Angleterre en 1790, 1796.
17. Letters of Espriella, 1807, vol. I, pp. 119–21; Cf. pl. 35.
18. R. Campbell, The London Tradesmen, 1747.

The RIVAL MILLENERS.
Printed for Rob.t Sayer, N.o 53 in Fleet Street, London.

From Sarah Woodcock, to the Girl,
That's doom'd the humble Mop to twirl.

Y.e Milleners delight on show,
And cry — 'Tis I will have that Beau.

183

65 *The Rival Milliners, after J. Collet*

The VICAR going to DINNER with the ESQUIRE.
Engraved from an Original Picture Painted by C.M.r John Collett.

66 The *Vicar going to Dinner with the Esquire, after J. Collet*

10 · The Professions

The Church and the Universities

The three learned professions are impeached together in a
conventional way in *The Triple Plea*, 1780, a mezzotint
after Collett with the same title and subject as two prints
of perhaps thirty years earlier. Doctor, lawyer and parson
dispute as to which 'should have the superiority' in de-
merit. The room is well furnished, all have prospered; on
the wall is a picture of three harpies: 'Behold these three,
too apt to poison, plunder, and delude mankind.' *The
Conspirators*, *c.* 1770, in the same series, is a burial scene in
a churchyard, attended by doctor, lawyer and cleric, all
are 'Grim Death's Purveyors'. But in general there is a
gradation of blame, lawyers get the worst treatment, the
clergy the most attention.*

*Cole (in 1765) thought otherwise, but he was not thinking of
prints: 'If a Parliamentary Enquiry into the Conduct of the learned
Professions was to be set on foot, I am certain, that which is *most
cried out against* [my italics], the Church, ought to be the last thought
of', *Paris Journal*, ed. F.G. Stokes (London: Constable, 1931, p. 372.)

As always, the dominant theme is the ancient and basic
one of the contrast between the higher and the lower clergy
– between pomp and penury. The range was in fact from
the Archbishop to the near-vagrant. A pair of mezzotints
after Dighton in 1782 speaks for itself: *A Master Parson
with a Good Living* [67], and *A Journeyman Parson with a Bare
Existence* [68]. The contrast was a target for anti-clerical
wit, but Churchmen, Johnson for instance, thought it in
the nature of things. It was part of the social fabric, bound
up with the dependence of the profession on patronage:
too many poor scholars seeking curacies, too many curates
seeking livings, too many poor benefices – one reason for
pluralities – the better ones largely a provision for the
younger sons of landed families. Hence the competition for
tutorships or chaplaincies in aristocratic households. 'The
parson knows enough who knows a duke.'[1] 'Attach
yourself to some great man, Sir! Many have risen to
eminence that way', was the advice of Martin Routh,
President of Magdalen College from 1791 to 1854.

67 *A Master Parson with a Good Living, after Dighton*

A MASTER PARSON with a GOOD LIVING.

68 *A Journeyman Parson with a Bare Existence, after Dighton*

A JOURNEYMAN PARSON with a BARE EXISTENCE.

VICAR and MOSES.

69 *The Vicar and Moses, Rowlandson*

That Orders were taken by some very unsuitable people was a natural result of social conditions. There were sinecurists who held a living and employed a curate. But that the parson was the chief civilizing influence in many parishes can hardly be doubted.[2] Dr Percy while still 'a little rector' told Johnson 'it might be discovered whether or no there was a clergyman resident in a parish by the civil or savage manner of the people'. (Non-residence was frequent, often because there was no habitable parsonage.) Parson Adams and Dr Primrose had their prototypes. Except as a diarist, Parson Woodforde was a typical country parson – sociable and charitable. *The Vicar going to Dinner with the Esquire* [66], 1768, sour, uncharitable, and married, is Woodforde's antithesis, except in dining with the squire.

The words 'living', 'benefice', 'incumbent', 'preferment'* reflect the mainly secular life expected from the most reputable clerics. Finding many dilapidated churches and ill-conducted services on his tours, John Byng reflected (1791), 'the day must come when this country will be convulsed by interior emotion, on the claims and oppressions of the clergy, their non-residence and neglect of duty'.[3] But there was one clerical activity that flourished – the sermons, vapid and somniferous as they were.† The

---

*Curate, one entrusted with the care of souls, originally meant any ecclesiastic, *Oxford English Dictionary*.

†'Dry, methodical, and unaffecting, delivered with the most insipid calmness', Goldsmith, *Essays*.

---

desire to have sermons – or at least one – in print, was widespread. Some were anxious to buy sermons, preferably printed in script, to read in the pulpit. Sermons could be best-sellers. Enormous quantities were printed, sometimes written in Grub Street. Even Charles Churchill left two volumes, posthumously printed. Parson Adams journeyed hopefully towards London with 'no less than nine volumes of manuscript sermons as well worth an hundred pounds as a shilling is worth twelvepence'. Parson Davey of Lustleigh, Devon, tried to get his sermons, preached 1771–81, printed. When he found it would cost him £2,000 he bought a press, and, helped by his maid, printed them in twenty-six octavo volumes.[4]

The toping, drunken parson was a favourite subject. He was embodied in illustrations to a popular song by George Steevens, *The Vicar and Moses*,[5] in what was almost a folk-print. This [69] was Rowlandson's version in 1784. There are at least four variants, not counting a barbed adaptation in 1831 (p. 185). The Clerk, Moses, goes to fetch the Vicar to bury an infant, and stays to drink with him till past midnight when they stagger out to go to the church. It seems odd that the names of Goldsmith's saintly Vicar and his son should have been given to these sots, but since Steevens was 'one of the wisest, most learned, but most spiteful of men',[6] a gibe at the sentimentality of the book was probably intended. Vicesimus Knox deplored the print's popularity 'among the vulgar'. 'It is often hung on the walls of farmhouses' and will inevitably diminish the respect for the clergy among those 'who from their infancy are accustomed to behold the parson as an object of derision, a glutton and a drunkard'.[7] Pert young Betsy Davey sent a *Vicar and Moses* to Woodforde as a valentine (1789) in no friendly spirit. We shall find it decorating an undergraduate's room. It was a subject for pottery, the Vicar in the pulpit, Moses below.

Perhaps (at this time) there was not much animus in such prints: all classes drank to excess. 'An honest drunken fellow is a character in a man's praise', Defoe had written in 1702. But guzzling parsons were another matter, inevitably associated with the grievance of tithes, with the pig as the inevitable symbol. In popular prints there are reincarnations of Parson Trulliber (in *Joseph Andrews*). 'A tithe-pig parson' was a term of abuse. There were ironical prints of clerical meals on the Fast Days proclaimed from time to time, notably on 19 April 1793, at the beginning of the war with the French Republic, for 'God's blessing and assistance to our arms and the restoring and perpetuating peace, safety and prosperity'. That is the date of Newton's anticlerical burlesque, *Fast Day* [70]. In Isaac Cruikshank's more serious *A General Fast in Consequence of the War* a year or so later, there are contrasted scenes, one in Lambeth Palace, all pomp and plenty, one in Spitalfields, in a starving weaver's room. 'A fast,' wrote Coleridge, 'a word that implies prayers of hate to the God of love – and after these a turbot feast for the rich, and their usual scanty morsel for the poor . . .'[8]

Seven degrees of clergy by Woodward in 1790 illustrate a parody of Shakespeare's 'seven ages'. The last, 'Sans shoes, Sans hose, sans breeches, sans everything', is *The Welch Parson*, traditionally the poorest of the poor. A Welsh curate, required to make a return to Parliament of the distresses of his neighbours, did so, adding, 'But their distresses cannot be greater than mine are. I have a wife who is far advanced in pregnancy, I have around me nine poor children, for whom I never yet provided shoe or stocking. . . . My income is £35 per annum, and for this I do the duty of four parishes.'[9]

A parson's progress from undergraduate to bishop in twenty-seven stages is depicted in *The Clerical Exercise* in 1791, a large plate after Woodward, a satire on patronage. Before ordination the young man asks his patron for a living, becomes a sporting parson, toadies the squire, marries his daughter, grows obese and clerical, finally attends a levee and gets his bishopric. Woodward's parsons are of all types from the arrogant and carbuncled to the slim, sleek and fashionable.

Apart from the display of cash, there is little exaggeration in *The Morning Visit* [71], 1773, where a dean asks a peer for a bishopric, though it may libel the dean concerned, Josiah Tucker of Gloucester. All classes, except the lowest, asked or intrigued for places and promotion, for themselves, their relations, their protégés; and the most highly placed were the most ruthlessly insistent. Farington has two tales about patronage, possibly apocryphal, but entirely credible.[10] When Erskine became Chancellor (1806), he told a son-in-law who was a doctor 'to leave Physick and turn to Divinity'. 'Holland understood the hint, took *Orders* and has already [January 1807] two or three livings.' Dr Samuel Goodenough had a school of fifteen boys at 150 guineas a year. 'Three or four sons of the Duke of Portland were educated there, but the Duke *never paid for them*.' But he did much better. He first presented Goodenough with a living, then obtained for him a canonry of Windsor, 'and lastly the Deanery of Rochester, the whole amounting to between two and three thousand pounds a year'. The *Dictionary of National Biography* confirms all but the school fee aspect (the authority for this was a drawing master at the school) and adds the Duke's final favour in 1808, the bishopric of Carlisle. Dr Goodenough was a scholar and F.R.S. but he was undoubtedly a pluralist. 'The parson knows enough who knows a duke.'

A feature of the period was the number of eccentric, unclerical clerics, who took to journalism or politics. Leaving out Sterne, examples are Cornelius Ford (p. 43), Parson Horne (afterwards Horne-Tooke), Charles Churchill, Bate (afterwards Bate-Dudley), 'the fighting parson'. Among other things Bate was duellist, playwright, journalist. He was the 'certain clergyman of extraordinary character' discussed by Johnson and Boswell in 1784, 'who by exerting his talents on temporary topicks, and displaying uncommon intrepidity', had 'raised himself to affluence'. The affluence departed, but for his 'most confidential services', the Regent made him a baronet in 1813 and gave him a stall at Ely. His demand for the deanery of Peterborough was defeated by Liverpool.[11] The only comparable doctor known to me is John Wolcot

70 *Fast Day*, R. Newton

71 *The Morning Visit*, anon.

– Peter Pindar – and he was in Orders. There were medical authors and men of learning in plenty.

Bonstetten, Gray's young Swiss friend, gives us a glimpse of Cambridge in 1770: 'Gray lived there, buried in a kind of cloister where the fifteenth century still lingered. The town of Cambridge with its isolated colleges was nothing but a cluster of monasteries where mathematics and some of the sciences had taken the shape and dress of medieval theology, beautiful monasteries with long silent corridors, solitary figures clad in black, young lords rigged out like monks in square caps, everywhere memories of monks alongside the glories of Newton.'

And, on academic boorishness, 'Long frozen faces, measured gait, bows with your hat on your head. . . . Here you only meet people formally, in the morning you ask permission to see someone in the evening, there are calls. . . . You will find three or four ladies sitting on chairs, while men with long black gowns occupy the sofas and easy chairs. . . . In France and with us silence is the most embarrassing thing in the world. . . . It is only in England that people know how to be silent; I have sometimes seen fifteen people sitting in a circle and saying nothing to each other for a quarter of an hour.'[12]

Bonstetten knew nothing of undergraduate life and seems to have met none but Gray's acquaintances. The university had its hierarchy corresponding more or less to that of the world outside. There was a gulf between Gentlemen Commoners (Fellow Commoners at Cambridge), not to speak of the lordlings in their gold-tasselled caps, and Servitors (Sizars at Cambridge). The former were rich, idle and privileged. The latter, if without patronage, over-crowded the market for curates, but with a patron and talent could rise high in the Church, bishoprics being divided between men of birth and men of ability.

College life was a favourite subject with amateur caricaturists, their designs usually etched by professionals. In the seventies Bunbury of Clare, Orde of King's, Topham of Trinity produced interesting Cambridge prints. *A School of Athens* after Orde [72], published in 1773 (after he had been a Fellow), is a satire on Cambridge in the setting of the old Provost's Lodge, looking over the Senate House and St Mary's Church, with Athene and her owl enshrined in a niche. The Provost presides, a scribe records the qualifications of the 'Professors of Arts and Sciences' who are collecting in the room; a dancing-master and a fencing master are prominent, others look as if they were more at home with horses and dogs than with books; all are probably portraits, the Provost being William Cooke, D.D., a former headmaster of Eton and a pluralist, of whom Cole says some very harsh things.

Two of Bunbury's Cambridge scenes, published in 1773 and 1774, are probably based on memories of Clare. *The Hopes of the Family—An Admission at the University* [73] and *The Xmas Academics* [74], four Fellows at a (dishonest) game of whist. By the Elizabethan statutes (valid in theory), cards were forbidden except during the twelve days of Christmas. More personal aspects of University life are the subjects of some prints sent by Cole to Walpole, with comments. There is one of 'Louse Hallifax' – afterwards Bishop of Gloucester – so called 'from his affectation of getting among the Heads of Colleges' – then an august and remote body. The spoils of a proctor (a woman's hat spiked on a halberd) and a practical joke are illustrated in *Venus turn'd Proctor* [75]. Cole explains: 'Mr Purkes [Purkis] of Magdalen College, Proctor in 1773, to whom some wag advertised that a basket of game was coming to him . . . which turn'd out to be dead cats and dogs &c. It is an handsome likeness of him. He stands in the attitude of the Venus of Medici in which posture he would frequently place himself before his Friends. Indeed he is a most consummate vain coxcomb always talking of uniting the Gentleman & the Scholar. . . . The People thought it wrong thus to expose a worthy man, for he was noways vicious but a good tutor & a no bad Scholar, yet others thought his vanity deserved it.'[13]

In *O Tempora, O Mores* [77], *c.* 1785, after Rowlandson, three undergraduates are discovered, by a horrified parent and tutor, dead to the world after a carouse. The room shows that their interests are wine, women and song. Prints on the wall illustrate contempt for the Church (for which one or more may be designed): 'The Vicar and Moses' and 'Dr Thumpcushion', a fat College Fellow embracing a woman.

The new century brought reforms to both universities. *The Rake's Progress at the University*, 1806, etched by Gillray, probably drawn by an undergraduate, probably of Cambridge, belongs to a more modern world. In five scenes it illustrates a sequence of College crimes committed by a well-meaning youth (he reads the 'Freshman's Guide'). He is seen emerging from 'the Fellows Bog', he walks upon 'the sacred grass', he brings a dog 'within the College walls'. And finally 'Expulsion waits that son of Alma Mater/Who dares to show his face in boot or gaiter'. And expelled he is [76].

A SCHOOL of ATHENS
dedicated to the illustrious LIGHT-RETRESS of her fame ... PROFESSORS of Arts & Sciences.
the UNIVERSITY of CAMBRIDGE.
O Matre pulchra filia pulchrior!

72 *A School of Athens, after T. Orde (afterwards Orde-Powlett, or Baron Bolion)*

THE HOPES OF THE FAMILY —— AN ADMISSION AT THE UNIVERSITY.

73 *The Hopes of the Family – An Admission at the University, Bunbury*

THE X.MAS ACADEMICS.
A COMBINATION GAME AT WHIST.

74 The Xmas Academics, Bunbury

75 Venus turn'd Proctor, anon.

76 The Rake's Progress at the University, Pl. V, Gillray

O Tempora,O Mores!

77 *O Tempora, O Mores, after Rowlandson*

Medicine

With all its archaisms, feuds and jealousies, the medical profession was the least harshly treated, the most progressive. But it attracted – understandably – a good deal of mistrust. Walpole was attacking medicine when he wrote 'Sure the devil's three names of Satan, Beelzebub and Lucifer, were given to him in his three capacities of priest, physician and lawyer!'[14] Besides the stereotypes – chiefly obsolescent physicians in consultation – medical history makes an impact, things were happening.[15] To begin with the stereotypes: *Dr Gallipot with his Wig of Knowledge* [78], 1774, is a bedside scene with the doctor weighing guineas in a scale. This looks like a satire on fee-grabbing, but it is a fact that John Hunter, anything but a fee-grabber,* took such a scale with him on his rounds, so presumably did others. (The scale was a result of the recent Coin Act against light guineas.)

The multiplication of doctors at a consultation was customary, but could be an aspect of fee-grabbing. In prints they range from three to six, as in *The Consultation* [79], after Rowlandson, *c.* 1785. In *Doctors Differ and their Patients die*, two doctors fight furiously while the moribund patient sits in a high-backed chair, gazing at space. It was supposed that, with only two, the junior must give way to the senior, but it was given out as a ruling of the College in 1753 that either the junior must submit, or a third be called in. Angelo records his experiences when he 'convened' three. 'They felt my pulse regularly every day for a week; they regularly closeted themselves to talk of the wind and the weather, or scandal and politics, for about five minutes'; each ordered a different remedy, 'took a guinea apiece and drove off to the next sufferer'. 'The multiplicity of them [doctors] has puzzled the case' – that of her little daughter – wrote Lady Pembroke in 1783.

Bath was of course a happy hunting ground for doctors, and they are prominent in Anstey's *New Bath Guide* (1766). Rowlandson's consultation over a gouty patient there, with the nurse asleep in her chair [80], 1798 – the doctors' dress old-fashioned by some thirty years – might have been an illustration of Anstey's lines:

> But so as I grew ev'ry day worse and worse,
> The doctor advised me to send for a nurse,
> And the nurse was so willing my health to restore,
> She advised me to send for a few doctors·more,
> For when any difficult work's to be done,
> Many heads can despatch it, much better than one.

Gout is pre-eminently the disease of the century. Next is hypochondria – melancholia, the English spleen – a cause of the alleged addiction of Englishmen to suicide, called by Dr Cheyne *The English Malady*, a book twice recommended by Johnson to Boswell. In *The Hypochondriac* in 1788 'the sage M.D.' discovers that the cause is

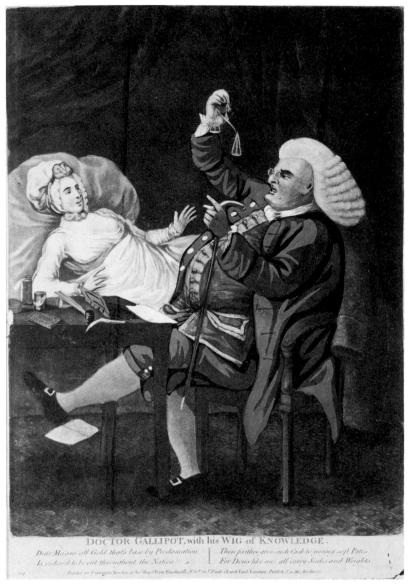

78 *Dr Gallipot with his Wig of Knowledge, anon.*

DOCTOR GALLIPOT, with his WIG of KNOWLEDGE.

---

*He took no fees from unbeneficed clergy, authors and artists. In his consulting room he saw his poor patients first.

79 *The Consultation, Rowlandson*

80 *Comforts of Bath, Pl. I, Rowlandson*

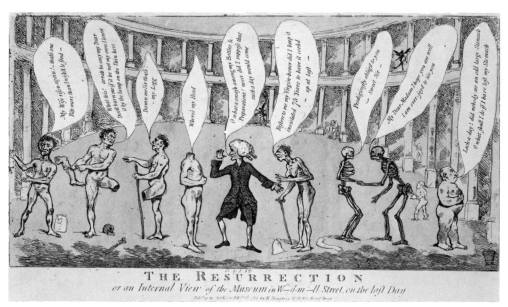

81 *The Resurrection or an Internal View*
of the Museum in W—d—ll Street
on the Last Day, (?) Rowlandson

93

82 *The Anatomist Overtaken by the Watch in Carrying off Miss W—tts in a Hamper, W. Austin*

83 *The Siege of Warwick Castle, anon.*

miserliness (shown over the fee) and arranges with the nurse for a potent and final remedy, 'the pitying bolus'.

The great development of the century was the advance of the surgeons after they had at last in 1745 separated themselves from the Barber-Surgeons and formed a Company of their own. Schools of anatomy and dissection, and some brilliant operators, Cheseldon, Percival Pott, and above all John Hunter, turned the craft into a profession. William Hunter's famous 'Museum' in Windmill Street, opened in 1770, is the scene of Rowlandson's macabre *The Resurrection or an Internal View of the Museum in W—d—ll Street on the Last Day* [81] with William Hunter in the foreground. These anatomical collections are now in the Hunterian Museum in Glasgow.

It became increasingly difficult to get enough subjects for dissection. Besides 'the Surgeons' mob' at Tyburn (p. 47) there were the resurrectionists who operated in graveyards. *The Anatomist Overtaken by the Watch in Carrying Off Miss W—tts in a Hamper* [82], 1773, clearly indicates some grisly tale. The Anatomist has dropped a paper, 'Hunter's Lectures'. The brothers would go to any length to get an interesting subject, but it was John, the most famous anatomist and surgeon of the century, who organized the extensive body-snatching necessary for the school. He dealt with the brigand bands and 'almost certainly' body-snatched himself.[16] Nevertheless, 'More than any other man he helped to make us gentlemen'.[17]

Before this, the matter of the status of the surgeons had precipitated a 'battle' between the College and the Licentiates. The latter were outraged in 1767 at a by-law that no one who had ever practised surgery could become a Fellow. Some Licentiates found themselves excluded from a dinner and a meeting at the College, then in Warwick Lane. A body of them broke in, blows were exchanged, squibs and prints followed. This was the subject of Foote's play, *The Devil upon Two Sticks* (1772), a farcical but barbed satire on the profession, in which the eccentric President of the College, Sir William Browne, was mimicked by Foote. While the battle goes on, the doctors neglect their patients, so that the weekly tale of London deaths (recorded in the Bills of Mortality) declines. But Foote qualified his satire: 'In some of the professors, a science, noble salutary and liberal; in others, a trade, as mean as it is mercenary; a contemptible combination of dunces, nurses, and apothecaries.' According to the play the invaders were routed by the College fire-engine. They brought an action against the College and lost it. In *The Siege of Warwick Castle* [83] the President is Death, the Licentiates, with Folly for their leader, are 'surgeons, apothecaries and quacks', but their chief crime is to be Scots.

A later battle was between the two kinds of surgeon, the minority, skilled and dignified, and those who were of the petty shopkeeping class, remnants and successors of the Barber-Surgeons. The Company was negligently allowed to lapse in 1796; leading surgeons petitioned for it to be replaced by a College, and were violently opposed by humbler practitioners. A rabid speech by Thurlow in the Lords defeated the petition: 'the merciless cruelty of these

regulations could only be supported by a surgeon'. Hence *The Battle of the Barbers and Surgeons* by Isaac Cruikshank. The combatants exchange insults: '. . . why I let as much blood for a penny as you charge a guinea for'. The matter was settled in 1800 by a Charter establishing the Royal College of Surgeons of London – a landmark, though till after 1858 both Colleges represented privilege and social status rather than brains.

Jenner's introduction of vaccination for smallpox in 1796 was eagerly accepted and violently resisted. There were vested interests (the old inoculators), and medical jealousies. Controversy raged, reflecting avarice, intrigue, calculated ridicule, popular enthusiasm. Graphic satire was strongly anti-Jenner. Out of a number of vaccination prints between 1801 and 1812 only one is Jennerian. In Gillray's *The Cow-Pock – or – the Wonderful Effects of the New Inoculation* [V] there is a good portrait of Jenner. In this blend of realism and fantasy the scene is the Smallpox and Inoculation Hospital at St Pancras: institutions for the gratuitous vaccination of the poor had multiplied. When Oxford gave Jenner the M.D. degree in 1812 (the first for seventy years), it was supposed that his election to the College of Physicians would follow. But no, he could not be admitted unless he underwent an examination in classics. He had been honoured by almost every other medical body in the world.

By the end of the century, it was mortifying that while lawyers, clerics, soldiers and sailors, some from humble beginnings, had achieved seats in the Lords, no physician had done so, despite their gentility, their 'sociable and agreeable dispositions', and their wealth. 'The office of a physician,' wrote Dr Thomas Percival, 'can never be supported but as a lucrative one.'[18] Baronetcies and knighthoods were less gratifying now that surgeons had received these honours.*

As in the legal profession, it was the lower grades that were gaining ground. Apothecaries were acting in every respect as doctors. 'I ever thought a good honest Apothecary a much safer person to apply to than half the Physicians and Surgeons in the Kingdom', Cole journalized in 1766, 'but there is the Difficulty; an Apothecary, by the influence the Physicians have over them, dares not prescribe . . . for fear of the Physician . . . tho' he may know in his own Judgment the Physician has mistaken the Case, & knows little of the matter. And to such a pass are we come, that the Fees of these Gentry are so exorbitant and excessive. . . .'[19]

The typical country doctor was an apothecary with some knowledge of surgery and midwifery, and was often as poor as the London doctor was rich – dependent on his horse or his legs – though some did well: Mr Perry of Highbury 'set up his carriage'. *The Village Doctor* [84], 1774, is comic realism, with the apothecary's sign and the placard, 'Probe – Surgeon and Man-midwife'. Mr or Dr – the style was important. Parson Woodforde calls his medical man Mr or Dr indiscriminately and once at

*The first surgeon baronet was Caesar Hawkins in 1778. The first medical peer, in 1897, was a surgeon, Lister.

least, 'Mr *alias* Dr'. In 1775 an Aberdeen doctor brought an action for damages against the infirmary there for calling him 'doctor of medicine' instead of physician, and lost his absurd case.* Jenner, a country doctor and technically a surgeon (he was a pupil of John Hunter) bought an M.D. degree from St Andrews (by post) when he began to practise at Cheltenham.

Outside the hierarchy there were the unqualified, practising among the poor, like Johnson's humble friend Robert Levett, who survives through Boswell, and in Johnson's lines '. . . officious, innocent, sincere, of every friendless man the friend'. Levett excepted, they are a nameless forgotten crowd. Very different were the quacks, patronized by the quality, notorious for fantastic advertising and ill-gotten wealth:

> These creatures, nature meant should clean our streets,
> Have purchas'd lands and houses, country seats.[20]

Only a few star performers can be noticed. Easily first was James Graham and his Temple of Health and of Hymen, with its Goddess of Health. From the Adelphi he moved to Pall Mall, with his two gigantic porters and the famous Celestial Bed, a cure for sterility at an enormous fee. Graham was 'The Emperor of the Quacks' played by Bannister in Colman's *The Genius of Nonsense* (Haymarket 1783) 'which faithfully represented the Bottle Conjurer of the Adelphi'.[21] He also used electricity and magnetism and was a compound of quack, visionary and fashionable doctor. In *The Quacks*, 1783, he competes with Katerfelto, a German, who was quack, travelling showman and conjurer, with a slogan, 'Wonders, Wonders, Wonders'.

Then there was Buzaglo, a Jew, who first attracted attention as an inventor of heating apparatus, and then set up, very successfully, as a gout doctor, professing to cure by muscular exercises only, helped out by 'wedges and pegs'.[22] His famous establishment is the subject of Sandby's *Ballet Arthritique*, 1783. Under his direction men with their limbs strapped into wooden cases are performing exercises in painfully contorted attitudes. At the turn of the century, and typical of changes since the days of the Celestial Bed, was Benjamin Perkins from Connecticut (son of Benjamin Perkins of the Perkinean Institute), who advertised (1796–1802) his patent Metallic Tractors at five guineas a set. In Gillray's *Metallic-Tractors* he is operating on a patient whose grossly carbuncled nose bursts into flame. A newspaper advertisement is displayed '. . . just arrived from America the Rod of Æsculapius. Perkinism in all its Glory – being a certain Cure for all Disorders; Red Noses, Gouty Toes, Windy Bowels, Broken Legs, Hump Backs. Just discover'd, the Grand Secret of the Philosopher's Stone with the true way of turning all Metals into Gold.' A typical example of Gillray's ways with puffing advertisers. The astonishing thing, recently discovered,[23] is that Perkins almost certainly commissioned this, was certainly pleased with it, paid for it and ordered twelve copies, asking for secrecy. Is this the first impact of Transatlantic advertising on England? Dr Haygarth had already exposed Perkins in his book *Imagination as a Cause and a Cure of Disorders of the Body*, showing that wooden imitations of the tractors had effected more 'cures' than Perkins's device.

There were also the travelling quacks who set up a stage with a zany or mountebank to attract attention – doctors of the poor. 'Dr Bossey' (i.e. Garcia, a Jew) is said to have been the last, at the end of the century. The travelling dentist who extracted teeth by beat of drum, survived much longer. His Elizabethan predecessor had been 'Kind Heart the Tooth-Drawer', one of the *Cries* of London (the music survives). By 1800 science had scarcely touched dentistry, though there were fashionable practitioners in London. A pair of Bowles mezzotints in 1784 are probably documentary, *The London Dentist* and *The Country Tooth Drawer*. The fashionably dressed dentist in his handsomely furnished room inserts his implement into the mouth of a middle-aged woman, while a female friend registers anguished sympathy. A Negro page in livery holds a case of instruments. The other scene is a smithy with a lighted forge. The farrier tugs with both hands at the pincers in his victim's mouth, pressing his foot against her leg. She is an old woman sitting on a low stool. Leather-aproned men look on, without sympathy; one holds her head. Parson Woodforde called in the village farrier to extract a tooth. Rowlandson's *Transplanting of Teeth* [VII], 1787, satirizes a practice, not abandoned till the turn of the century, by which the teeth of the poor were transferred to the jaws of the rich, often with lethal results to the latter.[24] The print was perhaps inspired by a forgotten novel:[25] a young chimney sweep describes the miseries of his little sister who had 'nothing but naked jaws since she was nine years old'. Dentists charged more for a 'live' transplantation than for a complete set of false teeth and these might cost up to £500.*

---

*Boswell was counsel for the Infirmary. The doctor, John Menzies, was a St Andrews M.D. *Boswell: The Ominous Years* (see Ch. VIII, n. 15), pp. 62, 100, 148.

*Human teeth were more costly than manufactured ones; the battlefields of the Peninsula were raided by dentists' emissaries, and 'Waterloo teeth' filled many mouths, E. S. Turner, *Call the Doctor*, (London: Michael Joseph, 1958), pp. 128–9.

THE VILLAGE DOCTOR.

Pub June 8th 1774 by H Humphrey Bond Street

84 The Village Doctor, (?) H. Wigstead (attributed to Rowlandson)

97

The Law

From medicine to the law is (despite the College) from the most forward-looking to the most conservative of the professions, tangled up in medieval survivals, complicated by legal fictions and pleadings. Its treatment in satire is also peculiarly traditional. To quote *The Times* (28 January 1856) 'Of the three learned professions, the medical has attained the highest character for disinterestedness. Hard things are said of the cupidity of the clergy . . .; still harder things are said of the lawyers, who are supposed to eat the contested oyster, while the plaintiff gets one shell, the defendant the other.' The ancient parable of the oyster pervades the legal prints. Pope's lines are *Verbatim from Boileau*:

> *Two trav'lers found an oyster in their way . . .*
> *'There take,' says Justice, 'take you each a shell,*
> *We thrive at Westminster on fools like you,*
> *'Twas a fat oyster – Live in peace – adieu.'*

This is the theme of *A Sharp between Two Flats* [86], a Bowles mezzotint of 1791: 'A Pearly Shell for Him and Thee – The Oyster is the Lawyer's fee'.

Throughout this century and the Regency, despite the efforts of Romilly and others, there is no hint of blame for the harshness of the criminal law.* Injury to property,

---

*A possible exception is the rope round the judge's neck in Hogarth's *Royalty, Episcopacy and Law* in 1724. See M.D.George, *English Political Caricature to* 1792 (Oxford: O.U.P., 1960), pp. 76–7.

especially landed property, inspires a pictorial chorus of hate. The Court of Chancery was 'aptly described' as 'a great machine for grinding down the landed interest into three per cent consols and then distributing it in costs'.

The Devil was gradually disappearing from the satirical print – attacks on Napoleon excepted – but he remained perennially associated with the lawyer. The lawyer's 'last circuit' was a traditional subject repeated from decade to decade – he rides to Hell on a skeleton horse. In this one [85], 1782, the quotation from *Hamlet*, beginning 'Where be his quiddits . . .', implies a barrister's sophistries – what Johnson called, defending it, 'the artefice of the Bar'. *The Old Bailey Advocate bringing off a Thief* about 1789 is on the same theme; he tramples on Truth and 'by flow of jaw' helps the felon 'to escape the law'. In Foote's play *The Lame Lover* (1770) the function of a barrister, according to the predatory Mr Sergeant Circuit, is 'to wrest as much land from the owners, and save as many thieves from the gallows, as any practitioner from the days of King Alfred'. Wilkes was fond of saying that 'the name of a lawyer is another name for a scoundrel'.

The First Day of Term was another traditional subject, with lawyers of all ranks from the Chancellor to clerks converging on Westminster Hall like birds of prey. In a mezzotint of 1782 with the subtitle, *The Devil among the Lawyers* [87] the allegations are forgery, bribery, excessive costs and a Chancery suit begun in 1699 and 'not yet finished'. Attorneys had a specially bad reputation. There was Johnson's famous remark, 'he did not care to speak ill of any man behind his back, but he believed the gentle-

THE LAWYERS LAST CIRCUIT.

Where be his quiddits now? his quillets? his cases? his
tenures? and his tricks? Why does he suffer this rude knave
to knock him about the sconce with a rotten jaw-bone, and will
not tell him of his action of battery? — — — *Hamlet.*

Published April 25 1782 by J.R. Smith No.83 opposite the Pantheon Oxford Street London

85 *The Lawyer's Last Circuit,* (?) *after Rowlandson*

man was an attorney'. But the attorneys were in fact turning their despised calling into a profession, and climbing the social ladder at least as successfully as the apothecaries. By the end of the century the term solicitor (previously restricted to those who practised in Chancery) was replacing attorney with its pejorative associations. Already in 1739 they had formed the Society of Gentlemen Practitioners in the Courts of Law and Equity which was the direct ancestor of the Law Society founded in 1827.[26] And though lands were lost by litigation, reckless extravagance and gaming were more common causes of ruin. The attorney–solicitor was becoming more and more essential to the landed interest for conveyancing, settlements, mortgages, loans, and general rescue from disaster. And of course to trade. Mrs Thrale found Charles Scrase 'a good attorney and a true friend' (he had lent money to the brewery), and 'loved, esteemed and honoured' him next to Johnson.[27]

Rowlandson's barristers are personifications of corrupt senility, greed and arrogance. *A Counciller* [88] probably dates from 1780; his wig, like that of his colleagues, has the black patch of a Sergeant, a superior order of barrister from whom the judges were chosen.

A SHARP BETWEEN TWO FLATS.
A Pearly Shell for HIM and THEE. ____ The OYSTER is the Lawyers Fee

86 *A Sharp between Two Flats, after Dighton*

Notes to Chapter X

1. W. Cowper, *Tirocinium*, 1784.
2. Cf. N. Sykes, *Church and State in the Eighteenth Century* (Cambridge: C.U.P., 1934).
3. John Byng, *Torrington Diaries*, ed. C. B. Andrews, vol. II (London: Eyre & Spottiswoode, 1935).
4. Tindal Hart, *The Eighteenth Century Country Parson*, (Shrewsbury: Wilding, 1955), p. 41.
5. *Roxburghe Ballads*, vol. III, p. 313.
6. Boswell, *Johnson*, vol. III (Oxford: O.U.P., 1934), p. 281n.
7. *Winter Evenings* (1787), British Essayists, vol. XXXVIII, p. 131.
8. *Essays on his own Times*, 1850, vol. II, p. 45 (February 1795).
9. A correspondent of *Archaeologia Cambrensis*, 1873, quoting the *Annual Register 1788*, where I have failed to trace it.
10. *Farington Diary*, ed. James Greig, vol. IV (London: Hutchinson, 1922–8), pp. 76, 83.
11. A. Aspinall, *Politics and the Press* (Home & Van Thal, 1949), pp. 169–71.
12. V. de Bonstetten, *Souvenirs* (Paris, 1831), quoted F. Wilson (ed.), *Strange Island* (London: Longmans, 1955), p. 106.
13. *Horace Walpole's Correspondence*, ed. W. S. A. Lewis and D. Wallace, vol. I (Oxford: O.U.P., 1937).
14. To Sir Horace Mann, 9 January 1775.
15. My chief authorities are C. Wall and others, *History of the Society of Apothecaries of London*, Wellcome Historical Medical Museum, 1963, vol. I; *The Evolution of Medical Practice in Britain*, ed. F. N. L. Poynter (London: Pitman, 1961); E. S. Turner, *Call the Doctor* (London: Michael Joseph, 1958); J. Kobler, *The Reluctant Surgeon* (London: Heinemann, 1960). Unfortunately, Sir G. Clark's *History of the Royal College of Physicians*, vol. II, 1966, appeared after this book was in print.
16. J. Kobler (see note 15), p. 66.
17. *Hunterian Oration*, 1877.
18. Thomas Percival, M.D., *Medical Ethics*, 1803.
19. W. Cole, *Paris Journal*, ed. F. G. Stokes (London: Constable, 1931), p. 372.
20. George Crabbe, *The Borough*, 1810.
21. Henry Angelo, *Reminiscences*, 1904, vol. I, p. 97.
22. According to Christopher Anstey's *Election Ball*, 1776.
23. Draper Hill, *Mr James Gillray the Caricaturist* (London: Phaidon, 1965), pp. 140–1.
24. J. Kobler (see note 15), pp. 132–42.
25. *The Adventures of a Rupee*, Helenus Scott, 1782.
26. E. N. Williams, *Life in Georgian England* (London: Batsford, 1962), pp. 59–61.
27. *Thraliana*, ed. K. C. Balderston (Oxford: O.U.P., 1952), pp. 330, 364, etc.

The FIRST DAY of TERM __ or, The DEVIL among the LAWYERS.

"The Lawyers are met, a terrible shew"

Printed for & Sold by BOWLES & CARVER.   No.69 St.Paul's Church Yard, LONDON.

87 The First Day of Term – or the Devil among the Lawyers, after Dighton

A COUNCILLER.

90 *A Poney Race, after G.M.Woodward*

A PONEY RACE.

From the Seven Years War to Trafalgar and after, the sailor is the subject of innumerable prints – often charming – his 'Farewell', his 'Return' (found also on mugs and punch-bowls), his adventures and misadventures. There is much sentiment and comedy, relatively little satire. Our print-shop sailor is usually on shore, either with money to burn and bent on pleasure, and of course a prey to harpies, or sadly maimed and begging for alms. The punning title of *A Rich Privateer brought safe into Port by Two First Rates* [III], 1782, a Bowles mezzotint, tells its story. In this brothel scene one woman dips her hand into the sailor's hatful of guineas, another has grabbed his watch and seals, while a typical 'landlady' brings up a bowl of punch. The rollicking sailor on shore comes splendidly to life in Rowlandson's drawing of 'The King and Queen on their way to Deptford to launch a man-of-war' [134].

For the other side of the picture there is *The Sailor's Return or Valour Rewarded* [89], 1783, after some resounding naval victories, where two cruelly maimed men beg in a London street. We have seen two others defeated by an admiral's 'Inflexible porter', and there is Rowlandson's

drawing of *Naval Veterans*, dragging the model of a ship through the streets asking for alms, like the 'frozen out gardeners' who paraded with the tools of their trade.

With the war against Napoleon prints of the sailor ashore multiply; he is treated with affectionate ridicule – his sea-lingo adapted to civil life, a speciality of Woodward, as in *A Poney Race* [90], 1807, one of many of the sailor on horseback. First sailor: 'Hallo you Swab lay to a bit . . . I've lost part of my upper rigging . . .'. *Sailors Rigging out Poll* is a scene in a Monmouth Street shop with much dialogue. 'Why Poll . . . you look like a Bond Street Frigate steering towards Pall Mall. . . .'

While the Navy is represented chiefly by Jack Tar – 'Poor Jack' – the commissioned ranks are more prominent in army prints. The plight of the officer on half-pay roused sympathy and indignation. Booth's distresses (in *Amelia*, 1751) illustrate the fate of the officer without interest or private means; an appeal to a 'peer with very considerable interest' is in vain: 'With regard to the personal merit of these inferior officers, I believe I need not tell you,' says the peer, 'that it is very little regarded.'

91 The Comforts – and – Curse of a Military Life, T.Colley

The Comforts – and – Curse of a Military Life [91], 1781, is inscribed: 'To the Commander in Chief and Secretary of War – Under all Administrations. Gent^m. You have been found callous to the Meritorius claims of Veteran Soldiers and remain heroically unmoved by their memorials unless accompanied by a Bribe to your Secretarys or a Vote in a dirty Borough. . . .'

The impact of the American war on social life is discoverable in a spate of prints on militia camps from 1778 (till France declared war no impact is traceable). Camp topics are visitors in search of amusement – the camps attracted sightseers in crowds –, soldiers' womenfolk and unsoldierly soldiers. The camps were part of the defences of the country (threatened with invasion in August and September 1779), and aids to recruiting. *The Camp* by Tickell was popular for two seasons at Drury Lane, its chief attraction being a realistic view by Loutherbourg of Coxheath Camp near Maidstone. 'I like the life very well,' a young officer wrote from Coxheath in September 1779, 'it is however rather too much of a lounge.'* *A Visit to the Camp* [92], 1779, is by Bunbury.

Gillray, son of a soldier who lost an arm at Fontenoy, had sympathy for the rank and file and a sardonic eye for the officer. His famous *A March to the Bank* [93], 1787, a daily event after the Gordon Riots, is ostensibly a satire on military arrogance. But, with a side thrust at the foppish officer, it is really aimed at the City authorities, who had

---
* *Pembroke Papers*, ed. Lord Herbert, vol. 1 (London: Jonathan Cape, 1939), p. 240.

seized on a complaint by a citizen that he had been pushed off the pavement to request the Secretary at War to order the men to march in single file. But the soldiers had complained of *their* treatment in the City, and the request was refused. At length the City asked for the withdrawal of the guard; the King's illness intervened, the matter was allowed to drop, though not without protest from the City, and the guard still goes there daily, but not on foot.

During the war with the French Republic, Guards officers evoked pictorial squibs from Gillray. In *Hero's recruiting at Kelsey's; – or – Guard-Day at St James's* [IX], the scene is a famous 'fruit shop lounge' (such shops were a London feature) in St James's Street, and there is satire for the commissions given to boys (with interest in high places). The lank elderly officer is one Captain Birch who must be the persistent and derided suitor of one of the Miss Wynnes as recorded in *The Wynne Diaries*.

Camps, and 'expeditions' however 'secret', were a great opportunity for sightseeing and beanfeasting, notably the 'Grand Expedition' to the Scheldt in 1809, when the transports lay in the Downs waiting for a wind, while Sir William Curtis, Alderman, friend of the Prince and butt of the caricaturists, sailed about in his yacht, taking 'delicate refreshments . . . to the military and naval commanders'. In *An Affecting Scene in the Downs* [94], one of George Cruikshank's earliest plates, the heading to a broadside, Curtis takes leave of Castlereagh, a reputed incident at the sailing of the ill-fated expedition.

92 *A Visit to the Camp, Bunbury*

A VISIT to the CAMP

93 *A March to the Bank, Gillray*

94 *An Affecting Scene in the Downs, G. Cruikshank*

95 *Blowing up the Pic Nics – or – Harlequin Quixotte attacking the Puppets*, Gillray

The theatre, always a major print-shop preoccupation, became so more than ever when Sheridan succeeded Garrick at Drury Lane. Garrick's farewell to the stage was a landmark. His intention to retire was made known to his friends in December 1775; in January the sale of Old Drury to Sheridan and his partners was arranged, and the splendid property was launched on its road to ruin. But first Garrick appeared in a series of farewell performances of his most famous parts, the last of all on 10 June. Garrick played Don Felix in Mrs Centlivre's *The Wonder*; his short farewell speech was interrupted by a burst of tears. Players and audience felt that the 'musical entertainment' could not take place. The curtain fell on 'the excited plaudits of the most brilliant and enthusiastic audience that had ever filled that historic house'.[1] Graphic satire's tribute was the dedication (1 January 1776) 'to David Garrick Esq.' of a handsome four-guinea collection of 'Darly's Comic Prints of Characters, Caricatures, Macaronies, &.' by Mary Darly, decorated with medallion profiles of Garrick. She had etched his portrait as Abel Drugger.

In the prints the standard themes persisted; for instance, that of contrasted audiences. Rowlandson's *Comedy Spectators. Tragedy Spectators* [96], 1789, illustrates the rapt attention of the less fashionable part of the house, and the tears that flowed so easily. The tragedy is *Romeo and Juliet*. The Shakespeare revival prospered, with its adaptations and perversions, while pantomime and spectacle kept all their popularity and spread to the minor theatres. *Dr Faustus* was revived at Covent Garden in 1768, where there was another variant in 1793, *Harlequin and Faustus*.

The old theme of the neglect of the drama for spectacle was fully illustrated and it survived in the pages of *Punch* till the monopoly of the two Patent Theatres ended in 1844. That the English were Shakespeare enthusiasts was repeated by foreign visitors, but, according to Wendeborn, the Prussian who had lived many years in London, songs and dances had to be introduced between the acts to keep the audience awake. And in Colman's *Old Brooms* (1776) a Frenchman asks 'Vat signifie your triste Sha-kes-peare . . . You mak-a de dance, and de musique, and de pantomime of your Sha-kes-peare, and den he do ver well'.

National interest in the theatre and its attraction for graphic satire were stimulated by the star character of the chief performers. These were, first Sheridan, as Manager, playwright, Prince's friend, politician, and wit; then the Kemble family; and ultimately, Kean, with many others of good magnitude including prima donnas (Billington and Catalani), and Mrs Jordan. When both theatres had been destroyed by fire (1809), both John Bull and the fashionable world were involved in the contrasted dramas of their restoration.

The theatre was rather less disorderly than before, but 'King, Lords, and Commons, o'er the Nation sit;/Pit Box and Gallery, rule the realms of Wit'.[2] A minor but most characteristic 'riot' at Drury Lane was witnessed by Dr Campbell, an Irish parson, who recorded his astonishment at a scene 'that strongly marked the English character'. It did not go beyond an hour and a half of uproar and missiles, chiefly apples and oranges, after which the farce was heard, but not in silence. By custom, the prologue and epilogue were dropped after the ninth night. On the tenth night of *Braganza** neither was on the bill, but the prologue was called for and delivered. The epilogue was not. Tumult followed. No propitiatory explanations that Mrs Yates was sick and in bed could appease 'the savages of the gallery', who clamoured for their 'rights' – her absence was 'an insult'. Among Campbell's neighbours in the pit there were noisy disputes between the clamourers and those who wanted quiet: 'The smallest fraction of such language w^d have produced a duel in the Dublin theatre. . . . And the millionth part of the submissions made by these poor players w^d have appeased an Irish audience. – Yea if they had murdered their fathers.'†[3] In the classic riot of 1809 (p. 112) it was an outrage when Kemble asked 'What is it you want?' instead of 'What is your pleasure?'

Overcrowding was worse than ever. *The Pit Door* [97] after Dighton in 1784 shows what could happen when Mrs Siddons was to play a favourite part. It is Euphrasia in Murphy's *The Grecian Daughter*. Disorder in the foyers was endemic, but of a different and very characteristic sort. Rowlandson's *Box Lobby Loungers* [98], 1786, is a Covent Garden scene, with rakes, beaux, bold courtesans, and a bawd with her playbills and basket of fruit. This was a nuisance said to have become worse by 1818, but perhaps only more conspicuous in a less tolerant world. Elizabeth Heber's reactions on a visit to Paris in 1802 are revealing. She found the decorum in the theatres 'very striking', 'not a whisper to be heard and every body in a crowded house attentive only to the performance; no rioting in the lobbies, or, in short, any impropriety of behaviour'.[4]

Another landmark was Mrs Siddons's triumph at Drury Lane in October 1782, followed by the eminence of the Kemble family. Jealousies were acute, and attacks on her

---

*A successful verse tragedy by Robert Jephson, extravagantly praised by his friends, including H. Walpole, who wrote the epilogue.

†It is irresistible to compare this with the memorable riot in the Abbey Theatre, Dublin (1907) over Synge's *Playboy of the Western World* who was totally discredited because, after all, he had *not* murdered his father.

COMEDY   SPECTATORS

TRAGEDY   SPECTATORS

96 *Comedy Spectators. Tragedy Spectators, Rowlandson*

97 *The Pit Door, after Dighton*

The PIT DOOR.   La PORTE du PARTERRE.

were vocal, fostered by the rivalry between the two theatres. In *The Rival Queens of Covent Garden and Drury Lane at a Gymnastic Rehearsal* [99] the Garden Queen is probably Mrs Yates – both played Euphrasia in the 1782–3 season – and the backers are probably the ladies' husbands: an anonymous critic, believed to be Yates, had supported Mrs Yates's claim, while Henry Siddons had written newspaper puffs for his wife, and was Evander in the play. Here the fool's cap is for Mrs Siddons, the laurel for her rival. The print was re-issued as *The Rival Queens or Mrs S—ddons and Mrs C—f—d Boxing for the Theatrical Laurel*: Mrs Siddons had openly wished that Mrs Crawford would retire and leave the field to herself. In 1816 (p. 205) she was to be again satirized, as Roxana, in Lee's tragedy, but more woundingly – confronted by a younger woman.

Like Reynolds, Gillray depicted Mrs Siddons as the Tragic Muse: in *Melpomene* [100], 1784, she is accused of shameless greed; the calumny reflects an incident in October 1783, when she was hissed off the stage after an accusation of taking large sums in Dublin for acting in benefits for distressed players. In Edinburgh, in the previous May, nine performances had brought the then unprecedented sum of £975, hence the money bags. A reputation for stinginess, not completely baseless, clung to her: she had known great poverty and was anxious to provide for her children. In this age of many spendthrifts and some misers thrift was not admired.

The Kemble family had an aloof dignity that attracted satire, even spite. John Kemble is Henry V in his own adaptation of the play in *How to Tear a Speech to Tatters* in 1789. His sister is more maliciously attacked in *How to Harrow up the Soul* with inscriptions blaming her for parsimony and mechanical gestures. Stephen Kemble, a year younger than John, was a gourmand who could play Falstaff without padding. Though more Manager than actor, he did play Hamlet when he was eighteen stone, and Dighton's *Hamlet in Scotland* [101] is more realistic than might be supposed. He wears the Danish Order of the Elephant and the traditional black velvet for the part.

Mrs Siddons, Mrs Jordan, and Miss Farren, in different ways, all contributed to the improved status of the actress (it is true that in 1730 Mrs Oldfield had been buried in the Abbey, but the Dean had forbidden a monument). Mrs Jordan, 'the Muse of Comedy', though beloved, was at times an irresistible target. Ultimately, her liaison with the Duke of Clarence gave her prestige, but in 1791, when she left Richard Ford (by whom she had four children) for the Duke, she was a print-shop victim. Their domestic life, devoted to their large family, conquered scandal, but not ridicule. The question became, 'if he kept her or she kept him'. Their published letters now show that both contributed to the chronically insolvent household at Bushey in a modern middle-class way.[5] Gillray symbolized this in 1797, when there were three out of their ten children, in *La Promenade en Famille – a Sketch from Life* [X], a Bushey Park scene. He drags the infants in a go-cart, while she studies a favourite part, Pickle in *The Spoil'd Child*. She was, says Leigh Hunt, 'neither beautiful, nor handsome,

BOX LOBBY LOUNGERS

98 Box Lobby Loungers, Rowlandson

99 The Rival Queens of Covent Garden and Drury Lane at a Gymnastic Rehearsal, anon.

*The Rival Queens of Covent Garden and
Drury Lane Theatres, at a Gymnastic Rehearsal !*

nor even pretty, nor "a lady", nor anything conventional nor *comme il faut* whatever, she appeared something superior to requisites of acceptability'.[6]

Miss Farren was acceptability personified. Lord Derby's attentions to her had been a print-shop theme since 1781; the long succession of prints on the decorous courtship began with Bunbury [102], an opportunity for his favourite topic of bad horsemanship. 'Lord Derby is still in pursuit of Miss Farren,' Hare wrote to Lord Carlisle, 'the caricature has had the good effect of mending his seat on horseback, which is entirely changed.'[7] At last, in 1797, Lady Derby died (he had refused to divorce her, determined she should not marry the Duke of Dorset), Miss Farren made her stage farewell, and married Lord Derby, all in seven weeks, and was favourably received at Court. Gillray's brilliant travesty of the cameo known as the Marlborough Gem, *The Marriage of Cupid and Psyche* [103], is one of a spate of satires.

By the nineties Sheridan had long been deep in debt, the finances of his theatre in confusion. The rebuilding of Drury Lane, supposedly unsafe, made things worse.* The new theatre was too big, and so was Covent Garden, recently enlarged, and this aggravated the admitted decline of the drama towards melodrama and spectacle. John Byng, seeing Mrs Siddons as Queen Catherine in the newly

*The last performance in the old theatre was on 4 June 1791, the first in the new one (Henry Holland's), 12 March 1794.

opened theatre, mourned for 'Old Drury'. 'The nice discriminations of the actors' feelings are now all lost in the vast void of the new theatre. . . .'[8] Box office successes were more necessary than ever, and the theatre lurched from one sensation to another, with Sheridan in the limelight.

His *Pizarro* in 1799, adapted from Kotzebue's *The Spaniards of Peru*, was more than a theatrical sensation. It hit the public taste, but its great popularity had patriotic implications: Spain=France, Peru=Britain, and a long speech by Rolla (Kemble) roused enthusiasm: 'They follow an adventurer, whom they fear. . . . We serve a monarch whom we adore.'* This tribute to George III from a Foxite outraged Fox and his friends; others deplored the prostitution of the talents of the author of *The School for Scandal*. Sheridan was accused of selling himself; prints multiplied, and the most effectively cruel was *Pizarro contemplating over the product of his new Peruvian Mine* [VIII] by Gillray. In fact the play was a gold mine for Drury Lane.

The next sensation was Sheridan's war against the fashionable amateurs of the Pic Nic Society. This had been organized by Colonel Greville to give public performances in a little theatre in the Tottenham Street Rooms. Pic Nic connoted the arrangement by which each member contri-

*In 1803 the speech was widely circulated on placards and broadsides as *Sheridan's Address to the People*, part of a flood of loyal papers issued under the threat of invasion. In the Second World War it was printed in *The Times* in their 'Old and True' series, also under threat of invasion.

100 Melpomene, Gillray

101 Hamlet in Scotland, Dighton

buted provisions for their suppers. Sheridan organized a Press attack: they were infringing the monopoly of the Patent Theatres and, as players in an unlicensed theatre, were threatened with proceedings for vagrancy – a great opening for caricaturists in 1802–3. Gillray's *Blowing up the Pic Nics – or – Harlequin Quixote attacking the Puppets* [95] is characteristically double-edged. After rehearsing Fielding's farce, *Tom Thumb* (the vast Lady Bucks as Dollalolla), the amateurs are feasting on their little stage, when they are terror-struck by an invasion of the professionals, led by Sheridan. He is Harlequin (with an empty purse), masked because of his anonymous newspaper paragraphs; the sparks from his swirling pen are the fruits of his Press campaign. Kemble, Mrs Siddons and Mrs Billington (the prima donna) follow at the head of a massed army of undistinguished players under the banners of the dramatists they neglect: Shakespeare (torn to show the mutilation of his plays), Otway, Rowe, with Kotzebue and Schiller (tricolour to imply the revolutionary character of German drama), Jonson, Congreve, Addison. Garrick's ghost rises through the boards. This particular attack reflects an outcry prophecying divine judgement on the Pic Nics for Sunday rehearsals. Sheridan triumphed, the Pic Nic enterprise collapsed.

A far bigger sensation followed – the astonishing rage for Master Betty, Young Roscius (1791–1874). After successes in Ireland and Scotland he appeared at Covent Garden (1 December 1804) at fifty guineas a night (while Kemble had £27 16s. a week),[9] later raised to seventy-five guineas. From 28 December he appeared on his off nights at Drury Lane. London went mad. Troops were called out to control the struggle at the doors. The Boy was lionized by society and patronized by *both* the Prince and George III who introduced him to the Queen. Pitt adjourned a debate for one of his performances. 'Expect no news of any kind,' Lady Bessborough wrote, 'for nothing but the Boy is talked of.'[10] This was more than a fashionable triumph. Master Betty was John Bull's pet, so depicted in the prints. The main theme of the satires is the discomfiture of the Kembles, especially John. In *The Theatrical Caesar! or Cassius and Casca in Debate* [104] the Boy bestrides both theatres; John Kemble misquotes to his brother Charles ('the envious Casca' not Brutus) '. . . he doth bestride the narrow way like to a colossus – and we petty mortals crawl under his huge legs, and peep about to find ourselves dishonourable graves'. Kemble became ill, and Farington notes 'there is no doubt that the extraordinary admiration of young Betty's performance, held out as . . . a superior pattern, has had an effect on Kemble's mind'.[11]

Gillray did not fall into line over the prodigy; the craze was an opening for a savage attack on Sheridan for his newspaper puffs for Drury Lane: *The Theatrical Bubble – Being a New Specimen of the Astonishing Powers of the Great Political Punchinello, in the Art of Dramatic Puffing.* An immense soap-bubble blown by Sheridan (a Falstaffian Punch) contains the arrogant boy striding over the heads of 'Garrick, Kemble, Cooke'. The cheering crowd respond with a shower of coins. Theatrical puffs paid for

102 [Lord Derby following Miss Farren], *Bunbury*

103 *The Marriage of Cupid and Psyche, Gillray*

The Young Roscius:

Drury Lane

Covent Garden

Why Man—he doth bestride
the narrow way like to a colossus
and we petty mortals crawl under
his huge legs, and peep about to find
Ourselves–dishonourable Graves.

J.B.
Pub. Dec 15 1804 by P.W. Fores
Nº 50 Piccadilly London.

Folios of Caracatures lent out for the Evening

The Theatrical Cæsar! or Cassius and Casca in Debate.

104 The Theatrical Caesar! or Cassius and Casca in Debate, anon.

in cash and free seats were a feature of the day, and in this line Sheridan was supreme: 'There is, and always has been, in this country' Cobbett wrote, 'a sort of family compact between the press and the theatre. . . . But you Sir, from some quality I suppose more than commonly aimiable, have long had the press in all its branches, completely at your command.'[12] Gillray accuses Sheridan also of defrauding his shareholders, and of stunts below the dignity of Drury Lane – a large dog lies behind him, Carlo, whose acting in *The Caravan* had just been a windfall for the theatre.*

The rage for juvenile performers spread. '*Roscii* and *Rosciae* sprang up like mushrooms.' In September 1805 Home's *Douglas* was played at the Haymarket, 'All the Parts by Young Ladies and Young Gentlemen from ten to fifteen years of age, Scholars at eminent Boarding Schools . . .'.[13] The chief *Roscia* was Miss Mudie; after leading roles in Dublin and the provinces she made her debut at Covent Garden (22 November 1805) aged eight and was hissed off. This was said to be Kemble's device for opening John Bull's eyes. Already, in February, the craze for theatrical infants had been ridiculed; in *John Bull in Lilliput or Theatricals for the Nineteenth Century*, John Bull plays the double bass for the tiny performers on their little stage; each child gestures self-importantly, regardless of the others, and, announces its identity – 'the little Siddons', 'the Infant Billington'. Master Betty was still playing at both houses in the spring of 1806, but *The Genius of Theatricals – Bringing John Bull to his Senses* in January, shows that extinction was at hand: John Bull sits on the ground, goggling at a tiny Roscius (Norval in Home's play) who is in flight. The 'Genius', a young woman floating on butterfly wings, has just removed a fool's cap with ass's ears from John's head, so that he sees at last that the boy is 'no bigger than a pinshead'. Kemble is about to raise him to his feet, watched benignly by Mrs Siddons.

Covent Garden was burnt down (20 December 1808), rebuilt with the help of subscriptions and with great expedition, and reopened 10 September 1809. Meanwhile (24 February 1809), Drury Lane had also been burnt to the ground. At the new Covent Garden pit prices were raised sixpence, boxes a shilling, galleries unaltered. Pandemonium followed in the greatest of all O.P. (Old Price) riots. The theatre was not materially damaged as on earlier occasions, but organized uproar prevailed – rattles, horns, shouts, stamping, songs, obscene noises. From 24 September to 3 October the theatre was closed while a committee examined the accounts; they justified the new prices. The issues then shifted and multiplied. 'No Private Boxes' – the third tier of boxes was reserved for subscribers, with anterooms and a separate staircase. This was an outrage. Placards were displayed showing gross immorality in the aristocratic boxes; 'No Catalani' (her fees were exorbitant), but Billington and English singers. 'No Pigeon Holes', the lunettes at each end of the top gallery. Rowlandson's *Pidgeon Hole* [105] came out fourteen months later, after

*The subject of a biography: *The Life of Carlo, the Famous Dog of Drury Lane Theatre With His Portrait*, 1804.

112

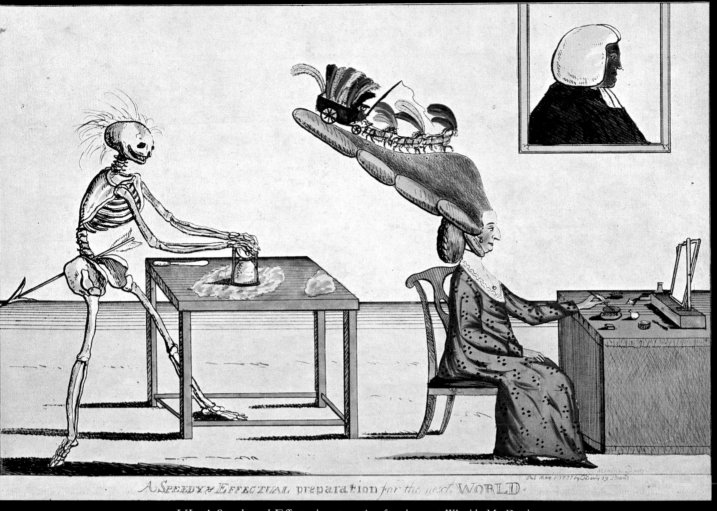

VI A Speedy and Effectual preparation for the next World, M. Darly

VII Transplanting of Teeth, Rowlandson

Pub.d June 4.th 1799. by H. Humphrey. 27 S.t James's Street

J.? Gillray, inv.? & f.t PIZARRO *contemplating over the product of his new Peruvian Mine—*

"Honor? Reputation? a mere Bubble!— will the praises of posterity charm my bones in the Grave?—psha!— my present
purpose is all!—O, Gold! Gold! for thee, I would sell my native Spain, as freely as I would plunder Peru."

VIII Pizarro contemplating over the product of his new Peruvian Mine, Gillray

PIDGEON HOLE, _A Convent Garden Contrivance to Coop up the Gods_,

Rowlandson Del.

Pub. Feb.y 20 1811 by Tho.s Tegg N.o111 Cheapside

105 Pidgeon Hole, Rowlandson

106 The House that Jack Built. I. and G. Cruikshank

This is the House that Jack Built

These are the BOXES Painted so neat, with snug room & sofa all complete, Where afignations are made by the Great that Visit the House that Jack Built

These are the Pigeon Holes over the Boxes Painted so neat, with snug room and sofa all complete, where afignations are made by the Great, that visit the House that Jack Built

This is the Cat engaged to squall To the Poor in the Pigeon Holes Over the Boxes painted so neat, with snug Room & sofa all complete, where afignations are made by the great, that Visit the House that Jack Built.

This is John Bull with his Bugle horn who Hissed the Cat engaged to squall to the Poor in the Pigeon Holes over the Boxes painted so neat with snug room and sofa all complete, where afignations are made by the great that Visit the Hous that Jack Built

This is Thief taker shaven & shorn that took up John Bull with his Bugle Horn who Hissed the Cat engaged to squall to the Poor in the pigeon Holes over the Boxes painted so neat, with snug room and sofa all complete, where afignations are made by the great that Visit the House that Jack

This is the Manager, full of scorn Who Raised the Price to the People forlorn, And directed the theif taker shave & shorn To take John Bull with his Bugle horn Who Hissed the Cat engaged to squall to the Poor in the Pigeon Holes over the Boxes Painted so neat, with snug Room & sofa all complete where afignations are made by the Great that Visit the House

Pub.t by J.W.Jones 50. Piccadilly London Sep.t 28 1809

28 Sep. 1809

The HOUSE that JACK BUILT

A STROLLING PLAYER.

Grant me great Mars! once more in arms to shine,
And break like lightning thro' th'embatled line,
Thro' fields of death to wirl the rapid car
Pub. Feb 16.1791. by S W Fores N3 Piccadilly.

And blaze amidst the thunder of the war.
Reustless as the bolt that rends the grove,
Or greatly perish like the son of Jove.
Alexander the great
16 Feb 1791

TRAGEDY.

107 A Strolling Player, anon.

Kemble had promised to raise the roof. The climax of fury was when a magistrate read the Riot Act from the stage, constables were brought in and rioters held to bail. The issue was now, 'the immemorial right of Englishmen freely to pronounce their judgment in the theatre, so long as they refrained from damage and violence. It was this right . . . which the violent conduct of the proprietors had violated in the most shameless fashion.' Thus Geijer, the Swede, a fascinated spectator. Throughout, the animus was against Kemble, though Harris, the Manager, owned more shares and was less conciliatory. It was the O.P. War, John Bull versus King John. Among the mass of contemporary literature, with many squibs and prints, Geijer's account is outstanding: 'There were hats with O.P. on them, an O.P. medal was struck worn on the breast. . . . There were O.P. fans, O.P. handkerchiefs, O.P. waistcoats and caps. O.P. was inscribed on all the walls of London, O.P. was put by the tradesmen into their advertisements along with other rigmarole to capture John Bull's credulity. . . . There was an O.P. dance . . . which consisted of jumping backwards and forwards on the benches. There was O.P. music for this dance. It was printed. I have it. It has an accompaniment of rattles. . . . In all my life I have not heard or read so much about British freedom. . . . One of the placards was characteristic . . . it was supposed to represent O.P.'s banner coat of arms. In the middle was a laurel crowned bull's head – emblem of John Bull. . . . Round about . . . were emblems, decorations of rattles, trumpets, horns and suchlike. Above, *God Save the King* and below "British Independence and Liberty".'[14]

It was Jubilee year – 12 October – and the repeated singing of the national anthem was part of the uproar. The most famous of the O.P. squibs was a parody of *The House that Jack Built* attributed to Horace Smith. Four illustrated versions survive, each a sequence of little scenes. This one [106], by Isaac Cruikshank, heavily stresses the Private Boxes: 'These are the Boxes painted so neat/With snug room and sofa all complete.'

Peace negotiations were conducted through Francis Place; the war ended in the almost complete surrender of Kemble. There was a dinner of reconciliation (14 December) and a performance of *Hamlet* next day, the first audible play in the new theatre. This lunatic – but well organized – frenzy was inflamed and exploited by Cobbett and the Westminster Radicals. But it diverted attention from the calamities of the 'Grand Expedition' to the Scheldt. This year, 1809, was also that of the grand scandal of Mrs Clarke and the Duke of York over the sale of army commissions, very fully illustrated and magnified in caricature, but ending in the discrediting of Mrs Clarke and the return (in 1811) to office of the Duke (who had resigned). These were the great sensations of the year (the fall of Austria at Wagram passed unnoticed), both were anti-ministerial, both actually favourable to the shaky Ministry.

The lot of the strolling player had been improved by better roads and the opening of provincial theatres, but the life was hard, and the calling still an outlet for stage-struck apprentices (Gillray was one) and unemployed

108 'Hamlet' in a Barn, R. St. G. Mansergh

OH QUI GOOSE-TOE!

He Danc'd like a Monkey, his Pockets well cramm'd;
Caper'd off with a Grin, "Kifs my A---- & be D----d.

Pub.ᵈ May 10ᵗʰ 1781 by W. Humphrey Nᵒ 227 Strand.

109 *Oh Qui Goose-Toe!*, (?) *N. Dance/Bartolozzi & Pastorini*

scene-shifters. *Hamlet in a Barn* [108], *c.* 1770, is an amateur's rendering of village barnstorming, patronised by 'Squire Dunderhead' and his lady. The passion for declamation and tragedy led to absurdities – actors, despising their audience, or sometimes ignorant, would jumble soliloquies from different plays. *A Strolling Player* [107], 1791, as Alexander the Great in the 1770 adaptation of Lee's *The Rival Queens* . . . is perhaps a portrait, almost certainly the truthful rendering of a type. John Byng found a company playing thrice a week at Biggleswade in 1791 (and producing playbills on the London pattern); the long programme was unendurable – *Romeo and Juliet*, comic songs, Dibdin's *The Waterman*. 'Except the pronunciation, the acting was of the nature of the lordly theatres.' But, 'more barnish slavery exists not; the company were starving; one fiddle and thirteen candles . . .'.[15]

The rage for amateur theatricals was another manifestation of the passion for the theatre. Not new – Frederick, George II's unloved son, was a great producer of plays. Children acted long before the *Roscii* and *Rosciae*. There is Hogarth's painting, *The Indian Emperor*, where small fashionables act Dryden's tragedy for a party of royal infants. In 1751 some of the quality hired Drury Lane to act *Othello*; the rage to see it was so great that the House of Commons was adjourned. Walpole's comment: 'They really acted so well that it is astonishing they should not have had sense enough not to act it at all.'[16] Hannah More, aged fifteen, wrote a moral play, *A Search after Happiness*, as 'a substitute for the very improper custom of allowing plays, and they not always of the purest kind', to be acted by young ladies at boarding schools. After an active circulation in manuscript it had sold ten thousand copies in many editions between 1773 and 1797.[17] We have seen the Pic Nics routed by Sheridan. At the other end of the social ladder were the spouting clubs in London, where the members met to declaim and rehearse. Thomas Holcroft, ex-stable-boy, when a servant of Granville Sharp the philanthropist, was dismissed for attending one. He graduated strolling player (1771–7), and finally, playwright. Murphy's popular farce, *The Apprentice* (1756) ridicules the stage-struck tradesman: 'What's a Spouting Club? a meeting of apprentices, clerks, and giddy young men, intoxicated with plays, and so they meet in public houses to act speeches, where they all neglect their business, despise the advice of their friends, and think of nothing but to become actors.'

In the early nineteenth century spouting clubs had been succeeded by the sordid 'private theatres' in the lowest of the London minor theatres, where, Dickens tells us, 'low copying clerks' and shop-boys paid considerable sums 'to exhibit their lamentable ignorance and boobyism' as Othello, Shylock, Richard III, etc. etc., female parts by prostitutes gratis. He pours contempt on these 'private theatres',[18] but he knew them well, and it is hardly credible that as a lawyer's office boy he had never played a part himself. Cruikshank's illustration in *Sketches by Boz* suggests preparation for *Macbeth*. Ranting and unseasonable declamation by the stage-struck was a favourite

caricature subject. Its spell-binding effect is shown by the fact that medical students, restive during a demonstration, used to be subdued by their lecturer's* delivery of the soliloquies from *Hamlet* or the death scene from *Richard III*.

All ranks went to the theatre. The Opera belonged to 'persons of quality', but it was accepted, as it had not been in Hogarth's day – prima donnas sang also in the theatres and the popular oratorios. The golden age of opera as a spectacle was from the early 1780s to the early nineteenth century: 'filled exclusively with the highest class of society', in the decorative 'full dress' of the period. A box, or a share in one, was almost obligatory for a woman of fashion: 'every lady possessing an opera box considered it as much her home as her house', and 'the best assembly in London' was in the coffee room after the performance.[19] When the Opera House was burnt down in 1789 Horace Walpole declared there was no need to rebuild it: 'the nation has long been tired of operas . . . dancing protracted their existence for some time, but *the room after* was the real support of both . . . to be crowded to death in a waiting room at the end of an entertainment is the whole joy.'

The importance of the ballet is spotlighted by the only sustained – but ineffective – protest against foreign performers in this period. The year was 1781. England and France were at war, there was a political crisis at home, and society went mad over two French dancers, Vestris father and son. Strong feeling was aroused by the huge sums paid to Frenchmen in war-time, but the Opera audience was unmoved – a theatre audience might have reacted differently. The King was blamed for going to the Opera instead of to a Drury Lane benefit for sufferers in a calamity in Barbados. For the benefit of Vestris *fils* the second reading of Burke's famous Bill of Economic Reform was postponed. 'To a great part of this House,' he complained, 'a dance was a much more important object than a war, and the Opera House must be maintained whatever becomes of the country.' An outburst of satirical prints illustrate the affair, including two charming ones, said to be 'very much like' attributed to Nathaniel Dance: Vestris *fils* dances at his famous benefit loaded with money bags. The title illustrates the phrase of the moment, '*Oh che gusto!*' rendered as *Oh Qui Goose-Toe!* [109]. The prologue at the opening of the Little Haymarket, delayed by the protracted Opera season, complained 'No more from Voice, or Ear, her profits flow,/The Soul of Opera fixes in Goose-Toe.' Paul Sandby's *Jason et Medée*, *Ballet Tragique*, with the elder Vestris between two ladies of the ballet, satirizes a notable performance on 19 June – 'The Grand Tragic Ballet' composed by Vestris and the subject of a quarto pamphlet, *Historical Account . . .*, 1781.

What would have happened if the dancers had appeared anywhere but at the Opera House? There was a warning in the calamity that befell Garrick in 1755. With great precautions he paved the way for an English version of *Les Fêtes chinoises* from Paris. The ballet master, Noverre, was Swiss with a German wife; out of sixty principals only

---

*J.F.Clarke, b. 1812; E.S.Turner, *Call the Doctor* (London: Michael Joseph, 1958), p. 149.

sixteen were French. War between the polite part of the house and the gallery followed. After six days of riot the plebs won with the help of an outside mob, to the slogan, 'No French dancers'. Much damage was done but Garrick's defence measures saved the theatre and his own house from destruction. War with France was pending, but the whole exquisite performance (décor by Bouchet) was alien to a public that would have preferred farce and acrobatics. Yet even in the Opera House 'the beaux in the pit' rioted when the ballet was not given on a Saturday night owing to the Sabbatarian Bishop of London's appeal for closure before midnight. They jumped on the stage, tore down the curtain, broke the chandeliers and reduced the House to 'total darkness'.[20]

When Mrs Billington (daughter of a German) returned to England she was acclaimed as an English prima donna; her singing of 'The soldier tir'd of war's alarms' (from Arne's *Artaxerxes*) at Covent Garden coincided with the Peace Preliminaries of 1801. Enthusiasm was unbounded. So it was remarkable that when John Bull, in 1807, has to choose between his 'two charmers' in *Bravuras, Rival Syrens – Or – John Bulls Rehearsal of Capt Macheath*, Mrs Billington is Polly; Angelica Catalani, Lucy in the *Beggar's Opera*; the latter dressed as Semiramide, the part in which she made her London debut in 1806. He sings '. . . Untill I heard Signora Pussy/*She* charm'd my *Ear* and pleas'd my *Eye*'. Till Catalani came Mrs Billington had been supreme. But the Italian's voice, acting and beauty were irresistible. We have seen her attacked by John Bull in the O.P. War, but reconciliation was speedy. When she finally left England in 1813, the mismanaged, insolvent Opera ceased to be fashionable in the old way.

Amateur music was a natural target for graphic satire, there was so much of it. Playing the harpsichord and then the piano was indispensable for Misses with pretensions to gentility. Compositions for these instruments were known as 'Lessons', the music master was as essential as the dancing master and the professions were sometimes combined. Music was linked with so many aspects of the social scene –

Catch Clubs, Glee Clubs, social climbing, husband hunting, the horrors of family music imposed on visitors, all are illustrated. We have seen the violin as a sign of idleness and dissipation in an undergraduate's room [77]. Only one example of the wide field is possible here. In a famous pair of plates by Gillray, *Harmony before Matrimony* and *Matrimonial Harmonics* [110 and 111], 1803, the harp is the instrument of allurement, the piano of malicious torture. The furniture of the two rooms tells the story. In the first there are emblems of amorousness, and a table-leg in the form of a satyr with a cloven hoof. In a few years the woman has coarsened, and there is a bottle of 'Hollands' (gin) beside her chair at the breakfast table. The man's good-humoured sprightliness has turned to sulky exasperation.

Notes to Chapter XII

1. A. Dobson, *Eighteenth Century Vignettes*, 3rd Series (Oxford: O.U.P., 1923), pp. 1–28.
2. Colman's prologue to Kelly's *Clementine*, Covent Garden, 1771.
3. *Dr Campbell's Diary of a Visit to England in 1775*, ed. J. L. Clifford (Cambridge: C.U.P., 1947), pp. 44–45, 111–13.
4. *The Heber Letters*, ed. R. H. Cholmondeley (London: Batchworth Press, 1950), p. 138.
5. *Mrs Jordan and Her Family*, ed. A. Aspinall (London: Arthur Barker, 1951).
6. *Autobiography*, 1850.
7. *Manuscripts of the Earl of Carlisle*, Historical Manuscripts Commission, 1897, pp. 555–6.
8. John Byng, *Torrington Diaries*, ed. C. B. Andrews, vol. IV (London: Eyre & Spottiswoode, 1938).
9. F. Reynolds, *Life and Times*, 1820, vol. II, p. 364.
10. *Correspondence of Lord G. L. Gower*, 1916, vol. II, p. 40.
11. *Farington Diary*, ed. James Greig, vol. III (London: Hutchinson, 1922–8), pp. 60f.
12. *The Political Proteus . . .*, 1804, p. 206. See *History of 'The Times'*, 1935, vol. I, pp. 47–48, 90–94.
13. J. Genest, *Some Account of the English Stage . . . 1660 to 1830*, 1832, vol. VII, pp. 643, 677.
14. E. G. Geijer, *Impressions of England 1809–10* (London: Jonathan Cape, 1932), p. 99.
15. John Byng, *Torrington Diaries*, ed. C. B. Andrews, vol. II (London: Eyre & Spottiswoode, 1935), pp. 306, 308–9.
16. To Sir Horace Mann, 13 March 1751.
17. M. G. Jones, *Hannah More* (Cambridge: C.U.P., 1952), p. 15.
18. *Sketches by Boz*, 1836.
19. Mount Edgcumbe, *Musical Reminiscence*, 1827.
20. *Wynne Diaries*, ed. A. Fremantle, vol. III (Oxford: O.U.P., 1935–40), p. 171 (15 June 1805).

HARMONY before MATRIMONY.

110 *Harmony before Matrimony, Gillray*

111 *Matrimonial Harmonics, Gillray*

MATRIMONIAL-HARMONICS.

THE HISTORIAN ANIMATING the MIND OF A YOUNG PAINTER.

112 *The Historian animating the Mind of a Young Painter*, Rowlandson

113 *The Chamber of Genius*, Rowlandson

THE CHAMBER OF GENIUS.

Want is the Scorn of every wealthy Fool
And Genius in Rags is turn'd to Ridicule — Dr. Solm.

Taste had been the first preoccupation of the *nouveau riche* who aimed at fashion; Tom Rakewell [3] had acquired a *Iudgement of Paris*, incongruously hung between portraits of fighting-cocks. In Lyttelton's *Persian Letters* (1735) there is a former 'citizen and tradesman', suddenly rich 'by some lucky hit in the more profitable trade of stock-jobbing, he has suddenly set up for a judge in architecture, painting, and all the arts which men of quality would be thought to understand'. Now, the increasing wealth of the middle classes had extended the zest for virtu. The founding of the Royal Academy in 1768 with the active patronage of George III was a landmark in improving the status of the artist. 'Since the arts have found protection from the Crown, the taste for virtu has become universal; persons of all ranks and degrees set up for connoisseurs, and even the lowest people tell familiarity of Hannibal Scratchi, Paul Varnish, and Raphael Angelo.'[1] 'The rage for these exhibitions is so great' Walpole wrote in 1779, 'that sometimes one cannot pass through the streets where they are. But it is incredible what sums are raised by mere exhibitions of anything; a new fashion, and to enter at which you pay a shilling or half a crown.'

Correspondingly, the cult of virtu in the *beau monde* was not what it had been. 'There being a fashion for antiques now in England,' Lady Pembroke wrote in 1779, 'is *quite a mistake*. They are admired according to their desert as usual by those who understand them.' She knows 'no Ladies or young men who think at all about them.'

There were two print-shop stereotypes of the artist – the portrait painter who flatters and thrives and the young aspiring artist in his attic, a 'genius', who paints 'History' in the grand manner. The first commonly derives from the Primrose family group, though the painter has graduated from itinerant drudge to obsequious prosperity. 'Portraits always have been and always will be popular in England', said Hogarth. In Bunbury's *A Family Piece* [114], 1781, the child-cupid is clearly a debt to Goldsmith. Rowlandson did a watercolour version of this, and another variant with Reynolds at the easel.

The painter who aims at high art is a sort of counterpart of the *Distrest Poet* (p. 30) though he usually registers eager confidence instead of gloom. *The Historian animating the Mind of a Young Painter* [112] by Rowlandson, 1784, reflects the still-accepted teaching of Jonathan Richardson: 'The historical painter must posess all the good qualities requisite to an historian . . . the talents requisite for a good poet . . .' and a very great deal more.[2] His is *The Chamber of Genius* [113], also by Rowlandson, dated 1812, but probably earlier. The Genius is often a victim of imperti-

nent intrusion, as in *A Meeting of Connoisseurs*, 1807, a large plate after J. Boyne the watercolourist. Five men have invaded the attic which is both studio and bedroom; four inspect a large canvas on the easel – subject, a classical Apollo with a sheaf of arrows, for which a tall Negro is posing. The fifth intruder alters the pose of the model, while the artist scowls gloomily beside his picture. His wife, holding an infant, turns her back on the unwelcome visitors. The room is bare except for three casts from the antique. This illustrates the poverty that goes with high art and the (resented) claim of the *cognoscenti* to dictate to the artist on the grounds of superior knowledge, prestige and rank. Haydon, most vocal of painters, is eloquent: 'No other professions are cursed with connoiseurs but Poetry & Painting. There are no connoiseurs in War, in Physic, in Surgery. . . . The professor's tactics of every other profession on Earth, who devote their lives to it, are supposed (& justly) to know more than those who fill a vacant day with wandering gabble or casual glance.'[3]

Portraits and 'History' with a sprinkling of dead game and live animals are displayed in the Great Room at Somerset House on the Opening Day in 1787 [115]. Reynolds with his ear-trumpet stands next to the Prince of Wales. The pictures are numbered and many can be identified from the Catalogue of the year, the more numerous portraits dominated by the two huge 'Historics' by the two R.A.s elect, 'The Assassination of David Riccio' by Opie and 'Walworth killing Wat Tyler' by Northcote, like a caricature of the grand manner.

It was, he said, to establish an English school of history painting that Alderman Boydell, print-seller and engraver, embarked on the grandiose enterprise of the Shakespeare Gallery (opened in 1789). This was the commissioning of paintings from leading artists to be exhibited and then engraved for an edition of Shakespeare, published by subscription. Like Hogarth, Gillray had strong views on art, and strong personal prejudices, and these were expressed in a violent attack on Boydell and his project in the remarkable print, *Shakespeare Sacrificed; – or – The Offering to Avarice* [116], 1789. The Alderman, in his furred gown, stands like a magician to direct the burning of the plays; the rising smoke supports a medley of figures travestied from the paintings already exhibited by Reynolds, West, Fuseli, Northcote, Barry, Opie.* Gillray expresses, as often, his contempt for puffing advertisements – these are being broadcast by Fame as bubbles and papers. The treatment of engravers by the Academy (exclusion till 1770, then

*All can be identified from the engravings, published in two volumes in 1805.

A FAMILY PIECE.

London, Publish'd October 15.th 1781, by W. Dickinson N.º 158 New Bond Street.

114 A Family Piece, Bunbury

ΟΥΔΕΙΣ - ΑΜΟΥΣΟΣ - ΕΙΣΙΤΩ

THE EXHIBITION OF THE ROYAL ACADEMY, 1787.

115 *The Exhibition of the Royal Academy, 1787*, H. Ramberg/P. S. Martini

SHAKESPEARE - SACRIFICED; _ or _ The Offering to AVARICE.

116 Shakespeare Sacrificed; – or – The Offering to Avarice, Gillray

117 *Titianus Redivivus; – or – The Seven Wise Men consulting the new Venetian Oracle*, Gillray

grudging admittance as A.R.A.s) is also condemned: a ragged boy with a palette pushes a boy with an engraver's tool outside the magic circle of the Academy. It is impossible not to see here, as elsewhere, Gillray's frustrated ambition for serious work in the grand manner. The pictures were painted and engraved, but the war checked the sale of prints, and Boydell was ruined.

Titianus Redivivus; – or – The Seven Wise Men consulting the new Venetian Oracle [117] is about 'the Venetian Secret', the chief topic at the opening of the Academy in 1797. To Gillray it was irresistible as a manifestation of brazen advertisement and ballyhoo, and an opportunity for art criticism of the most personal kind. An art student, a girl of twenty, professed to have discovered the secret of Titian's colouring, and sold it for ten guineas to those who pledged themselves to secrecy. Seven R.A.s were known to have bought it; West (P.R.A.) was believed to have had it free and there were many unidentified purchasers. Farington was supposed to have been the persuader; he and West were her chief patrons.

'Such industrious folly in contriving for the publicity of a quacking imposture, is, I believe, unparalleled in the history of the art.'[4] The purveyor of the Secret stands on a rainbow daubing at a picture of a large, pale goblin (Titian) on a large dark canvas. There is much symbolic detail and in the centre sit the seven R.A.s painting away as if in an art school. Their brushes, palettes and remarks convey Gillray's opinion of their work. Most conspicuous, on the right, is Farington. The others (right to left) are Opie, Westall, Hoppner, Stothard, Smirke, Rigaud. A pile of portfolios leaning against the headless statue of Apollo records the names of those Gillray wishes to commend: Cosway, Sandby, Bartolozzi (his master), Rooker (also an engraver), Turner (aged twenty-two), Loutherbourg (with whom he had collaborated in war pictures in 1793), Beechey and Fuseli.[5] In the foreground the ghost of Reynolds emerges, and three men run off to the right – blatant advertisers who find themselves outstripped. They are Thomas Macklin, who was commissioning paintings for an illustrated Bible, Boydell and West.

Since Hogarth's time, the status of the artist had greatly improved. Much was due to the Academy, much to Reynolds – his fortune, his relations with the Great, and with the literary-Bohemian world, in fact, to his social and intellectual gifts. He has been accused of Macchiavellian social climbing:[6] he certainly climbed successfully. Something was due to the closing of the Continent and the end of the Grand Tour, to changes of taste, and of course to the multiplication of patrons among the rich bourgeoisie. The Romantic movement had rescued landscape from neglect. Picturesque scenery had a ready market for reproduction in aquatint and book illustration.

The struggling artist is a perennial figure, but it was a favourite topic with Sir George Beaumont (patron, connoisseur, and amateur painter) that poets were always poor – he instanced Wordsworth, whom he greatly admired, and Milton – but that artists (*c.* 1808–15) were

paid too much; he feared the unqualified would be attracted to the calling by its rewards.[7] Farington records a conversation with West, Lawrence and Smirke in 1813 'upon the state of Artists in this country compared with what it was when Mr West arrived in England [1763], in respect of their personal manners and the degree of estimation in which they were held. He [West] said that in fifty years they had become a different description of men, as much more decorous in their deportment, and in their reception in Society. He observed that the establishment of the Academy had done much in giving dignity to the Arts, and that too much could not be done to preserve its importance.'[8] Even in 1841, even Haydon, bitter enemy of the Academy, agreed with William Collins R.A. that 'If it were not for the Academy, depend upon it, Artists would be treated like carpenters'.[9]

Literature was overwhelmingly dominated by Samuel Johnson, at least till after the great *Life* appeared. But the typical author, the stereotype, continued to be the Grub Street garretteer, especially the Poet immortalized by Hogarth. Disraeli's father (b. 1766) horrified *his* father by wanting to be an author: 'His idea of a poet was formed from one of the prints of Hogarth hanging on his wall.' Johnson exulted that patronage had ended, others deplored it. 'It is a shame', Boswell said in 1773, 'that authors are not better patronized.' 'No Sir . . . with patronage what flattery, what falsehood!' (Church patronage, however, Johnson defended – elaborately – and also the nomination borough: 'Influence must ever be the prerogative of property, and it is right it should be so.') To the patron had succeeded the bookseller-publisher. 'The author, when unpatronized by the Great, has naturally recourse to the bookseller. There cannot be, perhaps, imagined, a combination more prejudicial to taste than this . . . tedious compilations and periodical magazines are the result of their joint endeavours.'[10]

The penury and humiliation of bondage to the bookseller, and the still worse fate of rejection by him, are themes of *The Author* by Foote (Drury Lane, 5 February 1757): 'Patron! – The word has lost its use – a guinea subscription at the request of a lady whose chambermaid is acquainted with the author, may now and then be picked up. . . .' 'And yet the press groans with their productions, how do they all exist?' 'In garrets Sir. . . .'

The real John Cleland, threatened with arrest as the author of *Fanny Hill, Memoirs of a Woman of Pleasure*, wrote to the Secretary of State's Office in 1749 to apologize for 'the meanness of writing for a bookseller' and for being 'the author of a book I disdain to defend and wish from the bottom of my soul buried and forgotten'.* He deplores his present 'low abject condition, that of a writer for bread'.[11]

The Grub Street Macaroni [118], 1772, is seeking a patron, with a book hopefully 'Dedicated to my Lord S—'. He has rigged himself out in Monmouth Street, the mart for second-hand clothes (the shop label is still on his coat), in

_____
*Books lettered 'Fanny Hill' appear in prints to indicate depravity.

THE GRUB STREET MACARONI.

Dr Johnson

OLD WISDOM.
Blinking at the Stars.

118 *The Grub Street Macaroni, M. Darly*

119 *Old Wisdom. Blinking at the Stars, Gillray*

120 *A Chop House, Bunbury*

For defaming that Ge-
nius I could never em-
ulate by criticism with-
out Judgment; and
endeavouring to cast
the beauties of British
Poetry into the hideous
shade of oblivion.

MILTON
OTWAY
WALLER
GRAY
SHENSTON
LYTTELTON

I acknowledge my transgressions, and
my sins are ever before me ✳

*Vide The lᵗʰ Sermon at Sᵗ Dunstans.

Gillray

Apollo and the Muses, inflicting Penance on Dᵣ Pomposo, round Parnassus.

121 *Apollo and the Muses, inflicting Penance on Dr Pomposo, round Parnassus, Gillray*

old-fashioned dress which is too big for him. No one knew the miseries of Grub Street and writing for bread better than Johnson: from his own experience, and from his help to obscure garretteers: 'he listened to the complaints, the schemes, and the hopes and fears of a crowd of inferior writers, "who" he said . . . "lived *men knew not how, and died obscure, men marked not when*"'. In his own person he raised the status of the 'author by profession', much helped by the multiplication of reviews and magazines, and even by the generosity of some booksellers, notably Andrew Miller, whom he called 'the Maecenas of our age'.

The supremacy of Johnson, the uncouth son of a Litch-field tradesman, who had toiled in Grub Street, was a sign of a new age, very different from the age of Pope and Swift. The *Dictionary* (1755) established him as 'the Colossus of Literature'. His pension was an obvious target, and in

1763, with his £300 a year, he appears – with Hogarth and others – among '*The Hungry Mob of Scribblers & Etchers*'.[12] Churchill attacked him in *The Ghost* (1763): 'Pomposo insolent and loud, / Vain idol of a scribbling crowd . . .'. As a personality, famous not only in the world of letters, but in the club, the tavern, the drawing-room, and a familiar London figure, he sits with Boswell (both unnamed) in *A Chop House* [120], 1781, one of Bunbury's rare personal caricatures. *The Lives of the Poets* (1779 and 1781) attracted Gillray's satire in two important prints. In *Old Wisdom. Blinking at the Stars* [119], 1782, with an owl's body and ass's ears, Johnson stares short-sightedly towards the poets he had ventured to appraise: Pope and Milton, and two others. In *Apollo and the Muses, inflicting Penance on Dᵣ Pomposo, round Parnassus* [121], he is being scourged, and on his dunce's cap are the names of poets of *The Lives*. Two

Hero's recruiting at Kelsey's; – or – Guard-Day at St James's.

Pub.ᵈ June 9ᵗʰ 1797 by H. Humphrey, St James's Street

IX Hero's recruiting at Kelsey's; – or – Guard-Day at St James's, Gillray

La Promenade en Famille. — a Sketch from Life.

X La Promenade en Famille – a Sketch from Life, Gillray

TALES of WONDER!

XI Tales of Wonder!, Gillray

winged books credit him with 'the Milk of Human Kindness' as a man, and 'Envy' as an author. This was the print being discussed at Sir Joshua Reynolds's when Johnson arrived unexpectedly, and said, 'Sir, I am very glad to hear this. I hope the day will never come when I shall neither be the subject of calumny or ridicule, for then I shall be neglected and forgotten.'[13] Striking testimony to the treatment of celebrities in Johnson's England.

Johnson's death in 1784 evoked an unprecedented spate of biographies and anecdotes, and Boswell and Mrs Thrale (now Piozzi) came under attack for exploiting the great man. The most attractive of the Johnson prints are *Picturesque Beauties of Boswell*, twenty plates etched by Rowlandson after Collings in 1786 on the *Journal of a Tour to the Hebrides* (1785). They are admirable illustrations of cleverly selected passages, and satires on Boswell's seeming naiveté. Johnson has a heavy, not undignified, melancholy; Boswell (usually) a jaunty vulgarity. In *The Journalist. With a View of Auchinleck or the Land of Stones* [122] Boswell is attacked for boastfulness; he is, that is he claims to be, 'a Citizen of the World', he is lawyer, Scot, and feudal chief, proud of his barren acres and the 'Blood of Bruce'. His *Journal*, and *Ogden on Prayer*, and bulky 'Materials for the Life of Sam¹ Johnson L.L.D.' are much in evidence.

'I think', said Boswell (1776), and Johnson concurred, 'that ridicule may be fairly used against an infidel, for instance, if he be an ugly fellow, and yet absurdly vain of his person.' Gibbon is clearly indicated. Amateurs, including Lady Di Beauclerk, sketched his profile. He was cruelly caricatured as *The Luminous Historian* [123], 1778, a title altered to 'Vo-Luminous' on another impression. This illustrates Sheridan's recent reference to 'the luminous pages of Gibbon' in his famous speech against Warren Hastings. Gibbon heard the compliment, but asked his neighbour to repeat it and got the answer 'he said something about your voluminous pages'.[14] On the other hand, Gibbon scores in *Thou are weighed in the Balances, and art found Wanting* also 1788: Bishop Watson of Llandaff had published *An Apology for Christianity in a Series of Letters . . . to . . . Gibbon*. The Bishop and his massive works on theology and chemistry are outweighed by Gibbon and the six volumes (1776–88) of his *History*. . . . (Walter Scott's bulky volumes were to be similarly, but less reasonably, outweighed, p. 207.)

Another eighteenth-century historian was quite as much a public character as Gibbon. 'Macaulay's History', eight volumes of it (1763–83) was the now forgotten work of Mrs Catherine Macaulay, a 'female patriot' and 'a great republican', whose 'levelling principles' Johnson punctured by suggesting that they should be extended to her footman. At the age of fifty-seven (1778) she added to her notoriety by marrying a second husband, age twenty-one, who was moreover the brother of James Graham of the Celestial Bed. 'It having been mentioned' Boswell records

(1776), 'that a certain female political writer . . . sat hours together at her toilet, and even put on rouge . . . Johnson ". . . It is better she should be reddening her own cheeks than blackening other people's characters".' She is doing this in *A Speedy and Effectual preparation for the next World* [VI], a Darly print of 1777, which also ridicules the hairdressing of the day. She was then living at Bath, in the house of an absentee London rector, whose portrait is on the wall, and had just received six birthday odes from her admirers. 'Mrs Macaulay is one of the sights that all foreigners are carried to see', Walpole noted.[15] So much was she a notoriety that Foote put her on the stage as Mrs Margaret Maxwell, an aggressive blue-stocking with 'romantic republican notions'.[16]

No one succeeded Johnson as a public figure – clearly, no one could. The print shops were unaware of the beginning of a new age with *Lyrical Ballads* in 1798, but they could not miss the vogue for melodrama and tales of Gothic horror. M.G. ('Monk') Lewis became a literary notoriety with his blood-curdling romance, *The Monk*, which narrowly escaped prosecution for indecency in 1795, an early manifestation of 'Victorianism'. Later editions of this most popular work were bowdlerized by the author. Gillray's *Tales of Wonder!* [XI], 1802, satirizes, not the harmless anthology of the title (to which Walter Scott contributed ballads), but *The Monk* and its many imitations. The mother and daughter are evidently absorbed in the first edition, and the décor of the room expresses its unfitness for family reading. The taste for the 'horribly pathetic' (in which he saw a German influence) outraged Geijer: in 1810, 'One needs only to look at the books that lie open in the lesser bookseller's shops. They are nearly all ogre, ghost, robbers, murder stories, with an accompanying engraving of the altogether most horrible contents.'

Notes to Chapter XIII

1. *Fugitive Miscellanies* (1773), quoted *Johnson's England*, ed. A.S.Turberville, vol. II (Oxford: O.U.P., 1933), p. 38.
2. *Theory of Painting*, 1715.
3. *The Diary of Benjamin Robert Haydon*, ed. W.B.Pope, vol. I (Cambridge, Mass.: Harvard University Press, 1960), vol. I, p. 441 (13 May 1815).
4. Barry, quoted W.T.Whitley, *Artists and their Friends in England*, vol. II (London: Medici Society, 1928), pp. 209–12.
5. For the relation between Gillray and Fuseli, see Draper Hill, *Mr Gillray the Caricaturist* (London: Phaidon, 1965), pp. 147–8.
6. R.H.Wilenski, *English Painting* (London: Faber, 1943), pp. 135–45.
7. *Farington Diary*, ed. James Greig, vol. VII (London: Hutchinson, 1927), pp. 180, 241.
8. Ibid., p. 199.
9. *The Diary of Benjamin Robert Haydon* (see note 3), vol. V, pp. 57–58.
10. O.Goldsmith, *Present State of Polite Learning*, 1759, Chapter 10.
11. Quoted *The Sunday Times*, 16 February 1964.
12. M.D.George, *English Political Caricature to 1792* (Oxford: O.U.P., 1960), p. 122, pl. 32.
13. *Johnsonian Miscellanies*, ed. G.Birkbeck, 1897, vol. II, pp. 419–20.
14. *Life and Letters of Sir G.Elliot*, ed. Countess of Minto, 1874, vol. I, p. 219. Rogers's *Table Talk* tells a different version.
15. To Sir Horace Mann, 28 February, 1769.
16. *The Devil upon Two Sticks*, 1768.

THE JOURNALIST.

122 *The Journalist. With a View of Auchinleck or the Land of Stones, S. Collings/Rowlandson*

THE

Luminous Historian.

London; Published by W.ᵐ Holland Printseller N.º 50,
Oxford Street, August the 12ᵗʰ 1788.

123 The Luminous Historian, anon.

124 Coelum ipsum petimus Stultitia, P.Sandby

14 - *Passing Sensations*

Great events, war and peace, the loss of America, conquests in India, war with the French Republic, even the tremendous crises of the war with Napoleon, touched daily life less than one would imagine. Even this war was far from total war as we have known it. Haydon, enjoying the view from Primrose Hill (1810) – ladies, children, hay-makers, grazing cows, and, behind, 'the capital of the World, with its hundred spires' – could reflect 'What a change would Buonaparte make in such a scene of liberty and peace – could he but once put his withering foot on this dear island'.[1] Johnson had contended (in his 'clear your mind of cant' vein, 15 May 1782) 'Publick affairs vex no man'. And in December 1777: 'now the popular Clamour runs so high about our Disgraces in America [Saratoga], our Debt at home, our Terrors of a Bankruptcy, & Fears of a French War; what signifies all this Canting, says the Doctor? the World goes on just the same as it did; who eats the less, or who sleeps the less? or where is all this Consternation you talk of . . . but in the News papers. Nobody is thinking or feeling about the matter, otherwise than "tis somewhat to talk about".'[2] Mrs Thrale agreed. Certainly the routine and amusements of Society were undimmed.

'One effect the American war has not had, that it ought to have had; it has not brought us to our senses,' Walpole wrote, 'Silly dissipation rather increases. . . . The present folly is late hours.'[3] English indifference to Napoleon's triumphs was a recurring theme in Farington's *Diary*: 'Called on Dance [29 May 1806]. He talked of the Luxury of the Times in the midst of our difficulties & Said it resembled Old Rome – To get what each can for Himself or his associates is now the great object.'[4] Attention to earth-shaking events was always being wiped out by some passing obsession at home.

Theatrical sensations there were in plenty (the *Pizarro* one was basically political). Personal scandals were ruthlessly illustrated. There was the terrifying episode of the Gordon Riots in 1780; they evoked many prints, No Popery propaganda before and after the outbreak, and charming views of the camps established in London after the danger was over. The crisis of 1783–4 – the struggle of Pitt and the King against Fox and his friends – raged in the print shops as elsewhere. But there was a counter-attraction in the impact of the first balloon ascents. As usual the attitude of the caricaturists to scientific invention was derisive; the balloon was inevitably associated with the bubble – symbol of delusion and folly even before the South Sea calamity – and with flights to the moon, the lunatic and the moon-struck. It became a symbol for false hopes, sudden falls, popular follies. Moreover, the balloon was a French in-vention. An early, perhaps the earliest, balloon print was *The Montgolsier* [sic] – *A First Rate of the French Aerial Navy*, with an aeronaut, a cannon, and emblems of Folly. Dated 25 October 1783, it preceded the first ascent in a free balloon of a human-being – Blanchard's on 21 November. The prints are completely at odds with the prevailing enthusiasm (though they reflect it). 'Balloons occupy senators, philosophers, ladies, every body', Walpole wrote (2 December 1783), 'France gave us the *ton* and as yet we have not come up to our model'. From the first, the satirists envisaged military use: in *The Battle of the Balloons*, a popular print of 1784 two French engage two English ones, and we are told '. . . Such fights will be common (as Dunce to feel Rod)/In the Year of One Thousand Eight Hundred and odd'.

The outstanding early balloon prints are by Paul Sandby. He derides Lunardi's ascent from the Artillery Ground (15 September 1784) in *An English Balloon 1784*, 'Close to those walls where Folly holds her throne' (Bedlam). The balloon is a great grinning face, with ass's ears, wearing a fool's cap. Though burlesquing its shape, Sandby gives a realistic rendering of the bursting of Keegan's balloon (25 September 1784) in the garden of Foley House (now covered by Portland Place), while it was being filled with 'inflammable air' (hydrogen gas); this is *Coelum ipsum petimus Stultitia* [124]. Crowds flocked to see Lunardi's balloon when it was exhibited at the Lyceum in the Strand. There was a Balloon Coach between London and Bath, so called because it was faster than the mail. Ladies wore balloon hats. Many flights were made; the Channel was crossed (7 July 1785). . . . 'Of conversation the chief topic is air balloons', wrote Walpole to Mann (7 May 1785), '. . . nobody has yet broken a neck, so neither good nor harm has hitherto been produced by this enterprise'. But in July two Frenchmen ascended from Boulogne, their balloon caught fire at a great height and the craze subsided.

A very different sensation followed – the Prince's secret marriage to Mrs Fitzherbert, in her drawing-room in December 1785. By February it was the talk of the town. 'Oh but the hubbub you are to hear and to talk of, and except which you are to talk of nothing else, for they tell me the passengers in the street of all ranks talk of it.' Thus Walpole on 10 February. The print-shop windows were soon filled with ribald fantasies. *The Follies of a Day or The Marriage of Figaro* [XII], the title from Holcroft's version of Beaumarchais's famous play, is dated 13 March. Sometimes Fox and his friends (who were of course dismayed) abet the marriage, sometimes the Prince's less

125 A Peep behind the Curtain at Drury Lane, J. Sayers

creditable friends. Here, Weltje, the German Clerk of the Kitchen at Carlton House (and the Prince's factotum) marries the pair and the eccentric spendthrift, George Hanger, gives away the bride. Both figure prominently in marriage satires. Gillray's contribution was an elopement to the Continent managed by Fox and Co. The general theme is that the Prince is the victim of a designing widow. The shops continued to produce outrageous comments on the *ménage*. Debts (a notorious fact) and a rumoured infant were illustrated, as in *Love's Last Shift*, February 1787; contemporaries could not fail to recognize the title of Cibber's play, *Love's Last Shift, or the Fool of Fashion* – a book so lettered is in the *Figaro* print. In a squalid room the Prince and Mrs Fitz sit facing each other; an infant sleeps in a cradle; a calf's head roasts (or toasts) on a string before the fire. She mends the breeches he has taken off, and their attendants are Weltje (unpacking a basket of potatoes) and George Hanger.

That sensation was outclassed by the Regency crisis, which lasted from the autumn of 1788 to the King's unexpectedly rapid recovery in February. The struggle for power was between the Prince, his brothers and his friends, who hoped and asserted that the King could never recover (when Foxite Ministers would replace Pittites), and those who hoped and maintained that the illness was temporary, and that therefore a Regency (of the Prince) should have limitations. Though profoundly political, the crisis was also social, and bitter personal animosities were engendered and aggravated. A propaganda campaign organized by Sheridan, with newspapers bought and prints financed, had little or no effect on public opinion, though there were rats in high places who defected to 'the rising SUN' *A Peep behind the Curtain at Drury Lane* [125] imagines Sheridan's reactions on 26 December, when the audience called loudly for 'God Save the King' (then played only on special occasions) and when the huzzaing at 'Scatter his enemies' 'exceeded all imagination'.[5] With a conspiratorial scowl at the orchestra, Sheridan orders 'D—n 'em don't play God save the King'.

The Prince and his friends counted on victory. Mrs Fitz was to be a duchess (the prints make her a queen), royal dukes would be field marshals. Whig ladies wore 'Regency caps' with three feathers and '*Ich Dien*' in gold letters,[6] while the other side wore 'Constitution caps'. But with the national rejoicing at the King's recovery both parties wore loyal emblems. At the Drawing Room in March almost all the women wore caps with white feathers and bandeaux embroidered 'God save the King'. In *Restoration Dressing Room* [126] in April three Foxite ladies change their Regency emblems for loyal ones. Mrs Fitz, the Prince's feathers still in her hair, adjusts a garter: *Vive le Roi*. The ribbon favour on the floor is inscribed (ironically) 'Our Prayers are Heard, He Lives'. *Royal Dipping* in July [127] is an almost literal, and therefore comic, rendering of the scene at Weymouth, where the King went to convalesce in July 1789. 'Think but of the surprise of his Majesty', Fanny Burney recorded, 'the first time of his bathing; he had no sooner popped his royal head under water, than a

RESTORATION DRESSING ROOM

126 Restoration Dressing Room, (?) Kingsbury
127 Royal Dipping, J. Nixon

Royal Dipping.
Of purest Air, and healing Waves we tell
Where, welcome Maid Hygeia loves to dwell!
In Holland's Exhibition Rooms may be seen the largest Collection in Europe of Humorous Prints. Admittance, One Shilling.

London, Pub.d by Will.m Holland, N.o 50 Oxford Street July 15, 1789.

band of music, concealed in a neighbouring machine, struck up God save Great George our King.'

As these excitements died down attention could be given to the great events in France. In its early stages the Revolution was welcomed in England (it was compared with the glories of 1688), and enthusiasm for the fall of the Bastille was reflected in three simultaneous pantomimes. When the war came, prices rose, the volunteers were derided, and life went on as usual. The invasion and revolutionizing of Britain (still only a paper project) is burlesqued in *French Invasion or Brighton in a Bustle* [128] in March 1794. Martha Gunn the bathing woman is active, and Fox and Sheridan (pro-French) peer furtively from one of 'Smoker' Miles's machines. He was a Brighton character (d. 1797), for many years 'chief bather' there. When war returned after the brief interval there was a quite different attitude to the volunteers. For some months in 1803 they were heroes, the country was fully invasion-conscious, Boney was derided. Reaction followed and in 1804–5, when the threat of invasion had become more serious, scepticism or boredom had replaced the emotions of 1803.

Changes of costume have more than their usual social significance and were in fact sensations; they were recognized as corresponding to changes in manners and social attitudes. From the later sixties Macaroni fashions were the beginning of the end of typical eighteenth-century dress: wigs, full-skirted coats, wide cuffs. Shortly after this the hoop was in retreat and tight-lacing with it. Its demise has been attributed to the young Duchess of Devonshire after her marriage in 1774. From 1778 quasi-masculine dress for women in the fashion for the riding habit has been noted. (This was not for riding, there is talk of changing from a habit into a riding skirt, which was long.)[7] It succeeded the fantastic hair-dressing of 1776–7.

The sobering of dress for men began before 1780 – doubtless with the disappearance of Macaroni fashions when silks and embroideries had reached a peak of extravagance. In that year William Hickey found the bright colours and gold lace of his Calcutta outfit too garish for London; when he appeared in the theatre in a scarlet coat he was unkindly taken for the Lord Mayor's trumpeter. Somewhere about this time the umbrella superseded the sword, which disappeared, except for Court dress. Umbrellas, previously used only by women and Frenchmen, were tolerated in the London streets. This St James's Park scene [129] shows that they were in common use by 1784.* By this year the 'sparrow-tail' coat had appeared, but was considered foppish. Round hats – embryo top-hats – were innovations in 1781 and were connected with the driving craze. They went through many variations of crown and brim before they became cylindrical. Tight-fitting breeches became longer and longer, and by 1790 they were tied below the calf, on the way to pantaloons. Bucks and bloods wore exaggerated forms of this dress, with short hair – as

yet without political significance – and were known as 'crops'; the outstanding ones were Lord Barrymore and his two brothers, the Prince's raffish friends.

Plainer dress went with a lessening of formality in manners and a blurring of social distinctions. In January 1794 Lord Glenbervie reflected on changes which he dates from about 1790. Lord Auckland had just told him that (as an official in 1783) 'he never went to the Irish House of Commons but full-dressed', and was never seen on foot in the streets of Dublin. 'This formality, if otherwise adviseable, is so incompatible with present manners, that it would now be quite impracticable & ridiculous. At that time people still went full-dressed to dinner and to the Opera in London, and could not in decency go otherwise to the pit or boxes. . . . For these last three or four years, if a man has been to Court, he cannot go, without some singularity, to dine out or to an assembly without putting on a frock. . . . These sort of trifles, as they seem, have, and had, a deep connexion with all the more important modern changes, and striking root imperceptibly till about four years ago they blossomed with such luxuriancy to produce a monstrous crop of deadly fruit. I have heard Fox say the neglect of dress in people of fashion had he thought contributed much to remove the barriers between them and the vulgar and profligate, levelling and equalizing.'[8] Odd indeed from Fox, whose slovenly dress, plain blue coat and buff breeches (adopted *c.* 1778 from the American colours as a political gesture) had anticipated and sanctioned these changes.

It is to Fox and his friends that the beginning of the transformation of dress and manners is attributed by Wraxall: 'In 1777 society was subjected, indeed, to fetters from which we have emancipated ourselves – those of dress, etiquette, and form. The lapse of two centuries could scarcely have produced a greater alteration in these particulars than have been made by about forty years. That costume which is now [1815] confined to the levee or the Drawing Room was then worn by persons of condition with few exceptions every where and every day. Mr Fox and his friends, who might be said to dictate to the town, affecting a style of neglect about their persons and manifesting a contempt of all usages hitherto established, first threw a sort of discredit on dress. From the House of Commons and the clubs in St James's Street, the contagion spread through the private assemblies of London. But though gradually introduced, and insensibly perishing of a dropsy, dress never fell till the era of Jacobinism and equality in 1793 and 1794. It was then that pantaloons, cropped hair and shoe-strings, as well as the total abolition of buckles and ruffles, together with the disuse of hair-powder, characterized the men.'[9]

From 1793 cropped hair, worn as a political gesture, was a French fashion (though it had been a rakish, non-political one from 1790); those who paid the new tax in 1795 for a licence to wear powder were called guinea pigs. Their names were posted on church doors. In Gillray's *Leaving off Powder – or – A frugal Family saving the Guinea* [XIII] only the young man has welcomed the fashion; his sister

* James Macdonald relates how he used an umbrella in London in 1778; in three months it was tolerated by the mob and gradually came into general use, and 'now [1790] is become a great trade in London', *Memoirs of an Eighteenth Century Footman* (London: Routledge, 1927), p. 235.

FRENCH INVASION OR BRIGHTON IN A BUSTLE.

Publish'd March 1.st 1791. by I Downes N.º 240 Strand.

128 *French Invasion or Brighton in a Bustle, J. Nixon*

THE BATTLE OF UMBRELLAS.

Published as the Act Directs, by Harrifon & Co Nº 18 Paternofter Row, Sepr 1 1784

129 The Battle of Umbrellas, S.Collings/Thomas

is dismayed at the shame of her red hair. Southey, voicing a Spanish visitor to England, remarks 'the English costume is at present [1807] as totally unlike what it was thirty years ago as it is to the Grecian or Turkish habit'.[10] From about 1800 Beau Brummell, as the arbiter of fashion (till 1816) gave prestige and elegance to sober plainness, enjoining superfine cloth, perfect fit, and cleanliness – the starched neckcloth.

Changes in women's dress were equally striking. 'Habits' were followed in 1785–6 by inflated '*derrières*', a 'fashionable circumvallation of tow and whalebone', balanced by gauze-covered excrescences over the breast, together with huge wide-brimmed hats and big muffs, much caricatured and long remembered as monstrosities [35]. These extravagancies were short-lived. The next sensational change introduced a fashion that lasted, with variations, for over twenty years. The impact of the French Revolution on costume is a familiar fact – a reaction from the formality of

the *ancien régime*, followed by the high-waisted dress of the Directory and Empire which owed much to J. L. David and French notions of the dress of classical antiquity. At its most transparent – '*nudités gauzeuses*' – it was associated with Madame Tallien. What is less recognized is that it had an independent and earlier origin in England. Early in 1793 Lady Charlotte Campbell* had introduced the clinging high-waisted dress 'imitating the drapery of pictures and statues'. A slight swelling below the waist was given by a pad, and this was the subject of ribald newspaper comment, of a prologue and even of a farce, *The Pad* (Covent Garden, 27 May 1793): ' . . . an exact representation of a state of pregnancy . . . accompanied by a complete display of the bosom – which is uncovered and stuck out

---

* A beauty, b. 1775, daughter of one of the famous Gunning sisters, with 'the mania of being admired' according to Gouverneur Morris in 1795. As Lady C. Bury, she is known as a novelist, cf. below, p. 173, n. 11.

by the sash immediately below it'.[11] There were many caricatures, including *The Frailties of Fashion* (1 May) by Isaac Cruikshank, a park scene. The fashion reached Calcutta in July 1793, when Hickey noted 'a great importation of new ladies, the whole of them dressed in a style that appeared to us Goths as unbecoming as preposterous'. This was 'the no-waist system', from adopting which 'every girl appeared to be big with child'. These ladies had broken their journey at the Cape, causing a Dutch gentleman to exclaim 'Ah, God help their poor parents. How miserable they must be upon perceiving the situation their daughters are in.'[12]

By 1794 the pad had been modified, but not the clinging transparencies, satirized in *The Graces of 1794* [130]. According to *The Sporting Magazine* in July, 'Female dress of the present fashion, is perhaps the most indecent ever seen in this country. The *breast* is altogether displayed, and the whole drapery, by the wanton management of the wearers . . . is said to *cling* so to the figure that nothing can be said to be completely concealed. Well may it be necessary to veil the face.'

With a short lapse into shapelessness burlesqued in *Waggoner's Frocks and no Bodys of 1795*, the fashion for clinging draperies gained momentum and satirical prints multiplied. T. J. Mathias remarks 'the dress of the present period has warranted the caricatures of the day, particularly . . . "the dress of Ladies as it will be"',[13] that is, Gillray's print [131] 1796. 'The ladies of the present day . . . do not perhaps know they copy the fashion from Madame Tallien, who copied it from the Greeks.'[14] Lady Charlotte certainly anticipated her. But wherever it began, it was part of the spirit of the age, and also owed something to the new English muslins. Variations of the limp dress for women (Court dress excepted) held the field, till the sudden impact of Paris fashions when English visitors flocked to France in 1814 and 1815.

Notes to Chapter XIV
1. *The Diary of Benjamin Robert Haydon*, ed. W.B.Pope, vol. 1 (Cambridge, Mass.: Harvard University Press, 1960), p. 182.
2. *Thraliana*, ed. K.C.Balderston (Oxford: O.U.P., 1952), p. 192.
3. To Sir Horace Mann, 18 June 1777.
4. *Diary*, ed. James Greig, vol. III (London: Hutchinson, 1922–8), p. 240.
5. *Harcourt Papers*, ed. E.W.Harcourt, 1880–1905, vol. IV, p. 97.
6. Ibid., pp. 179, 180, 200, 216.
7. *Early Diary of Fanny Burney*, ed. A.R.Ellis, vol. II, 1907.
8. *Journals*, ed. W. Sichel, vol. 1 (London: Constable, 1910), p. 39.
9. N.W.Wraxall, *Historical and Posthumous Memoir*, 1884.
10. *Letters of Espriella*, 1807, vol. II, p. 327.
11. *Life and Letters of Sir G. Elliot*, ed. Countess of Minto, 1874, vol. II, p. 133.
12. *Memoirs of William Hickey*, ed. Alfred Spencer, vol. IV (London: Hurst & Blackett, 1925), pp. 114–15.
13. *Pursuits of Literature*, 1796, vol. II, 1.220n.
14. *Morning Chronicle*, 26 February 1796.

130 *The Graces of 1794*, I.Cruikshank

131 *Ladies Dress, as it soon will be*, Gillray

Ladies Dress, as it soon will be.

134 'The King and Queen on their way to Deptford to launch a man-of-war', Rowlandson

and Flanders; Switzerland was sometimes added but Germany was often omitted owing to the discomforts of travel. For generations the educational value of the Grand Tour had been hotly debated. According to Pope the young man 'gather'd ev'ry vice on foreign ground. . . . Spoil'd his own language and acquir'd no more'. 'They set out on their travels unlick'd cubs, and on their travels they only lick one another, for they seldom go with any other company. . . . They come home at three or four and twenty refined and polished (as is said in one of Congreve's plays) like Dutch skippers from a whale-fishing.'[5] Thus Chesterfield, who sent his son on the Tour when only fourteen. Adam Smith was contemptuous (1776). Cowper joined in the dispraise:

> From school to Cam or Isis, and thence home,
> And thence with all convenient speed to Rome,
> With rev'rend tutor, clad in habit gay,
> To tease for cash, and quarrel with all day. . . .[6]

Bunbury, who made the tour c. 1767–8, has recorded many impressions, *A Tour to Foreign Parts* [136] published in 1778, perhaps illustrates Chesterfield's acid comments: the oafish youth arrives at a French posting-inn holding a copy of the famous *Letters* (many editions between 1774 and 1777). The bear-leader stands behind. The squalid discomfort of French inns was a standing subject of complaint (Italian and German ones were worse but less was expected). The 'milk-churn' boots of the postillions invariably amused when first encountered. On her way to Spa in 1776 Mary Hamilton noted 'when I first saw a number of these boots standing upright in the inn-yard [Dessein's] at Calais & the postilions – just before they were to mount their horse, thrusting their legs in with shoes on their feet – I could hardly refrain from Laughing, & we were all amused at the novel sight of Postillions with long queues . . . & cocked and cornered hats.'[7]

'I was very highly diverted,' Nelson wrote in 1783, 'on starting *en route* from Calais with looking what a curious figure the postillions and their rats of horses, made together.' Bunbury sketched contrasted specimens of French, Italian, German and English ones.

The everyday sights of Paris were a special source of interest and surprise. The chief viewpoints were the *Pont Neuf* [137] and the *Place des Victoires*. These, with the quays, were the places where pedestrians had foot-ways.[8] The muff and the umbrella, used by men, always amuse. So does the long pigtail queue worn by the humblest people. The Dog Barber – *tondeur des chiens* – and the *limonadier* are recurring figures in English prints. There was nothing in Paris to compare with the crowded street-life of London; the streets were too narrow, too dangerous, too dirty, or else too empty. Johnson noted 'Nobody but mean people walk in Paris'.

Another viewpoint, also by Bunbury, is the subject of *Englishman at Paris, 1767* [138], published in 1782. He is the object of pitying surprise for his outlandish dress; all look at him, especially the *frizeur* with his umbrella. He is on foot and has neglected the common practice of English

visitors. 'When an Englishman comes to Paris,' Smollett writes (1763), 'he cannot appear until he has undergone a total metamorphosis. . . . It is enough to make a man's heart ake to see his wife surrounded by a multitude of *cotturieres*, milliners, and tire-women. . . . The good man, who used to wear the *beau drap d'Angleterre*, quite plain all the year round, with a long bob or a tye perriwig, must have provided himself with a camblet suit trimmed with silver for spring and autumn, with silk cloaths for summer, with cloth laced with gold or velvet for the winter; and he must wear his bag-wig *à la pigeon*. This . . . is absolutely indispensable for all those who pretend to any rank above the mere bourgeois.'

Even Johnson made purchases (costing thirty pounds) for his twenty-six-day visit in 1775, including 'a Paris-made wig of handsome construction'. And Horace Walpole (in 1765) was 'thrown into a cauldron with tailors, perriwig-makers, snuff-box-wrights, milliners, &c'. *The Englishman in Paris* [139], 1770, submits to the *frizeur*, beside him is a book, *A Six Weeks' Tour to Paris*. The picture on the wall is of two (French) monkeys, adorning an English bear. *The English Lady at Paris*, in 1771, after S. H. Grimm, is large, exuberant, complacent, vulgarly overdressed in a would-be French manner, much admired by her elderly husband, 'Mr Alderman Lovewife', by her maid and by a French footman. These visitors are not grand tourists. Till the revolutionary wars travel between the countries was checked but not stopped in war-time, but peace always released a pent-up flood. Walpole says that two years after the peace of 1763, forty thousand English were reported to have passed through Calais.

When the old notion of the Grand Tour as an education was superseded by holiday travel in search of the picturesque or mere novelty it was a sign of a new age. The change was linked with the French Revolution, with the cult of nature and the growing fashion for tours at home, and with the increasing numbers of middle-class travellers. According to Gibbon, the glaciers of Savoy (p. 218) had become an established expedition for (Grand) tourists by the sixties. The pioneer visit was made from Geneva in 1741 by William Windham and his tutor. The first recorded Swiss walking tour by undergraduates was in 1790, when Wordsworth and Robert Jones set off for the Alps in the spirit of Liberty. All this was not yet within the range of graphic satire. But the Englishman in France was a perennially popular theme.

The humours of French travel in 1790 are realistically treated in a set of four aquatints. *The Inn Yard at Calais* is 'Dessein's celebrated inn' as Arthur Young called it. Apart from tricolour cockades for the Englishmen, things seem as before; the friar (inevitable after *The Sentimental Journey*), the porter in ruffles and wooden shoes. In *Breakfast at Breteuil* the travellers are dressing, eating and drinking in haste; a picture of the attack on the Bastille hangs over the chimney-piece. In the last of the set, *Returning from a Review at the Champ de Mars in Paris* [140], with the *décrotteur* and the *limonadier* still in the picture, the review is clearly the *Fête de la Fédération* of 14 July 1790.

135 *Coach interior, Woodward/I. Cruikshank*

136 *A Tour to Foreign Parts, Bunbury*

VIEW ON THE PONT NEUF AT PARIS.

137 *View on the Pont Neuf at Paris, Bunbury*

In this same month Horace Walpole's letters to Mary Berry and her sister were filled with accounts of the misadventures of English travellers in France, begging them not to venture: he cannot understand their leaving 'the only country in Europe at present that one could wish to be in'. However, they went, spending two days of intensive sightseeing in Paris on their way to Italy. Even before the French declaration of war (February 1793) the English could be in danger from the populace as *aristocrates* or *espions*. There is nothing to suggest the Revolution in *Le Débarquement du Chevalier John Bull et de sa Famille à Boulogne sur Mer* [141] by Gillray after Bunbury, 31 May 1792. The indignant Britons are carried ashore by fishwives to be met by the usual hotel touts and French characters. When Frederic Reynolds was forcibly seized by *poissardes* at Calais in 1792 – at least forty, he says, wading out to the vessel – he attributed it to 'sansculottes principles'.

As never before intercourse with France was interrupted by the war, and more completely so after Napoleon's internment at Verdun in 1803 of Britons of (alleged)

military age. To view England from 1793 to Waterloo through social satires is to get the impression of indifference to what was happening abroad. There is much truth behind this. Jane Austen is far from being alone in suggesting it. 'If you were in the Isle of Thanet,' Mary Berry wrote to Walpole (28 September 1794), 'you would never . . . suspect that we were in the midst of a war such as Europe never saw before. Here every body is riding and driving and *phaetoning* and *currickoling* away. . . .'

But the urge to see the new France, and Buonaparte, and the loot of Italy, became intense. There was even a disposition to glamourize the First Consul, manifested in the portraits of the romantic hero of the Italian campaigns, based on Italian portraits, that filled the print shops. When the Preliminaries of Peace were signed (1 October 1801) London was illuminated, and according to Cobbett (who doubtless exaggerated) 'Nineteen transparencies [illuminated pictures] out of twenty were expressive of attachment to Buonaparte's person or the cause of France'. The Definitive Treaty (25 March 1802) was followed by a

ENGLISHMAN AT PARIS .1767.

M.º Bunbury del.

Publish'd 23.ª Feb.ª 1782.

J.ª Bretherton f.

138 Englishman at Paris. 1767, Bunbury

cross-Channel rush. The English print-shops concerned themselves with the approach of Fox and his friends to the First Consul at two levees. The prints were amusing and unkind. When Napoleon, as he was now styled – Emperor in all but name – used the short peace for wholesale acquisitions of territory and refused the expected lifting of the embargo on trade with France, there was a momentous swing of opinion. The French print shops began a theme which was to be greatly developed in 1814 and after, the uncouth manners and dress of British tourists. *La famille anglaise à Paris* [142] is a satire on the homely sightseers who went to France in 1802, and were different from those who went before the Revolution. Here the topic of the Briton in France ceases till 1814.

When the seaside gained upon the inland spa it was a sign of social change with analogies to the superseding of the Grand Tour by John Bull abroad. Of course it owed much to the increasing numbers of the middle classes, but if we consider the change in terms of Brighton versus Bath, the victory of the sea was largely due to the gaiety and fashion

brought there by the Prince of Wales. (All watering-places throve on the presence of royalty; George III (p. 134) gave prestige but not fashion to Weymouth from 1789.) The Prince went there first in 1782. In that year Cowper published *Retirement*:

> *Your prudent grandmammas, ye modern belles,*
> *Content with Bristol, Bath, and Tunbridge Wells,*
> *When health required it, would consent to roam,*
> *Else more attached to pleasures found at home,*
> *But now alike, gay widow, virgin, wife,*
> *Ingenious to diversify still life,*
> *In coaches, chaises, caravans, and hoys,*
> *Fly to the coast for daily, nightly joys,*
> *And all, impatient of dry land, agree,*
> *With one consent to rush into the sea.*

The hoys went to Margate, and Cowper had already expressed his aversion to the vulgar crowds they conveyed there. Generally speaking, the prints illustrate high life at Brighton, 'cits' at Margate, oddities and gouty invalids at

The ENGLISHMAN in PARIS.

Jn.° Collet pinx.   *J.° Caldwall fecit*

139 The Englishman in Paris, after J. Collet

Bath. All were 'watering places'. The seaside* began with sea-water as a variant of that panacea, spa-water. First at Scarborough at the end of the seventeenth century because it was a spa that happened to be on the coast. By the 1730s sea-bathing had begun there. The decayed fishing-town of Brighthelmstone gained favour when Dr Richard Russell established himself there (1750) and recommended sea-water for drinking and baths. Seaside places copied the inland spas: Assembly Rooms, balls, a Master of the Ceremonies, music, promenades, rooms for cards and gossip, subscription libraries, usually a theatre.

In 1722 Defoe had found 'Bright Helmstone' in danger of falling into the sea, which had recently devoured two hundred houses. By the sixties it was fashionable, with two libraries, and bathing machines. The first theatre opened in 1762. In August 1763 Gilly Williams found the best lodgings 'most execrable', the visitors, 'except our company', numerous and vulgar, but, 'I never liked any thing better'. And next year he wrote of the 'extraordinary exoticks' from France: 'Barbers, milliners, barons, counts, arrive here almost every tide, and they stay here till their finances are so exhausted that they depart upon the stage-coach and not in it.'[9]

Royalty – of the raffish sort – was there by 1781, the Duke and Duchess of Cumberland. In 1782 the Prince visited his uncle; in 1784 he was there for his health, but not in 1785. Therefore, according to the *Morning Post*, Brighton was filled with the dowdy: 'surely some of the Margate hoys have blundered . . . and landed their cargoes on the Sussex coast. . . . Some City beaus sport their gigs upon the Downs, and their persons upon the Steyne . . . they would fain be thought men of fashion . . .' By 1787 the Pavilion was habitable and the Prince, with Mrs Fitzherbert in her own house, was the established patron of the place. In 1789 Rowlandson and his friend Wigstead went there, and the latter wrote *An Excursion to Brighthelmstone*, with eight aquatints after Rowlandson. One is of the ladies hurrying down the cliff to the bathing machines; we learn that the Master of the Ceremonies controlled the bathing and 'had sent the gentlemen two hundred yards to the westward'. In 1763 Williams told Selwyn 'it would astonish you to see the mixing of sexes at this place, and with what a coolness and indifference half a dozen Irishmen will bathe close to those we call prudes elsewhere'.[10] The Brighton machines [128], unlike those at Margate, were without the hoods that covered the steps to the sea.† Female bathers, in the eighteenth century and after, were either nude or clothed from neck to heels in flannel.

In 1788 John Byng took a hasty look at Brighton and found it 'in a fashionable unhappy bustle, with such a harpy set of painted harlots as to appear to me as bad as Bond Street in the spring, at three o'clock p.m. . . .

*The *Oxford English Dictionary* dates the word from a doctor's advice in 1797: Walpole used it casually, 6 April 1774: 'the seaside, which has always been more serviceable than any remedy . . .', *Letters*, Vol. VIII, p. 437.
† By Thackeray's day there were 'white awnings', *The Newcomes* (1853–5).

RETURNING FROM A REVIEW AT THE CHAMP DE MARS IN PARIS.

140 Returning from a Review at the Champ de Mars in Paris (1790), after F. G. Byron

Elegant and modest people will not abide such a place.'[11] But he disliked watering-places. Pictorially speaking, the typical conveyance at Bath was a bath-chair or a sedan-chair, at Brighton it was the Prince's phaeton – or later, barouche, with a team of four or six which he drove under the tuition of Sir John Lade; and gigs and curricles were dashing madly over the Downs, then immediately behind the narrow strip of houses. Races (Brighton and Lewes), cricket, and the Prince's regiment, the Tenth Dragoons (afterwards Hussars) added to the gaiety. Then a new seaside fashion began, donkey-riding for ladies. This was the subject in 1805 of a popular song illustrated in *Taking an Airing at Brighton*, *The Donkeys or the Humours of Fashion*. Gillray etched an amateur's design *Morning Promenade upon the Cliffs, Brighton* [143] in 1806. The three groups are 'Kicking Sett', 'Active Sett', and 'Passive Sett'.

Margate was invariably denigrated as the resort of cits – it was not of course exclusively so. *The Margate Macaroni* of 1772 is an obese and overdressed vulgarian. In *The Return from Margate*, 1784, 'Alderman Guttle and his Family' arrive by stage at a London inn. *Voyage to Margate*, 1786 [144], is a scene on board a hoy, a most uncomfortable

form of travel with no cabin. *Landing at Margate* illustrates an article on the pretentiousness and gullibility of cits. Gillray, no disparager of cits, made elaborate notes for, but did not etch, a sequence of plates on 'John Bull and his Family' on a visit to Margate (he had been there for his health in 1807). It starts with 'a Fat Citizen' in a butcher's shop, and a journey by post-chaise. Margate scenes and diversions and the misadventures of the family are noted, with finally a long hotel bill presented by 'an insolent landlord' to Papa with an empty purse; the return 'the cheapest way [by hoy], all sick'.[12] Cowper compares Margate with Ramsgate in a letter to Unwin (1779): 'But you think Margate more lively. So is a Cheshire cheese full of mites more lively than a sound one. . . . I remember, too, that Margate, though full of company, was generally filled with such company, as people who were nice in the choice of their company, were rather fearful of keeping company with. The hoy went to London every week, loaded with mackerel and herrings, and returned, loaded with company. The cheapness of the conveyance made it equally commodious for dead fish and lively company.'[13]

By the turn of the century bathing had become a

149

Le Débarquement du Chevalier John Bull et de sa Famille à Boulogne sur Mer.

141 Le Débarquement du Chevalier John Bull et de sa Famille à Boulogne sur Mer, Gillray after Bunbury

recreation instead of an early-morning medical ritual, and the stylized formality of the spa was fading. Before this the attractions of the seaside cottage without the diversions of the spa had been discovered – Fanny Burney describes them in her 'Teignmouth Journal' of 1773.[14] Wigstead tells us there were lodgings and bathing machines at Rottingdean by 1789. The cult of nature and the picturesque was drawing people to the Lakes and the mountains (the pioneer visit was Gray's, in 1769). 'The Lakes, where the whole world are running every summer', wrote the Head Master of Harrow in 1779.[15] Wilberforce, who rented a house on Windermere from 1781 for 'solitude and quiet', gave it up in 1788: 'The Tour to the Lakes has become so fashionable that the banks of the Thames are scarcely more public than those of Windermere.'[16] The illustrated tour in search of the picturesque was popularized by the Rev. William Gilpin; he started with the Wye and South Wales (tour in 1770, the book in 1782), went on to the Lakes, the Highlands, to *Picturesque Beauty*, *Picturesque Travel* and to *Sketching the Landscape*. Rowlandson satirized Gilpin, his books, his travels, and his sketches, in the plates to *The Tour of Dr Syntax in Search of the Picturesque* (1812), verses by W. Combe, which first appeared in *The Poetical Magazine*

1809–10, as *The Schoolmaster's Tour* (Gilpin had been Master of Cheam School). It had sequels and imitations during the Regency and was often reprinted. Here is Syntax sketching Windermere on his horse Grizzle [145].

Every summer from the sixties, Britain was increasingly traversed by pleasure 'tours', usually by post-chaise, for scenery and sight-seeing: country seats, churches, ruins, prospects. 'Tours' became a favourite subject for book-making. 'A Tour indeed! I've had enough/Of Tours, and suchlike flimsy stuff', the bookseller told Syntax, to be reduced to obsequiousness when the tourist produced a letter from his 'noble patron'.

Bath, though brilliant and fashionable in the days of Beau Nash and after, was always noted for its mixed company. It was Nash, as Master of Ceremonies who (Goldsmith says) overcame the 'Gothic haughtiness' which had kept the nobility apart from the gentry at public entertainments. Nonetheless, Bath is the setting for a paper in *The World* 'On the art of not knowing people',*

---

*No. 46, 15 October 1756. The writer, Edward Moore, the only 'author by profession' among the *World*'s fashionable contributors, a failed linen-draper with noble patrons, may well have encountered something of the sort.

Landing of Sir John Bull & his Family, at Bologne sur Mer.

an 'invention of the age'. 'Persons of distinction . . . meet their inferiors in public places, and either walk, sit or stand close at their elbows, without having the least recollection of them, whom, but a week or a day before they had been particularly intimate with. . . .' The narrator, a clergyman 'of some fortune', came to Bath to enjoy the society of many friends there: 'I have dined several times with his lordship, have frequently drank tea with the ladies, and spent two months this summer with the baronet.' Even when playing cards at the same table they 'have not the least knowledge of me'.

Bath was a natural magnet for the *beau monde*, foreign grandees, the new rich, country squires, for gamesters and adventurers and of course for invalids (the same could be said of Brighton). 'These watering-places,' Walpole wrote in 1766, 'that mimic a capital, and add vulgarities and familiarities of their own, seem to me like abigails in cast gowns.' Early satirical prints (1777–8) are of oddities from Anstey's popular *New Bath Guide* (1766): Lady Pandora Macscurvy and General Sulphur, barbarians from the North. The gaucherie of performers at a Bath ball was a commonplace with London fashionables. Walpole even called the principal figures in Plate II of Hogarth's *Analysis*

of Beauty 'two samples of grace in a young lord [the future George III] and lady, that are extremely stiff and affected. They are a Bath beau and a country beauty.' One of Bunbury's most noted prints was *The Long Minuet as danced at Bath* [detail, 147], 1787. The long strip design shows ten couples in different stages of the dance; they are all meant to be ugly or awkward or both; today they have charm, even here and there a touch of grace. They include, according to the Latin inscription, an ox, a thief, a pig, and a parson. In his *New Prose Bath Guide* (1776) Thicknesse warns visitors against dancing in 'so public an assembly as Bath, unless they are quite sure they can dance with some degree of ease and grace'. Partners were introduced and ladies called out to dance by the autocratic Master of Ceremonies.

The classic passage on the mixed company at Bath, with its analysis of the new rich in the later sixties, is the diatribe on 'the general tide of luxury' which Smollett puts into the mouth of Squire Bramble: 'Every upstart of fortune, harnessed to the trappings of the mode, presents himself at Bath . . . Clerks and Factors from the East Indies, loaded with the spoil of plundered provinces [nabobs]; planters, negro-drivers and hucksters, from the American plantations, enriched they know not how; agents,

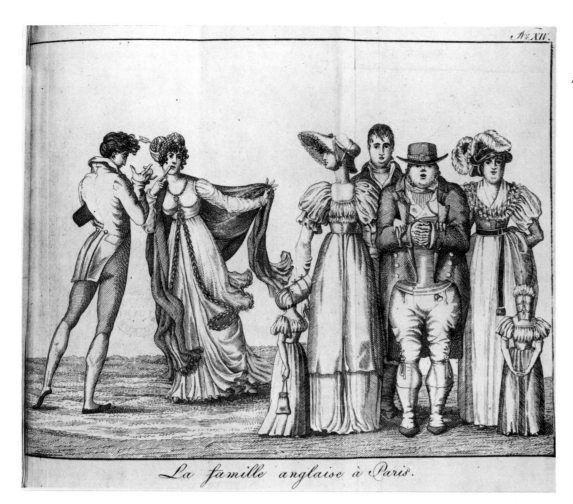

142 *La famille anglaise à Paris,*
after C. Vernet

La famille anglaise à Paris.

143 *Morning Promenade upon the Cliffs, Brighton, Gillray*

KICKING-SETT.   ACTIVE-SETT.   PASSIVE-SETT.

Morning Promenade upon the Cliff, Brighton.

commissaries, and contractors, who have fattened on two successive wars, on the blood of the nation; usurers, brokers, and jobbers of every kind; men of low birth and no breeding, have found themselves translated into a state of affluence, unknown to former ages ... and all of them hurry to Bath, because here, without any further qualifications, they can mingle with the princes and nobles of the land. Even the wives and daughters of low tradesmen, who like shovel-nosed sharks prey upon the blubber of these uncouth whales of fortune, are infected with the same rage of displaying their importance, and the slightest indisposition serves them as a pretext to insist upon being conveyed to Bath, where they may hobble country dances and cotillions among the lordlings, squires, counsellors and clergy.' He ends this interesting social stratification by concluding that 'a very inconsiderable proportion of genteel people are lost in a mob of impudent plebeians ...'.[17]

In Rowlandson's series of twelve plates, *The Comforts of Bath*, gout looms large: in the consultation in the sick room [80], at the fish-stall, where a gouty gourmand buys from a bath-chair [146], at a public breakfast, and in the final scene where cripples toil up or fall down the steep slope below the North Parade.

By the end of the century Bath was in decline. It had been in competition with Cheltenham from 1788 when the King went to take the waters, which Anglo-Indians believed good for their livers. In the new century there was a new exclusiveness that dimmed the public assemblies, though the old routine went on. The difference between the Bath scenes in *Northanger Abbey*, begun in 1798, and *Persuasion*, finished in 1816, is striking. Even the new buildings contributed to the loss of gaiety, by making the place a haven for spinsters and the retired. It so happens that two penetrating foreigners were at Bath in January 1810, both at the White Hart, both delighted with that famous inn. The Frenchman, Simond: 'The town looks as if it had been cast in a mould all at once, so new, so fresh, so regular. The buildings where the medical water is drunk, and where the

baths are, exhibit very different objects; human nature, old, infirm, and in ruins, or weary and *ennuyé*. Bath is a sort of great monastery, inhabited by single people, particularly by superannuated females.'[18]

Geijer, the Swede, less sophisticated, has many interesting things to say. He went to the Master of Ceremonies' ball. 'There was hardly any room for dancing, and no question of it. . . . Here were a multitude of made-up, painted hags' faces, enamelled with brand new smirks, figures sinking under the assaults of time and under the magnificence of raiment and diamonds and pearls.'[19]

Notes to Chapter XV

1. To Sir Horace Mann, 31 March 1761.
2. *The Farmer's Letters to the People of England*, 1771 (2nd ed.), p. 338.
3. *Torrington Diaries*, ed. C.B. Andrews, vol. II (London: Eyre & Spottiswoode, 1935), p. 321.
4. *Narrative of the Journey of an Irish Gentleman through England ... in 1782*, 1869, p. 57.
5. *Letters*, Chesterfield, 1892, ed. Bradshaw, vol. II, p. 580 (27 May 1757). Also the subject of his essay in *The World*, No. 29, 'On the little benefit accruing to Englishmen from their travels', 19 July 1753.
6. *The Progress of Error*, 1782.
7. *Mary Hamilton*, ed. E. and A. Anson (London: John Murray, 1925).
8. Dr J. Moore, *View of Society and Manners in France*, 1779, p. 33.
9. J.H. Jesse, *George Selwyn and His Contemporaries*, 1901, vol. I, pp. 266 7, 291.
10. Ibid., vol. I, p. 268.
11. John Byng, *Torrington Diaries*, ed. C.B. Andrews, vol. I (London: Eyre & Spottiswoode, 1934), pp. 371–?.
12. See Draper Hill, *Mr James Gillray the Caricaturist* (London: Phaidon, 1965), p. 136. Twelve drawings of 'The Journey to Margate' were sold at Humphrey's sale in 1835 (ibid.).
13. W. Cowper, *Correspondence*, ed. F. Wright, 1904, vol. I, p. 155.
14. *Early Diary of Fanny Burney*, ed. A.R. Ellis, 1889, vol. II.
15. *Pembroke Papers*, ed. Lord Herbert, vol. I (London: Jonathan Cape, 1939), p. 185.
16. *Life of William Wilberforce*, 1838, vol. I, p. 183.
17. *Humphrey Clinker*, 1771. Smollett last visited Bath in 1766, and left England in 1769.
18. *Voyage d'un Français en Angleterre pendant les années 1810 et 1811*, Paris, 1816.
19. E.G. Geijer, *Impressions of England, 1809–10* (London: Jonathan Cape, 1932).

VOYAGE to MARGATE

London Printed & Published by W.Hinton N.º 5 Sweetings Alley Royal Exchange Jan.ʸ 1785

144 *Voyage to Margate*, (?) I. *Cruikshank*

DOCTOR SYNTAX SKETCHING THE LAKE.

145 Dr Syntax sketching the Lake, Rowlandson
146 The Comforts of Bath, Pl. IV, Rowlandson

147 *The Long Minuet as danced at Bath* (*detail*), *Bunbury*

III   REGENCY

148 *La prière du soir, ami. Pl. to* E. Lami et H. Monnier, *Voyage en Angleterre*

The Regency opened in gloom, with prophecies of ruin and defeat. It was the year, 1811, the tide turned with the defence of the Lines of Torres Vedras, but that was not apparent. In that year Napoleon told Wrede, the Bavarian general, 'in three years I shall be master of the universe'. Prophecies of disaster from Cobbett and the Opposition continued till the Allies were in Paris in 1814, and were renewed during the Hundred Days till they were checked by news of Waterloo when the Radicals were 'galled exceedingly'. And when, in 1812, the Whigs did not get the office they had counted on (as the Prince's Friends) they launched a violent Press campaign against him, echoed and exaggerated in caricatures that reached a peak of grossness and scurrility. 'We all incurred the guilt if not the odium of charging his Royal Highness with ingratitude and perfidy. We all encouraged every species of satire against him and his mistress.' Thus Lord Holland, and the head-quarters of the campaign were reputedly at Holland House. The Regent's wife, previously attacked by the Whigs, was used by them as a weapon against him, and till her death in 1821 she was a recurrent storm centre.

Victory at last, so complete, so almost unimaginable, was expected to bring prosperity and plenty. Disillusion-ment was correspondingly great. By the end of our period the most basic of the changes since Hogarth's day was the growth of population, from (probably) under six million c. 1720 to the sixteen and a half million for England and Wales of the 1831 census, with a drift from the south to the Midlands and the north. The country was vastly richer and the chief beneficiaries were the financial, commercial and industrial interests the last a new kind of new rich.* The landed interest had done well too – that is, grandees, squires, farmers, parsons, but not labourers, except where local industries had pushed up wages. But the land was badly hit by the recession after 1815. The middle classes had prospered exceedingly. Lords were if anything less lordly – the peerage had been diluted and the barrier between aristocracy and plutocracy, never absolute, was less for-midable but more zealously defended. The old social geology of high life, middle life, low life was less stable and less accepted. This was the setting of a social phase

that pervaded the Regency, invaded the print-shops, and in one of its aspects, dandyism, survived the century.[1]

Old institutions remained static in a changing world, with inevitable stresses and strains. The first major break in the old system was Catholic Emancipation in 1829, forced on the King and the country by Wellington and Peel to avert civil war in Ireland. After this, Parliamentary Reform was inevitable. George IV's death, hard times, the 'Days of July' in France, brought in a Whig Ministry pledged to Reform. After two abortive Bills the third was carried owing to organized popular pressure in the wild excitements of the 'Days of May'.

The Regency was a strange mixture of the unregenerate eighteenth century and what was to be called Victorianism. One aspect of the latter was Evangelicalism, illustrated in this French view of family prayers in 1829 [148]. Another Frenchman's view gives the setting, but in a rather grander household (Lord Radnor's, 1835) with eleven or twelve women and eight or ten manservants who 'walked in formal order of hierarchic precedence. ... These twenty people took their places round the room and knelt down looking towards the wall. Near the fireplace ... the family knelt down too, and Lord Radnor read a prayer aloud, the servants giving the responses'.[2] Oddly, this was a pre-luncheon rite. Such family prayers (pre-breakfast or in the evening) were customary throughout the nineteenth century and were unkindly depicted by Samuel Butler. They began in the 1780s.

Another aspect of the Regency was prudery. Dr Bowdler published his *Family Shakespeare* in 1818 and added a word to the language. To Byron (in 1822) cant was 'the crying sin' of the time. 'We have nothing but cant, cant, cant', says Peacock's Mr Crotchet (1831). All this seems an in-congruous setting for that dominant character of the time, the dandy, a print-shop figure standing for anything from patrician insolence to proletarian aspirations.

Notes to Chapter XVI

1. See E. Moers, *The Dandy. Brummell to Beerbohm* (London: Secker & Warburg, 1960).
2. A. de Tocqueville, *Journeys to England and Ireland*, ed. J. P. Mayer (London: Faber, 1958), p. 82.

*In 1813 the Home Secretary told Parliament he had no objection to the appointment of magistrates for Lancashire of 'wealthy and respectable persons engaged in Trade, but not in manufacture'.

LONGITUDE & LATITUDE of S.ᵀPETERSBURGH.

149 *Longitude and Latitude of St Petersburgh, G.Cruikshank*

Social exclusiveness was a Regency preoccupation manifested and symbolized by the dandies and the subscription balls at Almack's with their lady patronesses, 'a feminine oligarchy, less in number but equal in power to the Venetian Council of Ten',[1] the seven 'Oligarchs of our Gynocracy' (*Don Juan*). The *beau monde* – 'the World' – no longer effortlessly supreme, had become self-conscious and defensive against the ever-increasing numbers and wealth of the middle classes and the 'monied interest', one aspect of the 'levelling and equalizing' that had pained Glenbervie in 1794. Social climbers multiplied in a fluid and expanding society, and barriers were erected. Stendhal's comment, after visits to England in 1817 and 1821, demands quotation: 'Society being divided as by the rings of a bamboo, everyone busies himself with trying to climb into the class above his own, and the whole effort of that class is put into preventing him from climbing.' Personalities doubtless contributed. Admittance to Almack's was largely controlled by Madame de Lieven and Princess Esterhazy, the Russian and Austrian Ambassadresses, with their diplomatic protocol and their un-English caste arrogance, and, above all, by Lady Jersey, 'Queen Sarah', with a determined animus against commerce. And Almack's had become a marriage market – 'nothing less than a great market place for beauty'.[2] For generations marriage had been becoming less a matter of family arrangement, more of personal choice.

> *All on that magic list depends*
> *Fame, fortune, fashion, lovers, friends . . .*
> *If once to Almack's you belong*
> *Like monarchs, you can do no wrong;*
> *But banished thence on Wednesday night,*
> *By Jove, you can do nothing right.*[3]

Exclusiveness was the *raison d'être* of Almack's, and as it gradually broke down the balls lost prestige and were formally ended in 1863. 'The palmy days of exclusiveness are gone by in England', the *Quarterly* remarked of Almack's in 1840, any attempt to restore an oligarchy 'we are quite sure would be ineffectual'.[4] In *Longitude and Latitude of St Petersburgh*, 1813 [149], by Cruikshank, evidently after an amateur, the tall thin woman and the short fat man are Madame de Lieven and Prince Pierre Koslovsky, who called himself '*l'aimable roué*', waltzing at Almack's. The setting shows the austerity that was a protest against the lavish entertaining of the new rich. It had been no feature of the earlier balls there (p. 66). The magnificence of rooms, décor and food had much impressed Dr Campbell in 1773: 'every thing in the most elegant style'.[5]

There are two excellent witnesses to the phase of exclusiveness: Captain Gronow, back from the Peninsula and Waterloo, one of some six who had vouchers for Almack's out of the three hundred Guards officers in London; and Prince Pückler-Muskau,[6] a Prussian and an acutely malicious observer who made a fortune-hunting visit to England in 1826–8. He describes Almack's: 'A large bare room with a bad floor . . . with two or three naked rooms at the side, in which were served the most wretched refreshments, and a company into which, in spite of the immense difficulty of getting tickets, a great many "Nobodies" had wriggled. . . . And yet Almack's is the culminating point of the world of fashion.' He saw this world as 'a peculiar caste, an *Imperium in Imperio* . . . not influenced by rank, still less by riches . . .' and attributes it to the English addiction to social striving. 'It is an almost universal weakness in England to parade acquaintance with the noble, the noble do the same with regard to the "fashionable" or exclusive.' He was impressed (like Mrs Piozzi) by the contrast with the Continent, where birth and status at Court were all-important. After further experiences of English life he expands this to describe 'an entirely new power . . . placed on the throne as supreme and absolute sovereign – Fashion . . . a goddess who in England alone, reigns . . . with inexorable sway though always represented to mortal eyes by a few clever usurpers of either sex' (Not so new; the gynocracy excepted, Fielding had noted it.) '*La mode chez eux*', wrote Stendhal, '*n'est pas un plaisir mais un devoir*'. The peculiarity of this phase was horror at contact with 'Nobodies'. (But Fielding had defined 'No body' as 'all the People in Great Britain except about 1200'.)

Gronow, looking back from the mid sixties, remembered that 'a worldly man or woman would, without scruple, cut their father or mother if they did not belong to the particular set which they considered good society . . . "Who's your friend", drawled Lord C—. "What," replied S—, "Oh a very good sort of fellow, one of my Cheshire farmers". It was his own father; a most aimiable and excellent man, and who had better blood and a larger fortune than any of the lordlings by whom his unworthy son was surrounded [in Hyde Park].' He adds, 'In these days of railways and monster parties, the folly of exclusiveness has very much died away; cutting near relatives is out of fashion – it is unnecessary in the whirl and bustle of life. . . . There is more self-respect among those who do not belong to the upper ten thousand.'[7] – a multiplication since Fielding's 1200 and Byron's 'twice two thousand for whom earth was made' (*Don Juan*).

There is remarkable agreement between the Briton and the Prussian. 'How unspeakably odious – with a few brilliant exceptions – . . . were the dandies of forty years ago. They were a motley crew, with nothing remarkable about them, but their insolence. They were generally not high-born, nor rich, nor very good-looking, nor clever, nor agreeable, and why they arrogated to themselves the right of setting up their newfangled superiority on a self-raised pedestal and despising their betters, Heaven only knows. They were generally middle-aged men, had large appetites and gambled freely, and had no luck. They hated everybody, and abused everybody, and would sit together in White's bay-window, or the pit boxes at the Opera, weaving tremendous crammers. They swore a good deal, never laughed, had their own particular slang, looked hazy after dinner, and had most of them been patronized, at one time or another, by Brummell and the Prince Regent.[8]

'The highest triumph of the English dandy [according to Pückler-Muskau] is to appear with the most wooden manners . . . and to contrive even his civilities so that they are as near as may be to affronts . . . to have the courage to offend against every restraint of decorum, to invert the relation to which our sex stands to women . . . to treat his best friends if they cease to have the stamp of fashion, as if he did not know them, "to cut them" as the technical phrase goes. . . .' Cutting had been Brummell's speciality: 'in the art of cutting, he shone unrivalled, he knew the "when", the "where" and the "how"'.[9] This was a development from the 'art of not knowing people' (p. 150).

The art of cutting is illustrated in a set of three plates after a clever amateur, M. Egerton, in 1827; *The Cut Celestial*; *The Cut Infernal* and *The Cut Direct*, with verses. In all a dandy riding or walking in London meets an acquaintance; he stares first at the sky, then at the ground; the last [150] 'requires little more than downright impudence'. The three cuttees are 'your dunning tailor', 'a story-telling uncle', and 'a respectable man with a shabby-drest wife and a poodle dog'.

We must go back to the dandy-impact on the print shops, the Press and the theatre in 1818–19, which has analogies with that of the Macaronies in 1771–2 (both were based on clubs (the Macaronies on the future Brooks's), both were fops, both gamblers, both reputedly effeminate). There was the usual time-lag. In April 1818 Lord Glenbervie* noted 'that term for a sort of fop is already worn out, so ephemeral are fashionable sobriquets and neologisms'.[10] How wrong he was. The Drury Lane pantomime for 1818–19 was *Harlequin and the Dandy Club, 1818*. The

*He had met Brummell at Calais in 1816 when he noted that he had been nicknamed 'the Dowager Dandy; the Tsar is the Military Dandy, some known character the Dandy Lion [Lord Petersham, so caricatured], Rogers [the banker-poet] the dead Dandy'.

prologue to *Brutus* (Drury Lane, 15 April 1818) describes the dandy:

> *France gave his step its trip, his tongue its phrase,*
> *The head its peruke, and his waist its stays . . .*
> *On the roug'd cheek the fresh-dyed whisker spread,*
> *The thousandth way of dressing a calf's head . . .*
> *The neckcloth next, where starch and whalebone vie*
> *To make the slave a walking pillory . . .*
> *What straps, ropes, steel, the aching ribs compress,*
> *To make the Dandy – beautifully less.*

There are three main categories of the print-shop dandy. First, caricatures of social notorieties, in which *The Genuine Dandy* is the Marquis of Worcester. Second, typical dandies, absurd, languid and effeminate nincompoops. Third, would-be dandies in some painfully squalid room, imitating the dress, manners and catch-phrases of their model. There are *Dandies Sans Souci*: prostitutes search two such dandies, who are dead drunk, to find no plunder, watch and seals are bogus. The companion print is *Dandies sans Six Sous*. In 1819 *The Dandies Coat of Arms* [151] etched by Cruikshank, symbolically summarizes the dandies of many prints, and in its crude way satirizes dandyism. The shield is a dandy's coat with a pinched waist, the centre seam bisects a little dandy, half-man, half-woman. The supporters are ape-headed dandies wearing fool's caps, each with a bottle of eau-de-cologne. The crest is a wig-block with ass's ears and blank features, blinkered by a high collar resting on a bulging breast supported by stays. The 'Order of Puppyism' hangs from the shield; a monocle dangles from a chain. Butterflies (p. 28) are prominent – emblems of worthless frivolity. If the dandy wore a wig, it simulated natural hair, as in Richard Dighton's *The Dandy Club* [152], 1818. Other accessories were chicken-skin gloves (yellow) and a neatly furled umbrella (its first appearance). The costume owed much to military uniform, especially to that of the Tsar – the pinched waist, bulging breast, high-shouldered effect of epaulettes. And Cossack trousers had a passing vogue. This dandy outfit was quite unlike – though partly deriving from – the elaborately inconspicuous dress of Brummell, the arch-priest of dandyism, who left England in 1816. It was also quite unlike the dress of George IV. And though in a famous caricature he is *The Dandy of Sixty* (in 1819, when fifty-seven, in field-marshal's uniform with cavalry boots and three rampant peacock's feathers in his cocked hat) he was not a dandy. Despite everything, there was still something of the youthful prince of Byron's tribute: ' . . . without alloy of fop or beau,/A finished gentleman from top to toe' (*Don Juan*).

Gradually the dandy sheds his eccentricities of costume, but remains a Regency figure, in prints as elsewhere, especially in fiction. Bulwer's *Pelham; or, the Adventures of a Gentleman*, 1828, is documentary. Pelham ('the puppy' as Thackeray called him) has at first the insolent and ultra-sensitive frivolity of his tribe, but emerges as a staunch and courageous friend and a keen politician with Radical views

Drawn by M.E.   London Published by Thos. McLean, 26 Haymarket   Aquatinted by H. Pyall.

THE CUT DIRECT!

150 The Cut Direct!, after M. Egerton

The Dandies Coat of Arms

151 *The Dandies Coat of Arms, G. Cruikshank*

– in fact, a romanticized Bulwer, who was a dandy, full of activity, literary and political. After violent attacks by Carlyle, first in *Fraser's Magazine*, then in *Sartor Resartus*, the author cut out excesses of effete aestheticism and effeminacy for the second edition (1839) – a good deal remains. There is a portrait of Brummell in the book, as Russelton, which the Beau called 'the grossest of caricatures'. Bulwer defended *Pelham* as substituting for Byronism the dandy pose, which was 'at least more harmless and more noble'. The book was a covert attack on dandyism according to Brummell, who glorified the uselessness of the man of pleasure as a protest against the bourgeois virtues of work and thrift (which had provided him with his own income).

Pelham was one of many 'novels of high society', mostly anonymous, sometimes *romans-à-clef*, between 1825 and 1850. The word 'exclusive' for a person first appeared in Ward's *Tremaine; or, The Man of Refinement*, 1825: 'She came out in full activity of Exclusiveness, a finished Exclusive.' Tremaine, the dandy, 'sat sufficiently often in the bay window of White's to conceive almost as high an idea of its powers as a judge has of the dignity of the bench'. He is cured of dandyism by love, religion, and life in the country. *The Exclusives*,[11] 1830, like *Almack's*, 1827, was an attack on exclusiveness when, as Pückler-Muskau thought, it had begun to wane. Certainly the Court of William IV was far from fashionable. But George IV, though fashionable, was far from an exclusive, and had become a recluse. At the Carlton House entertainments of 1812 which inaugurated the Regency 'the people invited were of all ranks and in no respect select'.[12] Sir Thomas Hammond* in 1831 thought the late King 'the *beau idéal* of a refined Monarch', but 'that he had by mingling with the low blood blackguards considerably broken down the barriers between high & low life, & had given them a shock'.[13]

The thronging crowds that were the excuse for exclusiveness are a main theme of Lady Susan O'Brien's notes on the social changes between 1760 and 1818 (for many intermediate years her runaway marriage to an actor had removed her from 'the World'). She begins with the Drawing Room. *Then*, once a week, sometimes crowded, 'but in general a well-regulated & elegant assembly of the best company. *Now*, held but three or four times a year & every body man or woman that can assume the name of gentleman or lady go to it. The crowds are so great & so little decorum attended to, that people's clothes are literally torn to pieces.'[14] She might have been describing Cruikshank's *Inconveniences of a Crowded Drawing Room* [XVI], dated May 1818 (Queen Charlotte's – one of her last).

Exclusiveness affected the parks – that touchstone of national *mores*. The old custom of walking in St James's Park with its jostling of classes had long since ceased with the change of the dinner hour from four or five to seven

---

*Hammond had been Chief Equerry and Clerk Marshal of the Household to George III and George IV for forty years, *The Diary of Benjamin Robert Haydon*, ed. W.B. Pope, Vol. III (Cambridge, Mass.: Harvard University Press, 1963), p. 50.

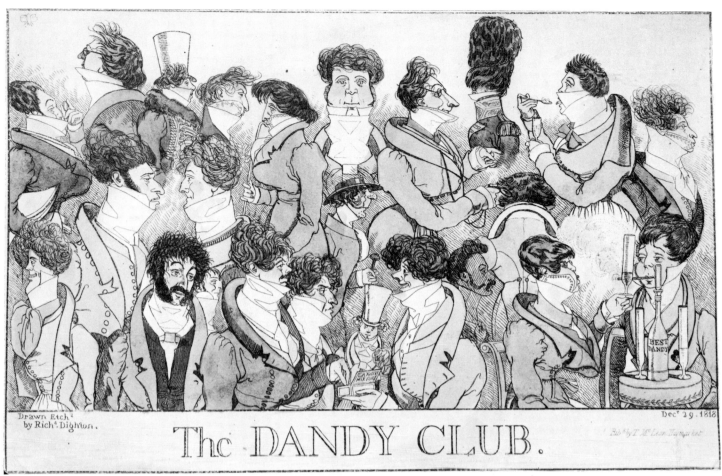

152 *The Dandy Club*, Richard Dighton

153 *Kensington Gardens (drawing)*, Rowlandson

154 *Tom Getting the best of a Charley*, R. and/or G. Cruikshank

155 *Tom and Jerry 'Masquerading it' among the 'Back Slums'*, R. and/or G. Cruikshank

or later (very late hours were a dandy affectation). Late hours, Lady Susan remarks, had altered everything. The 'Park hours' – in Hyde Park – were from four to seven: women in carriages, men driving themselves or riding; dandies, 'a line of men drawn up in battle array, and with impertinent nonchalance passing judgment on the women who drove before them', but even more concerned 'to show themselves ... to be admired'.[15]

Gronow, writing of 1814 and later, says that the company was composed of 'dandies and women in the best society; nor did you ever see any of the lower or middle classes intruding themselves in regions, which by a sort of tacit understanding, were given up exclusively to persons of rank and fashion'. And there was exclusiveness in reverse in Kensington Gardens. 'For some years', Madame de Lieven noted in 1820, 'that lovely garden has been annexed as a middle class rendezvous, and good society no longer goes there.'[16] She came to England in 1811. In that year Mary Berry found 'the complexion of these gardens is completely altered since I was there of a Sunday morning – always crowded with middling people, yet all the fine ladies used to come and show off their charms to the admiring mob, but now they have nothing to admire but one another'.[17]

Does this withdrawal pinpoint the onset of exclusiveness? Here is Rowlandson's drawing of Sunday morning in Kensington Gardens c. 1815 [153]. The 'rabble' had always been excluded: 'For the purpose of regulating the Company, servants are placed at the different entrances to prevent persons meanly dressed from going into the Garden.'[18]

Foreign visitors were deeply interested in English social stratification, no one more so than de Tocqueville with his probing questions. He elicited from Bulwer in 1833 a rather puzzling account of 'an immense revolution in the minds of Englishmen during the last half-century. Our aristocracy was great; it wanted to be fashionable, and that is one of the chief causes of its ruin. A line has been drawn between the upper and the middle aristocracy which, until then, had been united. The high nobility has set a tone and convention of its own; it has flaunted this superiority of convention, treated the middle aristocracy with arrogance and alienated it.'[19] Is this the division between exclusives and nobodies?

In the wild excitement over Reform, politics permeate social satire as never before. Almack's becomes a symbol of aristocratic insolence; in Seymour's *Lady Patronesses of Almack's versus Royalty*, November 1830, four of the seven ladies sit in close conference to decide that Queen Adelaide cannot be admitted: she intends going to 'the Gilt Hall, some vile place beyond Temple Bar [for the Lord Mayor's dinner that was cancelled]. She intends appearing in some vulgar stuff made by the *canaille* at a place called Spittlefields.' The Queen was patronizing English silks because of distress among weavers. These ladies, so grossly arrogant, ignorant and heartless, stand for the aristocracy, who, as borough owners, Cobbett reiterated, nominated the House of Commons, and, it was believed, appropriated places in Church and State, sinecures, pensions, and other fruits of taxation. The popular pressure behind Reform was based on this conviction. The abolition of rotten boroughs, Cobbett and others asserted, was the cure for poverty and distress. 'In consequence of the boroughs, all our institutions are partial, oppressive, and aristocratic. We have an aristocratic church, an aristocratic bar, an aristocratic game-code, aristocratic taxation, aristocratic corn laws, aristocratic laws of property ... all is privilege, proscription, monopoly, association, and corporation.'[20] As Bulwer told de Tocqueville 'there is an immense intellectual revolution taking place. In olden times the English thought that everything about their constitution was perfect, both advantages and abuses. Today everybody is looking for what needs mending.'[21]

Besides the dandy there was another typical Regency figure, the Corinthian or swell, largely a product of the astonishing popularity of Egan's *Life in London* which affected manners, conduct and language. The text was written for the plates, thirty-six coloured aquatints by Robert and George Cruikshank: *Life in London, or, the Day and Night Scenes of Jerry Hawthorne Esq and his elegant Friend, Corinthian Tom, accompanied by Bob Logic the Oxonian in their Rambles and Sprees through the Metropolis*, 1821. The success of the book was a social phenomenon. For the short run it was more popular than *Pickwick*. A list of ten stage versions between 1821 and 1840 is incomplete. In 1828 Egan listed sixty-eight piracies or imitations, including prints and songs. The plates were adapted to trays, snuff-boxes, fans and screens. Tailors advertised Corinthian fashions. Raffish young men imitated Tom and Jerry, especially their war on watchmen in *Tom Getting the best of a Charley* [154], a scene at Temple Bar, the most popular of the plates – it was copied on handkerchiefs.

The theme is high life and low life, the latter in places where swells went to 'see life', sometimes in disguise. The authors are the heroes of their book, transformed into a Corinthian and a country squire (the two Cruikshanks) and an Oxonian who is Egan, a sporting journalist. They are in the tradition of bucks and bloods with a spurious gilding of fashion. The plates show an intimate knowledge of pugilism, cockfighting, dogfighting (actually dog versus monkey), the Fleet Prison – none of clubs. High life is symbolized (on the wrappers) by Tom waltzing with a courtesan; and in *Highest Life in London* Tom and Jerry are in a quadrille at Almack's; the ornate décor showing that it is not from life. There are delicately drawn views of Vauxhall, the R.A., a gaming Hell, the salon at Covent Garden (p. 203) with Tom surrounded by courtesans.

The scenes that made most impact on the stage were the low-life ones, two especially. *Lowest Life in London* shows an East Smithfield alehouse where 'Black Sal' and 'Dusty Bob' (a dustman, 'Nasty Bob' in the book) dance a double shuffle. The other represents a rendezvous of professional beggars in St Giles, 'among the Cadgers in the "Back Slums"* in the Holy Land' [155]. Besides the inevitable ballad singer there are portraits – Billy Waters, the Negro

---

* The first appearance of the word, O.E.D.

fiddler, and Andrew Whiston, the crippled dwarf in a top hat who succeeded Billy as King of the Beggars (stage publicity dried up the alms on which Billy had prospered and he died in the workhouse). These four from actual life were the favourite characters of the best stage version of *Life in London*, Moncrieff's at the Adelphi, which had a record run despite attempts to stop it because it encouraged attacks on watchmen.

'Went to the Adelphi to see a new farce...', Mrs Arbuthnot, Wellington's friend, recorded in her journal (20 February 1822). 'I never had been at the place before. It is a very pretty theatre, but beyond everything vulgar I ever saw. It was crowded to an overflow, the people were hallowing and calling to each other from the pit to the gallery, fighting and throwing oranges at each other. The play itself was a representation of all the low scenes in London. ... In short it was a sort of very low Beggar's Opera, but it is impossible to describe the sort of enthusiasm with which it was received by the people who seemed to enjoy a representation of scenes, in which, from their appearance, one might infer they frequently shared.'[22]

Dedicated respectfully to George IV, the book surveys 'life' as lived by 'swells' ('I never was a gentleman, only a swell', says a character in *Midshipman Easy*, 1836). The women high-life characters are Kate and Sue (Harriette Wilson), notorious courtesans. In the theatre and in the widely circulated broadside version (a twopenny masterpiece 'in cuts and verse' of the Catnach Press), the low-life characters stole the show, though there was naïve admiration for the swells, shared by a youthful Thackeray. Egan called the broadside 'another wicked piracy'; it contains twelve cuts, the largest a spirited version of 'Upsetting the Charlies'.

Moralizing, a seeming concession to the spirit of the age, came with R. Cruikshank's print, *Emblematical Synopsis of Life in London* in 1826. In complete contrast with the book, raffish life is seen in terms of suicide and despair. The tiny scenes of low life have little connexion with the book. While dandyism and exclusiveness evoked criticism in novels of the 'silver fork school',[23] Egan's *Life in London* evoked street papers and popular farces that relishingly spot-lighted the low-life scenes. The book came out in parts, and Tom and Jerry made their first appearance at the peak of the near-revolutionary excitement of the Queen's affair in 1820.

Some diversions were common to Corinthians and dandies, notably high play. Rowlandson's view of *Gaming at Brooks's* [156] belongs to 1810 or later. The croupier

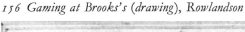

156 Gaming at Brooks's (drawing), Rowlandson

BOBBIN about to the FIDDLE — a Familly Rehersal of Quadrille Dancing, or Polishing for a trip to Margate.

157 Bobbin about to the Fiddle – a Family Rehersal of Quadrille Dancing, or Polishing for a trip to Margate, C. Williams

yawns, supper is going on in the background. Gaming Hells flourished in London and were occasionally raided from Bow Street. Dandies as 'Greeks' (card-sharpers) and their victims are depicted in Cruikshank's illustrations to verses called *The Greeks* and *The Pigeons* in 1817. All the Hells of London were outclassed when the ex-fishmonger Crockford opened his palatial building in St James's Street in 1828 (now the Devonshire Club). Crockford's was remarkable both as an exclusive and well-managed club with an aristocratic committee (including Wellington) and a Hell by which Crockford soon became a millionaire with consequent ruin to many.* 'One may safely say, without exaggeration,' writes Gronow, 'that Crockford won the whole of the ready money of the then existing generation.' Minor sharpers – 'Poor Famishing Rooks' – are depicted as ruined in Heath's *Greedy Old Nickford Eating Oysters* [XIV], *c.* 1829. Like the lawyer, the diabolical 'Old Nick' devours the substance of his clients in the appropriate form of

oysters. In the foreground his palace is symbolized by one of those 'grottoes' which London children built from oyster-shells on Old St James's Day (25 July) when they demanded 'a penny for the grotto'. It is placarded 'The St James's *Grotto* – This Fabric was raised on the Cost of many million Fat Oysters'. Lord Sefton, a dandy, who according to Creevey lost £10,000 in one year at whist, lost £200,000 at hazard as an habitué of Crockford's. In Disraeli's *Henrietta Temple* (1837), there is a favourable portrait of Crockford. 'Mr Bond Sharpe' speaks: 'there is not a man in this room who is not my slave. You see how they treat me. They place me upon an equality with them; they fool me to the top of my bent. And yet there is not a man in that room who, if I were to break tomorrow, would walk down St James's Street to serve me. . . . From the back parlour of an oyster shop my hazard table has been removed to this palace. Had the play been foul this metamorphosis would never have occurred.'

Though gaming flourished, card-playing as the inevitable evening occupation – the tyranny of cards so much complained of in the eighteenth century – was over. 'No cards are admitted' (at assemblies) Lady Susan O'Brien recorded, 'Music in which all are proficient has taken their place'. But there was no place for the music garden in an exclusive

---

*The rooms in St James's Street were used as a club only; the gaming was in a small adjoining house to the south, so that an indictment for gaming would not affect the club, Sir W. Fraser, *Words on Wellington*, 1900, pp. 64–5. The modern Crockford's is so called because its opening as a bridge club in 1928 was found to be just a century after that of the original. (Information from the P.R.O. of the Club.)

world. Ranelagh, which depended on fashion, had closed in 1803. Vauxhall survived to 1859, but was avoided by high life except for special events. Dicky Doyle drew the crowded scene there in the forties in his 'Manner and Customs of ye Englyshe' (*Punch*). The other surviving gardens descended in the social scale. White Conduit House ('Vite Condick Couse') lingered to 1849. Lysons described Bagnigge Wells *c.* 1810 as 'the resort of the lowest sort of tradesmen'; about 1840 it was that of 'the dandy dog's meat man' and his doxy.[24] Sadler's Wells had a miraculous survival by its transformation into a theatre. In 1896 it was a music hall, two houses nightly, admission 2*d.*, box a shilling.[25]

Two Regency innovations were the acceptance of the waltz and the cigar – as successors to the minuet and the snuff-box both symptomatic of the retreat from eighteenth-century formality. '*Now* [1818] there is a certain rudeness or carelessness of manners, affected both by men and women. Ladies pretty and young may go and seek their own carriages, & meet no assistance; persons with and without titles are called by their Xian names.'[26] The Regent must have contributed to the decline of the old formality. What monarch before George IV would have called his Prime Minister 'Arthur'?

The waltz reputedly came to English ballrooms in 1812, when Madame de Lieven introduced it at Almack's. But, according to Byron (*The Waltz*, 1812), it came from Germany 'while Hamburg yet had mails' – before the French occupation of Hanover in 1803. It also came from France. Farington noted (1802) the 'magical effect' of the 'Walse dance' at Tivoli, the Paris Vauxhall. 'The man makes a circle with his arms within which the woman turns round.' And in 1803, after dancing lessons in Paris, waltzes were being 'practised' at morning balls at Devonshire House.[27] Much earlier, in 1781, Prince Frederick (afterwards Duke of York) wrote from Hanover to the Prince 'when I return to England I must teach you two different kinds of dances from what we have the least idea of, the quadrilles and the waltzies'.[28] In 1816 the waltz acquired formal Court patronage at a Carlton House ball, when *The Times* (no friend to the Regent) 'remarked with pain that the indecent foreign dance called the *Waltz* was introduced (we believe for the first time) at the English Court on Friday last. This is a circumstance which ought not to be passed over in silence . . . [etc. etc.]'; it was 'an obscene display', and, 'the novelty is one deserving of very severe reprobation, and we trust it will never again be tolerated in any moral English society'.[29] There was a good deal of this kind of thing for many years, reminding us that Evangelicalism was gaining ground among all classes. The waltz was no novelty to the Regent. In 1805 at the Pavilion, when his band struck up a waltz, he waltzed round the table with one of his dinner guests.[30] Prints show great variety of contact between partners. The quadrille became the rage after Lady Jersey introduced it at Almack's from Paris in 1816, and in 1817 there was a spate of caricatures. *Bobbin about to the Fiddle – a Family Rehersal of Quadrille Dancing or, Polishing for a trip to*

Margate [157] mildly satirizes the lure of fashion for the middle classes. (Quadrilles were in fact rehearsed before fashionable balls.) This print illustrates the fact that the 'cit' as a subject of satire has virtually disappeared. His place is taken by the would-be dandy.

After 1820 (in prints) the cigar (or segar) is a dandy attribute, an instrument of selfish impoliteness and a status symbol. Smoking went out of fashion in polite circles early in the eighteenth century, though it lingered in the universities. The cigar brought it back, introduced by officers who had acquired the habit in the Peninsula; Anglo-Indians too had learned to smoke cheroots. It gained ground slowly; smoking was prohibited at White's till 1844; smoking in the streets was the height of bad form. Rawdon Crawley's misadventures will be remembered. Dining in 1826 with the Duke of Sussex, an inveterate smoker of German pipes, Pückler-Muskau noted that 'after the ladies left the table, cigars were brought in, and more than one smoked, which I never before saw in England'. *Corinthian Steamers or Costumes and Customs of 1824* [159], first published in 1821, is a park scene, in which dandies and smoking in the company of ladies are attacked. In 1830, in a drawing-room, a dandy puffs smoke towards the lady sitting beside him, saying, 'the only reasonable objection I can see to smoking is, that one runs a risk of singing one's mustachio's by it'. This is called *But One Objection to Cigar's*, and though realistic is barely credible.

The cigar is also a symbol of democracy on the march. In a workingman's coffee shop, in 1829, an indignant customer with a cigar exclaims 'Vot, not smoke I'll go to the Divan'.* Cruikshank's *Cigar Divan*, 1832, illustrates a new type of London lounge, with dandies at their most effeminate and hypochondriacal. A political squib of 1832, *The Triumph of Reform; a Comic Poem* is illustrated by a print of the decadent children of a solid countrified John Bull; two dandified youths smoke cigars, one daughter burns her mother's pattens, while another screeches at the piano.

Part of the high-life picture is the hierarchy of servants. The old stories of the lady and her footman have disappeared. The classic satire on the pampered menial (a cliché dating from the eighteenth century) is Cruikshank's '*Ignorance is bliss*' [158], 1828; one asks 'What *is* Taxes Thomas?' (Leech adapted it to politics in a *Punch* cartoon (16 November 1846). Peel: 'What *is* to be done with Ireland?' Lord John Russell, 'I'm sure I don't know'.) In R. Cruikshank's *Household Troops* four upper servants in 'worthy and confiding families' record ironically and sanctimoniously (but not brazenly as in *High Life below Stairs*) their dishonesties, perquisites, and extortions from tradespeople.

Low life is interwoven with the March of Intellect, as we shall see later. Its lowest depths are connected – as before – with gin: Rowlandson, Cruikshank and Seymour illustrate its lethal character. *The Dram Shop* [160], 1815, is a plate from Rowlandson's *Dance of Death*; while pretty prostitutes are being served, Death poisons the liquor at its

___
*The O.E.D. gives 1848 as the first use of divan in this sense.

source. In Cruikshank's *Gin Shop* in 1829 the theme of Death is taken further. The customers, dregs of the town, are within a man-trap set by Death, who waits for them in the guise of a watchman. The barmaid is outwardly pretty, but her fashionable dress, smiling mask, and gloved hand cover a skeleton, revealed by a grinning skull on her shoulder. The elaborate gas lighting foreshadows the gin palace. Inscriptions point the moral: 'To the Workhouse, to the Mad House, to the Gaol, The Gibbet'. We shall find the exploitation of the poor by the sale of gin an item in a wholesale indictment of a corrupt society (p. 182).

Notes to Chapter XVII

1. Grantley Berkeley, *My Life and Recollections*, 1866.
2. E. W. Bulwer, *Godolphin*, 1833.
3. Henry Luttrell, *Letters to Julia*, 1823.
4. Quoted, C. L. Graves, *Mr Punch's History of Modern England*, vol. 1, (London: Cassell, 1921), p. 209.
5. *Dr Campbell's Diary of a Visit to England in 1775*, ed. J. L. Clifford (Cambridge: C.U.P., 1947), p. 60.
6. *A Regency Visitor. The English Tour of Prince Pückler-Muskau described in his Letters*, ed. E. M. Butler (London: Collins, 1957).
7. R. H. Gronow, *Reminiscences*, 1889, vol. 1, pp. 226–7.
8. Ibid.
9. Trebeck, accepted by Brummell as a portrait, in T. H. Lister's popular novel *Granby*, 1826.
10. *Glenbervie Journals*, ed. W. Sichel, vol. 11 (London: Constable, 1918), p. 192.
11. Often attributed to Lady Charlotte Bury, Cf. p. 138, but probably not by her.
12. *Glenbervie Journals* (see note 10), 1910, vol. 1, p. 160.
13. *The Diary of Benjamin Robert Haydon*, ed. W. B. Pope, vol. 111 (Cambridge, Mass.: Harvard University Press, 1963), p. 508.
14. *Life and Letters of Lady Sarah Lennox*, ed. Lady Ilchester and Lord Stavordale, 1901, vol. 11, p. 290.
15. *The Exclusives*, vol. 1, pp. 162–3, quoted E. Moers, *The Dandy. Brummell to Beerbohm* (London: Secker & Warburg, 1960).
16. *Private Letters of Princess Lieven, to Prince Metternich*, ed. P. Quennell (London: John Murray, 1948).
17. *Berry Correspondence*, ed. Lewis Melville (London: John Lane, 1914).
18. *A Sunday Ramble*, c. 1774.
19. A. de Tocqueville, *Journeys to England and Ireland*, ed. J. F. Mayer (London: Faber, 1958), p. 55.
20. J. Wade, *The Extraordinary Black Book*, 1831, p. 223.
21. A. de Tocqueville (see note 19), p. 56.
22. *The Journal of Mrs Arbuthnot*, 1820–1832, ed. F. Bamford and the Duke of Wellington, vol. 1 (London: Macmillan, 1950), p. 144.
23. M. W. Rosa, *The Silver Fork School: Novels of Fashion preceding 'Vanity Fair'*, (Oxford: O.U.P., 1936).
24. Street ballad, quoted P. Cunningham and H. B. Wheatley, *London Past and Present*, 1891.
25. W. W. Wroth, *London Pleasure Gardens of the eighteenth century*, 1896, p. 52.
26. *Life and Letters of Lady Sarah Lennox* (see note 14), loc. cit.
27. *Berry Correspondence*, ed. Lewis Melville (London: John Lane, 1914).
28. *Correspondence, George Prince of Wales*, ed. A. Aspinall, vol. 1 (London: Cassell, 1963), p. 48.
29. Quoted, A. E. Franks, *Social Dance* (London: Routledge & Kegan Paul, 1963), p. 129.
30. *Creevey Papers*, ed. Sir Herbert Maxwell, 1904, vol. 1, p. 66.

158 'Ignorance is Bliss', G. Cruikshank

159 *Corinthian Steamers or Costumes and Customs of 1824, W. Heath*

160 *The Drum Shop, Rowlandson. Pl. to 'The Dance of Death'*

161 A View in Whitechapel Road, 1831, after H. T. Alken

The FOLLIES of a DAY or the MARRIAGE of FIGARO.

Published March 13th 1786 by S.W.Fores at the Caricature Warehouse Nº 3 Piccadilly.

Fitz. delin.

Herbert fecit

Price 2 6

XII *The Follies of a Day or the Marriage of Figaro, anon*

CHARLES 2.

Leaving off POWDER, – or – A Frugal Family saving the Guinea.

Pub. March 10th 1795 by H. Humphrey Nº 37 New Bond Street

J.Gy. des. et fec.

XIII *Leaving off Powder, – or A Frugal Family saving the Guinea, Gillray*

GREEDY OLD **NICKFORD** EATING OYSTERS

Leaving the poor Devils from minor Hells in a starving condition —

XIV *Greedy Old Nickford Eating Oysters, W. Heath*

Low life, more than high life, became involved in the great issues of social change. Two related themes pervade the second quarter of the century: 'the March of Intellect' or 'of Mind', and mechanical invention. Both are combined in 'March' prints – the phrase recurs in newspapers, speeches, verse, and caricature captions. In the prints it stands for learning and luxuries for the masses (to the neglect of their work), and in general for a sceptical attitude to 'progress'. Its classic exponent is Dr Folliott in Peacock's *Crotchet Castle* (1831): ''The March of Mind has marched in through the back parlour windows, and out again with my spoons.' To the unfortunate Rector of Camerton in 1828, it was 'the march of intellect with a vengeance' when two new maidservants departed after 'heavy complaints of their beds and accommodation' – 'like a farmhouse more than a gentleman's'. And two years later he confides to his journal (with much more on national decadence): 'Ideas are communicated through the medium of our newspapers with which the purer minds of their grandmothers were wholly unacquainted but according to the *march of intellect*, they were but ill acquainted with, or, in other words, had no knowledge of, the world.'[1] 'Old Bland' (the Dowager Lady B.), wrote Creevey from Devonshire House in 1825, 'is very great upon maidservants. She says, manufactures and *education* have destroyed the race.'[2]

The 'March' phrase was used approvingly for the rationalist view of progress: Thackeray wrote (anonymously) of 'the three cant terms of the Radical spouters', 'the March of Intellect', 'the intelligence of the working classes', and 'the schoolmaster abroad'.* To Hazlitt the phrase meant a wider interest in literature and art. '. . . the world of books overthrows the world of things, and establishes a new balance of power and scale of civilization. . . . Tut! we have read *Old Mortality* and shall it be enquired whether we have done so in a garret or a palace . . .? This is the true March of Intellect, and not the erection of *Mechanics' Institutions*, or printing of *Twopenny Trash* [Cobbett's], though I have nothing to say against them neither.'[3]

The March in fact was an aspect of democratization and industrialization, a shifting of social stratification, a sense that everything was on the move – feared, resented or welcomed. The happenings that sparked off a succession of 'March' satires were, first, the plan for London University,

'Cockney College', attacked in *John Bull* (3 July 1825) as 'the destruction of all Distinctions in Society. . . . The reign of Liberty and Equality' (the undermining of the hierarchy of Church and State that rested on Oxbridge). Second, Brougham's Society for the Diffusion of Useful Knowledge – 'Steam Intellect Society' as Peacock called it. Third, road travel by steam, an absorbing topic in 1825 and after. There were successful trials of Gurney's steam carriage in 1825, followed by journeys to Bath at fifteen miles an hour. A pair of pictorial prophecies appeared in 1828, after Alken, both called *The Progress of Steam*. One is *A View in Regent's Park, 1831*, a high-life scene with steam coaches, open carriages and men riding three-wheeled steam horses. The other, *A View in Whitechapel Road, 1831* [161], is cheerfully unfashionable, with two stage coaches, 'The Infernal Defiance' from Yarmouth and 'The Dreadful Vengeance' from Colchester. Both insides and outsides are enjoying 'Hot cakes Tea & Coffee' cooked *en route*. A tricycle cart sells 'Bread Served Hot'. Horses have vanished from both scenes and all the vehicles and tricycles emit clouds of smoke.

The Horses, 'going to the Dogs' [162], waiting to be made dogs' meat, is Cruikshank's contribution in 1829, where the coach is copied from a print of Gurney's 'New Steam Carriage' in *Bell's Life* (9 December 1827). The promise, or menace, of the invention was killed by penal road tolls in the interests of the horse. We shall find it as the symbol of the machine at its most devastating.

A less obvious but important background of the March was the Stock Exchange boom of 1824–5 and the crash of 1826. Attacks on inventions were common form, but they were barbed by these crises. The South Sea Bubble was unforgotten and company promotion was always suspect. There were solid reasons for the boom. Trade was expanding, agriculture recovering, inventions multiplying; taxation was reduced yet the revenue reached new heights. A speculative mania seized all classes; to the caricaturists all flotations were bubbles. Typical ones were canals, railways, gas, water supply, mines (in Ireland and South America), insurance. There was a popular belief that insurance schemes were paper, mines solid wealth: it proved otherwise. Theodore Hook wrote 'Bubbles of 1825': 'In these days of bubbles when ev'ry thing floats/Docks, bridges, insurances, gas-lights and boats . . .'. The railway was still regarded as a bubble. The Stockport–Darlington line had sparked off a minor mania, whose only solid result was the Manchester–Liverpool line, opened in 1830 with éclat and tragedy.

In *Bubbles for 1825 – or Fortunes made by Steam* each of the

---

*'Half-a-Crown's worth of Cheap Knowledge', *Frazer's Magazine*, February 1838. 'Schoolmaster abroad' (*pace* the *Oxford Dictionary of Quotations*) is from Brougham's speech of 20 January 1828: 'The schoolmaster was abroad [cheers] and he [Brougham] trusted more to his primer than he did to the soldier in full military array.'

162 The Horses, 'going to the Dogs', G.Cruikshank
163 March of Intellect, W.Heath

bubble-blowers on the platform has a bowl of froth at his feet, his 'nest eggs'. They are cannily silent while the deluded public clamour for shares in their bubble companies. The clamourers are of all classes from the fishwife upwards. Some of the projects were sound enough if they had not been bedevilled by speculation – instalments soaring to a premium, further instalments not forthcoming. A banking and currency crisis followed, many bankruptcies, much distress and an exodus of debtors to the Continent.

After the crash, steam was more than ever associated with the wilder aspects of invention. *March of Intellect* [163], 1829, combines the fantasies of invention with low-life luxury. The last is represented by the elegant street-seller's table, where a dustman devours a pineapple, his *vis-à-vis* an ice. In two adjacent sheds a boot is polished by steam and a giant steam razor operates on the Duchess of St Albans. From Greenwich Hill the 'Grand Vacuum Tube Company direct to Bengal' bridges an ocean conveying passengers in a coach, while from Bengal a suspension bridge reaches Cape Town. There are flying machines, an air-ship taking convicts to Australia; there is military transport by balloon, road transport by steam of various sorts, including a steam horse for assorted passengers (public transport), and a cat's-meat trolley. A hybrid neo-Gothic church ridicules modern taste and is fortified against the Anatomy Bill (p. 193) which Cobbett libellously called a Bill for making all parishes 'into a sort of joint stock company of Body Snatchers'. Cloud-borne castles in the air are 'Scheme for paying the National Debt'.

In *The March of Intellect* [164] another dustman sits by the fire in his ramshackle room surrounded by signs of extreme poverty, absorbed in a book, 'Introduction to the Pleasures of Science. Dedicated to the Majesty of the People'. On the mantelshelf is a bust of Shakespeare. There is a pipe in his fantail hat, but he smokes a cigar with an air of

THE MARCH OF INTELLECT

164 The March of Intellect, H. Heath
165 The Grand "March of Intellect", G. Cruikshank

The Grand "March of Intellect"

179

LONDON going out of Town. — or — The March of Bricks & Mortar!

166 London going out of Town – or – The March of Bricks and Mortar, G. Cruikshank

fashion, and has a monocle. The jest in such prints was to connect the remarkable movements for self-education and the emergence of a new working-class élite with low life and poverty, which, by tradition, were subjects of comedy. The dustman, still illiterate in the mid century,* was far removed from this élite. A 'March of Mind' street scene of about 1828 illuminates this. In implied contrast with the slatternly ballad-singer, street musicians perform operatic music; a harpist screeches the famous contralto aria '*di tanti palpiti*' from Rossini's *Tancredi*. A bricklayer's labourer (Irish) sits on his hod, deep in a big book from the 'St Giles's Reading Society' (an incredible institution, St Giles's being what it was). A coachman, absorbed in 'An account of the Road, Literary, Historical … &c', treads heavily on a screaming child. Behind is a shop, 'Breakfast & Reading Room', placarded with a long list of 'Works Within', which ends 'Reviews, Edinburgh, Quarterly, Monthly. All the Periodicals. All the Classics &c.&c.&c'.

*Among twenty men in a dust yard Mayhew found five only who could read, and only two who could write – imperfectly – 'these two are looked up to by their companions as prodigies of learning', *London Labour and the London Poor*, 1851, Vol. II, p. 178. See also above, p. 73.

This is realism, exaggerated. From about 1810 (after a reduction in the tax on coffee) coffee shops for working men multiplied, supplying newspapers to their customers (like the old coffee houses), and sometimes periodicals. They were both a cause and result of greater sobriety, and, according to Francis Place 'the cause of great improvement to the working people'. A journeyman tailor describes his satisfaction (*c.* 1815) at finding a warm and comfortable room, coffee and a newspaper for breakfast, and still more to find that by paying an extra 6d. a month he could read (in the evening) the monthly reviews and magazines, not apparently the quarterlies.[4]

Another aspect of the March was learning for children,* ridiculed by Cruikshank in 1828; in *The Grand 'March of Intellect'* [165] big-headed, bespectacled boys, with

*'March of Mind' derives from a poem with that title by Miss Mitford, written for an anniversary meeting in June 1814 of the British and Foreign School Society, previously known as the Lancastrian Society, schools founded by Joseph Lancaster. They were suspect to Churchmen and Tories and in rivalry with Dr Bell's 'Madras' system, or 'National Society for Educating the Poor in the Principles of the Church'. The conflict started a rivalry which long bedevilled English elementary education.

167 The Flight of Intellect, anon.

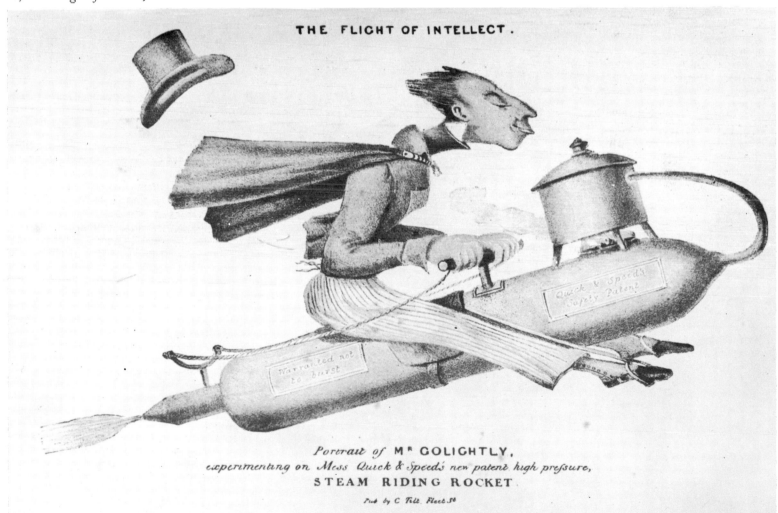

THE FLIGHT OF INTELLECT.

Portrait of Mr GOLIGHTLY,
experimenting on Mess Quick & Speed's new patent high pressure,
STEAM RIDING ROCKET.
Pub by C Tilt, Fleet St

This is one of the innumerable skits which appeared at the time of the introduction of Railways, and is specially directed against Stephenson's first locomotive, "The Rocket."

trumpets, drum and banners, goose-step after their leader. And, on the same sheet, in *The Age of Intellect*, a horribly precocious child teaches his grandmother to suck eggs – 'to extract the matter contained in this shell by suction'.

The 'March' metaphor was worked hard. Cruikshank's *London going out of Town – or – The March of Bricks and Mortar* [166], 1829, is a rendering of the ruthless devastations of the jerry-builder. New houses, still unfinished, are fissured by cracks. The scene is Hampstead (still rural); trees and hay-stacks are bombarded by bricks; smoke from older build-ings and from lime-kilns deepens the gloom. Industrial smoke had already in 1822 provoked an Act – needless to say totally ineffective – to make factories consume their own smoke. A Glasgow project to enforce it is illustrated with scepticism in Heath's *Glasgow Looking Glass* in 1825: *Consumption of Smoke*, 'Present' and 'future'. In one a factory is smothered in smoke, a single tree has lost its leaves. In the other the same buildings, smokeless, are surrounded by flourishing trees and admiring pedestrians.

Steam in graphic satire is fantastic, portentous, calami-tous (explosions of steamers), associated with travel by road and by air; as yet the railway was remote from the London print shop. But there is *The Flight of Intellect* [167], *c.* 1830, a 'Portrait of Mr Golightly experimenting on Mess Quick & Speed's new patent high pressure Steam Riding Rocket', that is, Stephenson's Rocket* engine which won a prize in 1829, followed by its triumph at the opening of the Liverpool–Manchester line. Today it seems prophetic, an odd anticipation of the jet engine.

Steam as a symbol of machine industry in its blackest aspects is combined with a wholesale attack on tax-eaters

who range from king, bishop, judge and general, through dandies and land-owners, to parish beadles. This is Seymour's *Heaven & Earth* [detail, 168], 1830, a year of unemployment and distress, gradually lessening. The cloud-borne tax-eaters in 'Heaven' are in an arc above their victims. The clouds rise from the coin-laden smoke of factories. Starving people on 'Earth' beg for parish relief; a beadle retorts, 'My good Voman, vot should you have children for – dont you know there's no more hoperatives never vanted'. Others appeal in vain to the New Police. A dense crowd besieges the factories with a placard 'We want Employment', but steam has made them redundant. Out of six factories three are 'Steamall Vacuum Gas Piston & Co'. The others are (prophetically) 'Silk wove by Steam', 'Gloves made by Steam', 'Bread Made By Machinery'. Beside the factories is a manufacturer's mansion, 'Engine Hall'. His carriages are two steam coaches, one standing at his stables, the other (cut off by the right margin), filled with people, ploughs through the unemployed. Another crowd clamours frantically towards a big retort or still inscribed 'Lethe Cheap Gin', with Death peering from behind it. *Their* prayers are heard and lucrative smoke from the still blends with the clouds above. This is remote from earlier scenes of poverty – frozen-out gardeners, or simply scenes of low life. It reflects the mood of the first six months of 1830 and foreshadows the bitterness of Reform Bill satires.

---

*The rocket depicted is evidently one of the Congreve rockets as used in the rocket battery which was the British contribution to the battle of Leipzig, the Battle of the Nations, in 1813.

Notes to Chapter XVIII

1. *Journal of a Somerset Rector, John Skinner, 1772–1839*, ed. H.Coombs and A.N.Bax (London: John Murray, 1930).
2. *Creevey's Life and Times*, ed. J.Gore (London: John Murray, 1934), p. 220.
3. *Conversations of James Northcote Esq., R.A.* (sixteenth conversation), 1830.
4. T.Carter, *Memoirs of a Working Man*, 1845, pp. 186–7.

168 *Heaven & Earth* (detail), R. Seymour

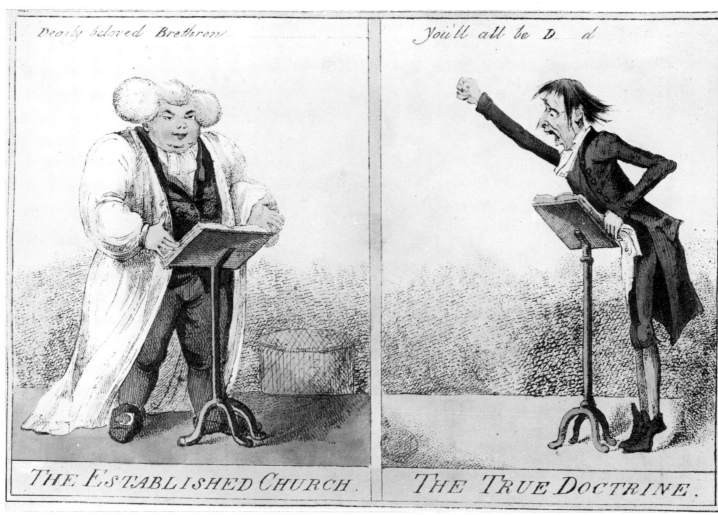

169 *The Established Church. The True Doctrine,* (?) *G. Cruikshank*

170 *Plucking a Candidate for Holy Orders,* (?) *G. Cruikshank*

19 - The Professions

The Church

The professions, even medicine, were about to come under attack as part of a corrupt social system, and the Church, even more than the Law, became public enemy number one. Measures of reform did nothing to appease opinion, but drew attention to abuses. The flowing tide of unpopularity had three main causes, and stages. First, Peterloo, the 'Manchester Massacre', in 1819 was precipitated by the folly (at best) or the savagery (at worst) of two clerical magistrates.[1] Then came the Queen's affair in 1820–21, when many of the beneficed, and especially of the higher clergy, were vocally anti-Queenite. After an interval of comparative calm, animus against the Church reached a peak when all the bishops but two voted against the Reform Bill which the Lords defeated in October 1831. 'The fate of the Church is sealed', wrote J. S. Mill (20 October). And Thomas Arnold wrote in the following June: 'The Church, as it now stands, no human powers can save.'

Before 1819 the attitude to the Church was much as before. The old theme of *The Master Parson and his Journeyman*, again by Dighton, reappeared in 1812. The obese bishop has a ticket for a 'Turtle Dinner' tucked into his waistcoat: the lean melancholy cleric standing beside him holds a Bible. Another ancient theme in a new form is the contrast between the placid complacent sermons of orthodoxy and the death and damnation oratory of Dissent, illustrated in *The Established Church. The True Doctrine* [169], 1818. Rowlandson's parsons (Dr Syntax excepted) are usually old-fashioned Dr Carbuncles – he did a number of Oxford drawings, where his College Fellows are elderly grotesques. *Plucking a Candidate for Holy Orders* [170], also 1818, lithographed by Cruikshank, is more realistic. There is an Oxford Almanack on the wall; the stout parson, so snugly fitted into his chair, looks with grimly appraising contempt at the dandyfied, dishevelled, dismayed Oxonian.

Anti-clericalism and active church-building are the context of *Coming out of Church* [171], c. 1828. The fat John Bull is outraged at applications for 'voluntary' contributions. The two demanding bishops who bar his way are Manners-Sutton of Canterbury, and Howley of London who was shortly to succeed his companion. Pictorial attacks on the Church multiplied in 1831, and a Sunday paper, *The Ballot*, published by Wakley from the *Lancet* office, produced a series of wood engravings called *Sketches of the Church* which included and transcended the old attacks on the pluralist and the tithe-grabber. 'The Vicar and Moses' (p. 86) is the caption for a drunken cleric who staggers past the altar, spilling a chalice, and snapping his fingers at the table of the Ten Commandments, and so at both God and Moses.

Finally, in *The March of Roguery ! ! ! ! ! !* [172] the ancient theme of the Four (or Five, or more) Alla, found on inn signs, is adapted to a wholesale assault on the social system. King and bishop go first as 'State and Church'; one says 'I rule', the other 'I pray'. 'Farmer' scowls at the bishop, saying 'I work for both'. 'Merchant' says 'I cheat you three'; 'Lawyer', 'I fleece you four'; 'Doctor', 'I poison you five'; 'Devil', 'I'll have all six'. This old gibe at the learned professions with added venom is by C. J. Grant, afterwards the illustrator of the unstamped penny papers which were expressions of working class and Chartist opinion – crude and forcible woodcuts, republican and anti-clerical.

171 *Coming out of Church, W. Heath*
172 *The March of Roguery!!!!!, C. J. Grant*

Medicine

At last the old-style physician has disappeared and doctors and their ways are approached in a different spirit. The medical student makes an appearance; medical education – its futilities and anomalies – and medical jobbery were topics of the day. The demand for subjects for dissection was unsatisfied and the grisly outcome (fully illustrated) was the Burke and Hare murders in Edinburgh in 1829. Body snatching, schools of anatomy and the senile surgeon are targets in *The Anatomist* [173] after Rowlandson, 1811. He is Professor Sawbone* who is to deliver 'A Course of Anatomical Lectures accompanied with Dissections ... tomorrow evening'. It illustrates the surprising fact that surgeons and students were allowed to take subjects for dissection to their rooms. Resurrectionists and derisory medical teaching in Glasgow were topics of Heath's *Glasgow Looking Glass* (the first caricature magazine) in 1825.

Socially speaking, the most remarkable career of any doctor of the period – of any period† – was that of Sir William Knighton (1776–1836), physician, friend, and confidant of George IV. His medical career too was not unremarkable. Beginning as an Assistant Surgeon to the Royal Naval Hospital, Plymouth, he studied at Guy's, collected a number of degrees (from the Archbishop of Canterbury, from Aberdeen, from St Andrews, and later from Göttingen); bought a house in Hanover Square, where he practised as an *accoucheur* and made £10,000 a year in this lucrative but despised branch of the profession. When Knighton was *accoucheur* to a mistress of Lord Wellesley the latter incurred a heavy debt which he was unable to pay. In true eighteenth-century fashion he met this by introducing Knighton in 1810 to the Prince of Wales, who made him his physician and found him 'the best-mannered medical man I have ever met'. In 1812 he was made a baronet. He gradually became indispensable to George IV, who wrote to him as 'the dearest and best of friends' and was 'most affectionately yours'. 'I am now beginning to be made his confidential friend,' Knighton wrote in 1819, 'in all those secret occasions which a life of pleasure and sensuality had exposed him to.' In 1822 he was gazetted Keeper of the Privy Purse and was acting as the King's private secretary, an office not officially recognized. He then gave up his practice, but seems to have occasionally visited V.I.P.s or their wives. He had soon turned the heavy debt on the Privy Purse into a balance. His ascendancy over the King became complete; he was indispensable to him, and also, at times, to Ministers who found their master most trying to deal with. In 1824 Madame de Lieven told Metternich he was 'the real Prime Minister'. Professor Aspinall comments 'it would be truer to call him the real sovereign'.[2]

*The earliest recorded use of Sawbones is by Sam Weller, 'I thought everybody know'd as a sawbones was a surgeon', E. Partridge, *Dictionary of Slang* (1837: *Pickwick*).

†In England. Struenzee (1731–72), a German doctor, as favourite of the King and lover of the Queen, made himself dictator of Denmark, was overthrown by a conspiracy and executed.

All this for a 'man-midwife' was an outrage to contemporaries. In 1823 he applied to be made a Privy Counsellor and the King wrote to Liverpool: 'you are already acquainted with my feelings relative to the admission of my invaluable friend Sir William Knighton to the Privy Council. The thing is so proper and so just that I wish to have no conversation on the subject.' But Liverpool refused. Mrs Arbuthnot comments: 'in the first place he does not think the accoucheur of all the ladies in London exactly fit to be in the Privy Council'. And a few days later she calls him 'a fellow who, fifteen years ago, carried pills and phials round the town of Plymouth'.[3] Here are some Knighton appellations: 'the apothecary',[4] 'the midwife', 'th'accursed midwife', 'the vagabond Knighton'.[5] Wellington (who called him the *Accoucheur*, or the Barber, or the Midwife, and once at least 'the gentleman midwife'), appreciated Knighton, and thought the Privy Council and a peerage within his deserts, *but*: 'The mistake in all this is his Belief that his being either Privy Counsellor or Peer will make him anything in Society in this Country. With a view to place in Society, I would prefer the simple *Barber* with his Talents & conduct, to being a Baronet or Grand Cross of the Guelph [which he was], or Privy Counsellor or Peer.'[6]

On George IV's death Knighton prevented Lady Conyngham from appropriating jewels. He is doing so in this print, *Slano* [174] by Heath, where the scene (at the Conynghams' place in Ireland) is the falling out of thieves – a baseless imputation. He and Wellington acted as the King's executors.

Medically speaking, the outstanding personality is Thomas Wakley, a Taunton apothecary's apprentice who became a London surgeon, and is as characteristic of one aspect of the period as Knighton is of another. He was Radical, aggressive, public-spirited. In 1823 he founded and edited the *Lancet*, using it to report lectures and to make war on the closed shop of the hospital doctors who charged high fees for instruction. Sir Astley Cooper, the leading surgeon and a wealthy philanthropist, had contrived the separation of the medical schools of Guy's and St Thomas's to provide posts for a nephew (Bransby Cooper) and a niece's husband. Wakley campaigned against this nepotism: a famous encounter began with a damning account in the *Lancet* of a bungled operation for lithotomy by Bransby Cooper, with an assertion that he owed his post solely to his uncle. Young Cooper brought a libel action for £1,000 damages and got £100, a sum that supported the main charge and was eagerly paid by subscription. The war between the *Lancet* and the Cooper was a print-shop theme, as in *Barney the Cooper or the Head of the Guy's performing his Last Operation* [XV], 1828. Bloodstained students from Guy's advance to Cooper's support – after the trial his pupils had voted him a testimonial in glowing terms.

As in John Hunter's day, the most reputable lecturers and anatomists (notably Astley Cooper) had dealings with the resurrectionists. The Burke and Hare murders threw a lurid light on the business. Knox, a brilliant and popular

A COURSE of ANATOMICAL LECTURES accompanied with Dissections will be delivered Tomorrow Evening by Professor Paulson

Price One Shilling

Pub.d March 12 1811 by Tho.s Tegg N.o 111 Cheapside.

Rowlandson Del.

THE ANATOMIST.

173 The Anatomist, after Rowlandson

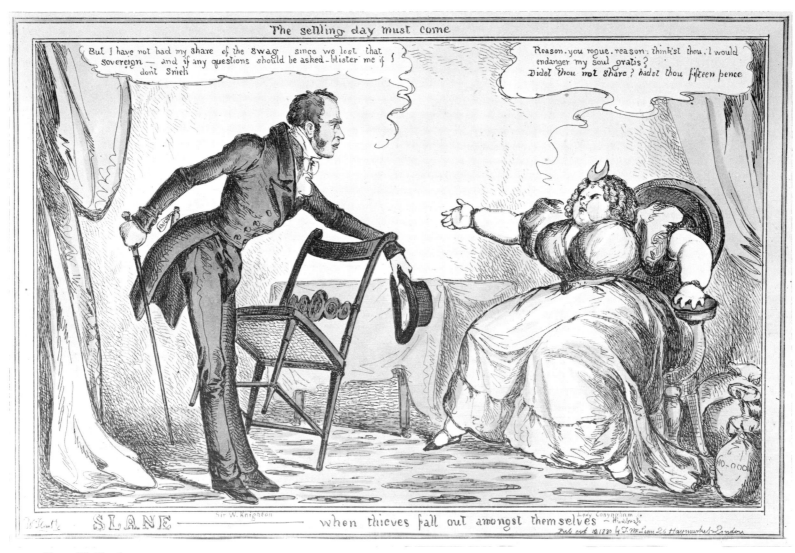

174 Slane, W. Heath

175 *The Central Board of Health, W. H. Merle/G. Cruikshank*

176 *Wretch's Illustrations of Shakespeare;*
Act IV, Scene 2ᵈ in King Richard III –
Time 1828, D. McNee

177 *Salus Populi Suprema Lex, G. Cruikshank*

178 More Don-Key's! It is well known that Asses are particularly fond of having their Back's Rubbed, H. Heath

XV Barney the Cooper or the Head of the Guy's performing his Last Operation, W. Heath

XVI Inconveniences of a Crowded Drawing Room, G. Cruikshank

lecturer, was pilloried in two sets of Edinburgh lithographs, *Noxiana* and *Wretch's Illustrations of Shakespeare*, where he is attacked as an instigator of murder. In *Act IV, Scene 2ᵈ in King Richard III – Time 1828* [176] Knox addresses the page – Hare – 'Knowest thou not any whom corrupting gold . . . ?' and Burke takes the part of Tyrrel, murderer of the Princes in the Tower. The result was an Anatomy Regulation Bill, dropped because of misrepresentation and unpopularity (p. 179), but after two London resurrectionists had been convicted of murder, the Anatomy Act (1832) still the basis of the law, ended the dreadful traffic – an item in the transition to a new age.

The first cholera epidemic in England (1831–2) coincided with the Reform Bill excitement. There was controversy among doctors, the Press and the public as to its existence, nature and treatment. As Wellington remarked 'there was great want of clearness in the distinction made by physicians between the words contagious, infectious, and epidemic'.[7] Local Boards of Health were appointed with a central one in London which met at the Privy Council Office and issued statistics. At this moment any Government appointment would have been attacked as jobbery. Wakley, in the *Lancet*, denounced *The Times* for its 'slanderous attacks' on the Board of Health, its 'utter ignorance of the history of epidemic and contagious diseases'. *The Times* had said that 'Choleraphobia was profitable to the medical profession'. In *The Central Board of Health* [175], 1832, by Cruikshank after an amateur, the four distinguished members of the Board are grossly caricatured and venomously attacked. They drink a toast 'May we preserve our health by bleeding the country'. A picture of smoke emerging from a bottle is the old symbol for hoax and humbug deriving from the 'Bottle Conjurer' of 1749. *The Times* (15 February 1832): 'The public will look in vain for a cessation of the official reports, while the Government employs agents to search for cases at high salaries.' This popular delusion and manifest libel is accepted in *A London Board of Health Hunting after Cases like Cholera*; six doctors search after smells in a filthy cellar where cat's meat is sold. (The filth is supposedly harmless.)

More justified, but wholly unregarded, was a verse broadside of 1832 illustrated by Cruikshank, *Salus Populi Suprema Lex* [177], on 'John Edwards Esq.', 'the Water King of Southwark', proprietor of the Southwark Water Works, which took its water from the Thames where one hundred and thirty sewers discharged themselves. He sits, as an ancient Welsh chieftain, enthroned above the filthy river; dwellers in Southwark demand 'pure water', 'We shall have Cholera'. Spectators on the south bank are indifferent and contemptuous – 'Oh never mind, any nastiness goes down here in the Borough'. The medical profession had not yet connected cholera with contaminated water.

Unnoticed, but important, is a landmark in medical education and the official progress of the apothecary: the Act in 1815 empowering the Apothecaries Society to examine and license all apothecaries and to prosecute unlicensed practitioners.

Quacks of course continued to practise and prosper. As before, the outstanding one seems oddly typical of his period. This was John St John Long, son of an Irish basketmaker who set up in London in 1827, after failing to make good as an artist, treating consumption by friction with corrosive liniment which was also inhaled. By 1829 he had established a lucrative and fashionable practice in Harley Street – a good address but not then a medical preserve. The *Lancet* denounced him in 1830 as the king of humbugs. Soon after, two women died from his treatment. In one case he was found guilty of manslaughter by a coroner's inquest, and was discharged on paying a fine, whereupon he drove from court in Lord Sligo's curricle, congratulated by 'noble' friends, and hooted by the populace. On the second occasion, after a coroner's manslaughter verdict he was acquitted at the Old Bailey. The *Law Times* thought a verdict of murder would have been justified. This is the subject of *More Don-Key's!** It is well known that Asses are particularly fond of having their Back's Rubbed* [178], 1830. Four asses, Long's patients, undergo his treatment of friction and inhaling. In the graveyard are the tombs of his victims. In the background, a beadle pursues Long with a coroner's warrant.†

---

*The original Don-Key (subject of very many caricatures) was John Key, the Lord Mayor elect, whose warning of plots of rebellion and assassination induced Wellington to cancel the 1830 Lord Mayor's Day dinner at the last moment.

†In 1831 he had the effrontery to publish *A Criticial Exposure of the Ignorance and Malpractice of Certain Medical Practitioners in their Theory and Treatment of Disease*. He died in 1834.

Nº 1. BLESSINGS of BRITTAIN — or A Flight of Lawyers — "A Darksome cloud of Locusts swarming down." Milton

179 Blessings of Brittain – or A Flight of Lawyers, C. Williams

180 Term Time, G. Cruikshank

Term Time

The Law

In this most traditional of themes the demerits of the lawyer are magnified in a completely traditional way, well suited to post-war attitudes. In *Blessings of Brittain – or A Flight of Lawyers* [179], 1817, a swarm led by the Chancellor (Eldon) and the other judges, followed by the barristers and their clerks, is represented as 'A Darksome cloud of Locusts swarming down'. It is the 'First Day of Term' (p. 98) and they are about to make their ceremonial entrance into Westminster Hall. There is a companion plate, a second *Blessings of Brittain* and a secondary evil – a descending swarm of tax-collectors and rate-collectors to rob John Bull. About 1820 the lawyer again rides his 'last circuit' to Hell tied back to back with Death on a skeleton horse, chased by demons and a demoniacal rider on the Pale Horse of *Revelation*.

In 1828 Brougham's long and famous speech on Law Reform, and the accumulated delays that had multiplied in Chancery under Eldon, made abuses in his court a burning question. *A Chancery Suit!!!* repeats the theme of 1749 (p. 38) with more sophistication and especial stress on the grievance of sinecures. A giant file (a spike for papers) bisects the design; a handsome country house is hooked at the top, at the base is the same house in ruins. The plaintiff is lured by an attorney with prospects of getting the property; he loses, and as before: 'How blest was I before I went to law/I fear'd no writ; I felt no bailiff's claw.' The defendant, still more ragged and dejected, soliloquizes: 'For tho' thou'st got the day, thou'st lost thy Clothes.' Two fat barristers appropriate spoils. A lengthy procession of officials, headed by the Chancellor, and with many holders of obsolete medieval office, winds round the design, its tail pointing to the Fleet Prison. Pückler-Muskau describes with gusto 'a very diverting caricature' with the same title; 'At first a young man handsomely dressed, and in high blooming health, fills the hat of a starved skeleton of a lawyer with guineas by way of retaining fees. A long procession of men and things follow, and at last we see the young man as a broken-down beggar, seeking alms of the lawyer, now grown as fat as a tun, which the latter scornfully rejects.'[8]

The ancient oyster reappears in Cruikshank's *Term Time* [180], one of a sheet of illustrations of 'Hard Times' in 1827. A lawyer stands outside Westminster Hall with a brief bag stuffed with papers in 'Noodle v Doodle', proffering a shell to each litigant: 'Gentlemen – It was a very fine oyster! – the Court awards you a shell each.' Prisoners crowd to a barred window with the age-old words – 'Pray remember the Poor Debtors'. Barristers hurry to the courts in Westminster Hall. Jarndyce v Jarndyce had many ancestors. Oysters – a whole barrel-full of them for guzzling barristers – figure in a *Punch* cartoon on the sensational and ruinous enquiry (*de lunatico inquirendo*) into the sanity of 'Mad Windham' in 1863.[9] Not only lawyers profited. The land for the Law Courts in the Strand, opened in 1880, was bought and cleared at enormous cost out of funds in Chancery from the estates of intestate litigants.

Notes to Chapter XIX

1. See G.F.A.Best, *Pillars of the Church* (Cambridge: C.U.P., 1964), pp. 246ff.
2. A.Aspinall, 'Sir William Knighton and George IV', *English Historical Review*, January 1940, on which this account is chiefly based.
3. *The Journal of Mrs Arbuthnot*, 1820–1832, ed. F.Bamford and the Duke of Wellington, vol. I (London: Macmillan, 1950), pp. 245, 246.
4. *The Creevey Papers*, ed. Sir Herbert Maxwell, 1904, vol. II, p. 104.
5. *George Canning and his Friends*, ed. J.Bagot, 1909, vol. II, p. 392.
6. *Wellington and his Friends, Letters . . .*, ed. seventh Duke of Wellington, (London: Macmillan, 1965), pp. 50f.
7. P.H.Stanhope, *Conversations with Wellington* (Oxford: O.U.P., 1938), (11 November 1831).
8. *A Regency Visitor. The English Tour of Prince Pückler-Muskau described in his letters*, ed. E.M.Butler (London: Collins, 1957), p. 297.
9. R.W.Ketton-Cremer, *Felbrigg*, (London: Hart-Davis, 1962), p. 265.

181 *A Milling Match Between Decks, W. Elmes*

In the phase of retrenchment and reform (which began before the words became the motto of the Whig Ministry that followed George IV's death) army officers were under attack as dandies and fops – expensive superfluities. Grotesque uniforms figure in Hyde Park 'Monstrosities', plates deriding the fashions of the day. (Exotic uniforms were a foible of George IV but uniform was not worn in England by officers not on duty.) Military dandies *par excellence* were the officers of the Tenth Hussars, the Regent's regiment till he became King. In 1824 they incurred a barrage of caricatures and adverse Press comment and were even the subject of a play at Covent Garden – *Pride shall have a Fall* – after complaints by a Cornet Battier that he had been insulted in the mess. Attacks subsided only when Battier – who seems to have been less than

sane – was utterly discredited over a duel, and 'even *The Times*' gave him up. One of the much-illustrated items in the indictment was arrogant bad manners in a Dublin ball-room, and 'Tenth dont dance' is still a catch-phrase. In *A Tenth Rejected – or – The Dandyfied Coxcomb in a Bandbox* [182], a parson on a quest for tithes is met by the farmer's wife who proffers 'a *Tenth*', a miniature hussar; the parson rejects it: 'I never tithe *Monkeys*.'

On the other hand, there was the bitter lot of the officer on half-pay, married, and without a private income: little if at all better than in Fielding's day. *Military Progress (Slow Movement) or the Reward of Merit*, 1822, 'by a Half Pay Officer' (W. Heath)* is a sequence of eight scenes. A young

---

*Heath was reputed 'ex-captain of dragoons', but he is not in the *Army List*.

182 A Tenth Rejected – or – The Dandyfied Coxcomb in a Bandbox, C. Williams

183 *Captain Dick Demi-Solde on a Wild Goose Flight to the Swan River*, (?) John Phillips

A MID — on   HALF PAY.

TOWER   HILL.

Eng.d & Pub.d June 1 1825 by C.Hunt, 18 Tavistock St.t Covent Garden.

184 *A Mid – on Half Pay. Tower Hill, anon.*

man, whose commission has been bought by subscriptions from his friends, marries 'sans six sous', goes on active service, distinguishes himself, is promoted lieutenant and ordered home on half-pay. The last two scenes show his struggles for a year or two and then the debtor's prison – Booth's lot (in *Amelia*) without the happy ending.

For the Navy, there are first some views of the grosser aspects of sea life, with the frustrations of the war with America. For example, *A Milling Match Between Decks* [181], 1812. 'With sailors carousing, rum flowing, and women on board, the scene below decks was an obscene compound of Gin Lane and the stews.'[1] Writing not of all sailors but of 'the outcasts of prisons' Captain Chamier says 'it was absolutely necessary to provide them on board with the only pleasures they sought on shore. Hence the introduction of women, dancing, and liberty-liquor.'[2] With at least equal truth there is a tragically realistic scene, *A Mid – on Half Pay. Tower Hill* [184], 1825 – a very different shoe-black from Hogarth's (p. 47). Naval retrenchment had been the order of the day, and Joseph Hume, its most vocal advocate, had complained that too many midshipmen were promoted. The one depicted, an oldster, unpromoted, was in fact the victim of a long-standing grievance, and the special irony of the print is that midshipmen had *no* half-pay. The career of a midshipman and the lottery of promotion are the subjects of three sets of aquatints, two (with text by John Mitford) in 1818 and 1819, and one by Marryat (etched by Cruikshank) in 1820. All are more or less autobiographical. In ... *Finding things not exactly what he expected* Master Blockhead (Marryat) is introduced to the midshipman's 'birth' or mess on the lowest (orlop) deck, a scene of 'wild disorder', darkness and discomfort. The youngsters lark inside the berth, the oldsters sit outside, as does one small boy blacking shoes from a jar of 'Day & Martin'. Marryat's autobiographical *Frank Mildmay* describes just such an introduction to the mess.

The plight of half-pay officers – both services – is reflected in a colonizing project which became a print-shop topic in 1829–30, the Swan River settlement in Western Australia. There were great expectations, large land grants, a rush of emigrants, and calamitous results for the pioneers. Among the applicants for grants were many half-pay officers and their fate is prophesied in *Captain Dick Demi-Solde on a Wild Goose Flight to the Swan River* [183], 1829. In a glowing account of the possibilities of the colony in the *Quarterly Review*, April 1828, there was a warning to isolated settlers. 'Those principally in our eyes are half-pay officers of the army and navy, whose applications ... we understand to be very numerous.' By 1850 to 'cut one's lucky' and 'go off to the Swan Stream', had become a slang catchphrase for the down and out who has to decamp.

In this year (1829) there seemed to be other hopes for poor Captain Demi-Solde, jobs as Inspectors and Superintendants in Peel's New Police. But all applications from commissioned officers were turned down. Peel explained why to Croker (who had urged that police pay was inadequate) in a way that spotlights differences between then and now (though with some inverted relevance to modern problems). 'I have refused to employ gentlemen – commissioned officers for instance . . . because I am sure they would be above their work. They would refuse to associate with other persons holding the same offices who were not of equal rank, and they would therefore degrade the latter in the eyes of the men. . . . A sergeant of the Guards at £200 a year is a better man for my purpose than a captain of high reputation if he should serve for nothing. . . .'[3]

The New Police were a landmark for caricature and comic art as for social life. The old night watchmen had been depicted so often as senile and venal incompetents, sleeping in their boxes, or the victims of bucks and bloods and swells. Their lanterns and staves were captured as trophies, for instance by Tom Rakewell (p. 43) (the tradition seems to have been transferred to the policeman's helmet). Contrariwise, watchmen (it is said) would produce broken lanterns to the constable of the night as evidence against the innocent. The first attacks on Peel's 'Blue Regiment' or 'unboiled lobsters' (a soldier being a lobster) in the Press and in caricatures were political. In one of these Wellington and Peel are Tom and Jerry in *A Slap at the Charleys or a Tom and Jerry Lark*; the latter delivers a boxer's knock-out blow at a poor old watchman, others have been felled, and some flee; a watch-box topples. But it was for social satire that the policeman was to be an enduring topic. An early, perhaps the first, comic policeman appears in Heath's *Drunkards on Duty* [detail, 185], 1830. The dishevelled Peeler addresses a pump; and his words are prophetically in character: 'Come move on there – its time you was in bed young woman, any body with half an eye could see you were in liquor.' Nothing here of the 'Police Establishment à la Bourbon', which, according to Cobbett, had 'laid the foundation of an Austrian slavery'.[4] (His companion is an officer in disordered uniform addressing a braying ass which he takes for a sentinel drunk on duty.) In 1833, in a savage little pamphlet written and illustrated by himself, *Cruikshank against the New Police*, Robert Cruikshank drew the first of many policemen feasting with the cook in the kitchen.

Notes to Chapter XX

1. C. Lloyd, *Captain Marryat and the Old Navy* (London: Longmans, 1939), p. 26.
2. *Tom Bowling, A Tale of the Sea*, 1841.
3. *The Croker Papers 1884*, vol. II, pp. 19–20 (10 October 1829).
4. W. Cobbett, *History of the Regency and Reign of George IV*, 1834, vol. II, par. 508.

185 *Drunkards on Duty* (detail), W. Heath

186 *The Brewer's Entire Saloon, W.H.Brooke*

The theatre continued to attract a flow of prints on the neglect of the drama and addiction to spectacle and performing animals, on the rivalries of the Lane and the Garden, and of the leading players. These ancient topics never failed, they were conditioned by the monopoly of the two Patent Theatres, an archaic survival that persisted till 1844. Meantime the major theatres were at best precariously solvent, the minors flourished on light entertainment. Only outstanding events can be touched on here. First, the re-opening of Drury Lane, burnt down in February 1809, five months after the destruction of Covent Garden. Rebuilding was slow, and the reactions that followed were very different from the O.P. frenzy. Large subscriptions were raised and a committee for rebuilding appointed, nominated by Sheridan and his friends, but determined that the Manager who had brought financial disaster should have no further concern with the theatre. The Chairman was Whitbread. Sheridan was paid £20,000 for his patent; his partners, including his son Tom, got another £20,000. 'The majority of the creditors are to accept 5s. in the pound, while Mr Sheridan, the bankrupt Proprietor, who has occasioned all this loss, is to retire with £40,000 in his pocket', complained the *Examiner* (20 October 1811).

The rebuilding committee was merged in a Committee of Taste, with Byron and Lord Holland as leading members, for running the theatre, which they did with much ineptness. The extremely plain exterior was derided as 'Whitbread's Brewery'. The Committee advertised for an 'Address' to be spoken on the opening night, 12 October 1812. Over one hundred were sent in, one from Whitbread. All were rejected, and Lord Holland asked Byron to produce one. This was spoken by Elliston, rousing a storm of protest from the unsuccessful, led by Dr Busby (Mus.D.) who had been accustomed to provide Elliston with prologues and epilogues. On 15 October, amid great confusion, he addressed the House from a box, was removed by Bow Street officers, recaptured by the audience, and at last got leave for his son to read his Address from the stage, saying, 'they would hear such a monologue as they had seldom heard'. Young Busby was inaudible, but the Doctor published his ludicrously bad verses in next day's *Morning Chronicle*, where a week later they were parodied (anonymously) by Byron. In the meantime Horace and James Smith had published (12 October) their famous *Rejected Addresses*, brilliant parodies of the authors of the day, including 'Architectural Atoms Translated by Dr B.', prophetically headed 'To be recited by the Translator's son'. All this and more is recorded and ridiculed in elaborate prints; the simplest is Cruikshank's heading to a verse broadside in which a reincarnation of Dr Busby of Westminster School flogs young B. for his bad verses.

Despite the Covent Garden precedent, the private boxes were accepted without demur. The feature of the new theatre was the 'grand salon' eighty-six feet long with apsidal ends faithfully depicted in *The Brewer's Entire Saloon* [186] with the addition of divans for prostitutes who register their gratitude to Whitbread, while Sheridan, as Harlequin, leans disconsolately against a statue of Apollo. Long-established custom being what it was, the place would inevitably be a rendezvous for courtesans. That 'the religious and decorous English' should tolerate such things astonished Pückler-Muskau in 1826; 'Between the acts they fill the large and handsome "foyers" and exhibit their boundless effrontery in the most revolting manner.' Recording in 1818 the outstanding changes witnessed in a long life, Lady Susan O'Brien ends the list, '*J'ai vu* 100,000 Bibles given to the people, & *Salons* built at our theatres for the reception and entertainment of prostitutes and their attendant swains. This one may call neutralizing.'[1] The Bibles were distributed by the British and Foreign Bible Society, founded by Evangelicals in 1804. The contrast reflects conflicting aspects of Regency life, but the innovation was more in the religion and decorum than in the 'boundless effrontery' (p. 107). It is noteworthy that there was an impression in England of 'the broad, naked and *shameless profligacy of foreign manners*'.[2] Haydon, in Paris in 1814, though familiar with London streets and theatres, could write of the *Palais Royal*: 'The blaze of the lamps, the unrestrained obscenity of the language, the indecency, the bawdy bloody indecency of the People, bewilder & distract you. Such is the power & effect of this diabolical place, that the neighbourhood, like the country around the poison tree of Java, is mad by its vice and infected by its principles.'[3]

Drury Lane, faced by bankruptcy, was saved, but not by the Committee. Their Manager, Arnold, discovered Kean acting in Dorchester and engaged him. His triumph (first as Shylock, 26 January 1814) was immediate. On his nights only the theatre was filled. When his Richard III was announced Covent Garden challenged him with a simultaneous performance by C.M. Young. The contest was between two schools, the Kemble declamatory manner, and Kean's natural (and inspired) acting. 'Young's attempt to compete,' pronounced the *Examiner*, 'was declared by all good judges . . . perfectly ridiculous.'

Kean's brilliant, chequered career, his eccentricities and misfortunes, were a godsend to the caricaturists to the end

187 *The Theatrical Atlas*, G. Cruikshank

of his life. In *The Rival Richards, or Shakespeare in Danger* the two actors, each with his theatre behind him, struggle for possession of a reincarnated Shakespeare. The salvation of Drury coincided with Napoleon's last brilliant campaign and the allies' entry into Paris (31 March). In *Three Great Actors* (19 May) Kean, as Richard, stands between Wellington and Blücher. As *The Theatrical Atlas* [187], and as Richard,* he is the sole support of Drury Lane; a tiny Whitbread, encased in one of his beer-barrels, registers approval.

But the precarious finances of the theatre, and Sheridan's importunities, worried Whitbread literally to death, and he killed himself (July 1815). The Committee's efforts at management ended in 1819 with Elliston's appointment as Grand Lessee and Manager. The lamentable publicity of Kean's affair with the wife of Alderman Cox (1824-5) made him both unpopular and ridiculous – hooted off the stage, attacked in the Press and a print-shop victim. It is memorable as the occasion of Macaulay's famous words: 'We know nothing so ridiculous as the British public in one of its periodical fits of morality.'[4]

At the other house, Mrs Siddons, who had retired in 1812, made two of her occasional reappearances in June 1816, playing Lady Macbeth. 'Players should be immortal', was the *Examiner*'s comment, 'If their own wishes and ours could make them so, but they are not.' By this time Miss O'Neill was the leading tragic actress at Covent Garden, and Mrs Siddons is cruelly compared with her in *Theatrical Jealousies – or The Rival Queens*. Once again, Mrs Siddons is the doomed Roxana in Lee's tragedy. John and Charles Kemble peer anxiously at their sister.

Except for Kean, comedians were the popular stars.

---

* The figure travesties J. J. Hall's portrait of Kean interrogating Stanley on the approach of Richmond.

Charles Mathews, a wonderful mimic, gave 'At Homes' or 'Monodramas' written by himself, at the Lyceum Theatre from 1816, which seem to have anticipated Ruth Draper. Sitting at a table, he impersonated all the characters by voice, expression, and costume accessories (from under the table), and achieved 'an entire and instant transformation'. According to Leigh Hunt, the 'At Homes' 'for the richness and variety of his humour, were as good as half a dozen plays distilled'. One of these was the first known instance of humour or satire applied to the language and 'domestic manners of the Americans',* the product of a successful visit to America in 1822-3. This is the subject of Cruikshank's plate, *The Mathew-orama for 1824 – or – 'Pretty Considerable D—d Particular' Tit Bits from America....* Outside a shack, or 'hotel', is its 'Independent Landlord' in a rocking chair, indifferent to the hunger of his guests. The many characters include 'a real Yankee' with a gun, looking for his slave, Agamemnon, who is a jovial Negro with a fiddle; two dandified and impolite English tourists, an Irish fortune-hunter; a Colonel (a Kentucky shoemaker); a moronic German-American judge (at the table); and another 'particularly cool landlord'.

---

* The writer of a thesis on the subject had come to this conclusion after much research. Mrs Trollope's book was published in 1832. Mathews, on a second visit to America, acted this Monodrama and provoked a storm.

Notes to Chapter XXI

1. *Life and Letters of Lady Sarah Lennox*, ed. Lady Ilchester and Lord Stavordale, 1901, pp. 290ff.
2. Rev. J. W. Cunningham (evangelical Vicar of Harrow), *Cautions to Continental Travellers*, 1823 (2nd ed.), *Pamphleteer*, vol. XXI, p. 471 (his italics).
3. *The Diary of Benjamin Robert Haydon*, ed. W. B. Pope, vol. 1 (Cambridge, Mass.: Harvard University Press, 1960), p. 359.
4. *Edinburgh Review*, 1831, on Moore's *Life of Byron*.

188 *The Great Unknown lately discovered in Ireland, R.Cruikshank*

Scott and Byron are the literary personalities of the print shops – Byron more as a social notoriety than a poet. Scott dominates the scene, though perhaps less than Pope and certainly less than Johnson had done. But then he was not a London character, though he had a wider public than either. An elaborate design in 1812, *The Genius of the Times*, rashly attempts literary criticism and prophecy. Climbing Parnassus, and nearest to the temple of Fame, is Scott, carried on the back of his publisher. Byron is being hauled up in a cask of Whitbread's Entire. Eight writers are doomed to the waters of Lethe: five of them can be identified by the books they hold: Wordsworth, Coleridge, Southey, Leigh Hunt and Godwin. There is also a group of best-sellers, who turn aside and make no attempt to climb; Monk Lewis is the most prominent of these. Sheridan staggers tipsily at the bottom of the hill.

In 1817, according to Glenbervie, the great topic of discussion in clubs and elsewhere was who wrote 'Waverley etc.', and the latest opinion was that it was 'a [non-existent] brother of Sir Walter Scott in Canada, or his wife'. The secret was not formally revealed till 1827; it had long been divined by Scott's Edinburgh friends, but till the last there were doubts. Was it possible that he could produce the novels as well as his acknowledged works, while carrying on his profession as a lawyer and his extremely active social life? In *The Great Unknown* lately discovered in Ireland* [188], 1825, Scott stands with his son outside Trinity College, Dublin; the pile of books on his head is topped by *Waverley*. In *The Unknown Known*, a little Edinburgh print, in February 1826, he has four sets of legs, belonging (presumably) to the lawyer, the author, the publisher, and the laird. One of his most exacting undertakings, after the crash of 1826, was the nine-volume *Life of Napoleon* a much-praised *tour de force* for which Wellington gave him information. In *The Balance of Public Favor* [189], 1827, Scott with his bulky *Napoleon* is outweighed by little Tom Moore with his little prose tale, *The Epicurean*, which he had contrived to get published the day before Scott's book was to come out. 'The Likenesses are very strong and good', Lady Holland wrote to her son, describing the print, 'the joyous air of Moore is very well represented'. *Abbotsford* (June 1831) is a callous rendering of fact: Scott toils at *Count Robert of Paris* while Death with his javelin looks from the doorway. After two strokes in 1830 Scott worked desperately at his last two novels in the interests of his creditors. He died in 1832.

*The earliest known reference to 'the Great Unknown' is by Ann Scott in 1818, J.G.Lockhart, *Life*, 1838, Vol. IV, p. 202 (information from Sir Herbert Grierson).

Scott was attacked, in prints, for the large sums he made by his poems. In *Rival Candidates for the vacant Bays* in 1812 there are twelve candidates from Byron to Busby. Scott, in armour, says 'Three thousand pounds I've made a joke by/A six weeks scrawl entitled *Rokeby*'. (He had refused the laureateship and suggested Southey.) But the typical poet continues to suffer in a garret, and a little copy of Hogarth's Poet headed the 'Poet's Corner' in *Bell's Life*. In a set of *singeries* in 1828 by Thomas Landseer (brother of Edwin), *Monkeyana . . .*, satirizing contemporary man, one is *Distressed Poet; or, Three Weeks in Arrears*; in desperate poverty, the ape-poet trembles before his ape-landlady: he cannot pay the weekly shilling for his garret but is engaged on 'Lofty Projects' for Covent Garden theatre.

Interest in the world of art declined, partly no doubt because the spirit of the age had changed, partly because

189 The Balance of Public Favor, J. Doyle

THE BALANCE OF PUBLIC FAVOR.

London, Published by Thomas McLean 26 Haymarket.

A SKETCH OF THAT CURIOUS LITTLE

PIMLICO
STATU QUO

IOHN. NASH
ARCHITECT SITTING ON HIS (EGG) Dome of Buck.m Pal.

190 *A Sketch of that Curious Little Architect sitting on his Egg,*
W. Heath

Cruikshank and his contemporaries did not share the aesthetic interests of Gillray and Rowlandson, not to speak of Hogarth. The outstanding artist of the period – not the best but the most publicized (by himself), the one who attracted caricature – as 'The Quack Artist' – was Haydon (1786–1846). His claim to be a great genius, as a history painter, the one hope for High Art in England, his campaign against the Academy, the exhibitions of his vast canvases, his patronage (at one time) by 'rank, beauty and fashion', his misfortunes, his highly successful lectures on art, made him a public figure – he calls himself 'the most prominent man'. His *Autobiography* and his *Journals* have given him another sort of fame from that of his lifetime. *R.A.'s of Genius reflecting on the true line of Beauty at the Life Academy Somerset House* [192], 1824, is a fantasy on Haydon's 'genius', and his contention that the Academy was a close corporation of portrait-painters, hostile to High Art. The R.A.s sit like students to draw the model. Haydon stands in the foreground, a pupil at his feet, the only one who can paint. His *bête noire*, Shee, sits at the feet of Sir Thomas Lawrence, P.R.A., whom he was to succeed in 1830. Behind Lawrence is the late President, Benjamin West, who died in 1821. The setting and the model are after Rowlandson, the portraits by Robert Cruikshank. This is one of seventy-two aquatints to *The English Spy*, an imitation of *Life in London* extended to the provinces.

'Taste' was no longer obligatory to the man of fashion. George IV's taste, now so generally admired, was ridiculed and deplored. The Pavilion as transformed by Nash was a sensation: 'His palace or pavilion or Kremlin, or mosque – for it bears all these names and deserves them', Madame de Lieven wrote in 1820. Satires on the King's fishing in Virginia Water illustrate the exotic *chinoiserie* of the Fishing Temple – but without doing it justice; the public were rigidly excluded. The climax of condemnation was for Nash's transformation of Buckingham House into Buckingham Palace – derisively Pimlico Palace. This is the subject of two illustrated parodies of 'The House that Jack built'. One, *The Palace that N—h built, c.* 1829, opens with a view of the east front and the 'egg-cup' dome or 'ball in cup' (on the west front, but visible) which was regarded as the acme of absurdity. A dandy sketches it, a dustman cocks a snook. *The Times* (29 May 1828): '. . . some demon has whispered "Visto have a taste" as if there were a Royal way to architecture, and a man could take it up as easily as playing with a cup and ball . . .'; the building is 'that polyangular monster of depravity', and its demolition is called for. The quotation was barbed; the context was

For what has Visto painted, built and planted?
Only to show how many tastes he wanted.
What brought Sir Visto's ill-got wealth to waste?
*Some demon whisper'd Visto have a taste.**

Here is *A Sketch of that Curious Little Architect sitting on his Egg* [190], 1830. Behind all this, and violently expressed, was anger at the expense of repeated alterations, the subject of two Select Committees (1829 and 1831). In 1830 a thousand men were at work to get the palace finished by the King's birthday in August; he died in June. The dome was removed on Victoria's accession; Nash's Marble Arch, removed to Cumberland Gate in 1850, was the gateway to the east front; it was to have been topped by an equestrian statue of George IV (now in Trafalgar Square), which is derided in 'The Entrance, the Triumphal Arch', and other illustrations to *The Palace that N—h built*. The most memorable satire on Nash is Cruikshank's *Nashional Taste!!!* [191], 1824, with the architect spiked on the spire of All Souls, Langham Place, which had been condemned in Parliament and the Press.

---

* Alexander Pope, *Epistle to Burlington*, 1731, cf. p. 22. 'Visto' was Sir Robert Walpole, builder of Houghton.

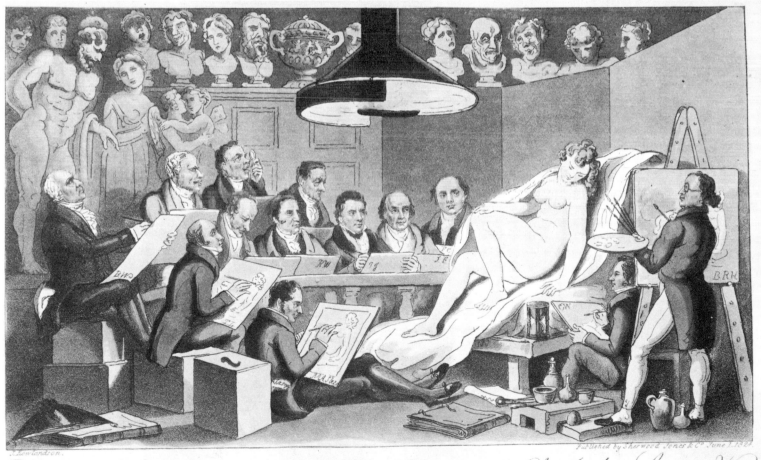

193 *Amusements des Anglais à Paris, anon.*

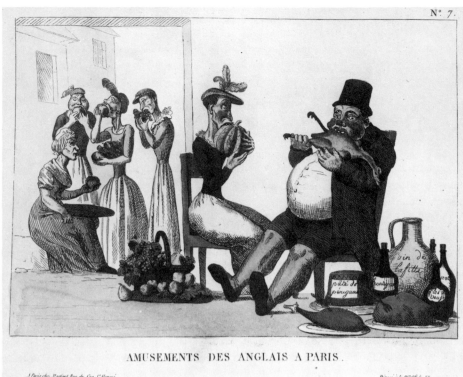

194 *A Swarm of English Bees hiving in the Imperial Carriage, G. Cruikshank*

The sensations that followed each other so rapidly were mainly political. The sensation of sensations – victory in 1814 – had its minor attendant sensations. One was the impact of Paris on the English, and of the English visitors on the French. The French reaction to the influx – and to defeat – was a spate of prints ridiculing the dress and manners of their visitors. First, a set of '*Scènes anglaises Dessinées à Londres*' by a *soi-disant* '*français prisonnier de guerre*'. The topics are traditional. He begins with *Les Dames anglaises après diné* [sic], their silent morose boredom at the tea-table while the men sit long over their wine. *L'après dinée* [sic] *des Anglais*, the men in various stages of drunkenness, displays the gross dining-room manners* that had long shocked foreigners.[1] Then there is *Le Boxeur blessé* . . ., one of those street encounters for which the bystanders made a ring, long a subject of praise (liberty, fair play) or blame (brutality), and probably obsolescent if not obsolete.† *Amusements* [sic] *des Anglais à Londres* – suicide from ennui. All this leads up to the climax, *Amusements des Anglais à Paris* [193], which speaks for itself. This last is one of the many prints on British gormandizing and gaucherie, bad French, bad manners, gross overtures to the ladies of the ballet, and the all-pervading subject of English costume. It is noteworthy that such prints could be openly sold in Paris during a military occupation, and be bought by the visitors. (There seem to have been none on the dreaded Prussians.) There was also a popular farce by Potier, *Les Anglaises pour rire*, and all this (with a prelude in 1802) seems to be the beginning of the Continental caricature stereotype of the gawky ill-dressed Englishwoman with projecting teeth and large feet. *Promenade d'Anglais* and *Promenade Anglaise* [195] reflect the English passion for the promenade – the French did not walk for pleasure – French ladies did not walk in the street. Among the very many French prints on English modes and manners there are the sightseeing family standing to stare and fellow countrymen greeting each other as if on a desert island.

A minor facet of victory, after the visits to Paris, was a sudden revolution in feminine fashions, despite male protests. When Napoleon was (supposedly) safe in Elba, costume became almost an international question. English women astonished Parisians by small plain hats or bonnets, sometimes with a floating gauze veil, an almost normal waistline, coloured silk spencers worn with skirts, usually white, and so plain and skimpy that in French eyes they seemed to slant inwards to the feet. French bonnets towered, decked with flowers, feathers and ribbons; high-waisted dresses flowed outwards, much flounced and trimmed. Newspapers implored English ladies not to adopt French fashions. *The Champion* (5 June 1814) addressed verses 'To the Ladies of England':

> *Beauties!* . . .
>
> *Attend the friendly stanza*
> *Which deprecates the threaten'd change*
> *Of English modes for fashions strange*
> *And* French extravaganzas. . . .

English fashions are 'Domestic – simple – chaste – sedate'. (An interesting development since 1793 and after.) In May Ward wrote to Mary Berry from Paris: 'The women are chiefly distinguished by a sort of bonnet three stories high and by far the most horrible superstructure that was ever piled upon the human head. . . . The rest of the dress by no means atones. . . . It is a slovenly confused looking thing.' French prints suggest that the English were dressed for walking and sightseeing, while Parisians were always *en toilette*. But the result was a revulsion from the domestic, simple, chaste, sedate; a fashion for enormous bonnets, pinched waists, inflated sleeves, short projecting skirts – a complete reversal of the feminine contour since 1793, which lasted, with many variations, for many years.

Another aspect of victory in 1814 was the visit of the allied grandees in June. The occasion was marred by the manoeuvres of the disgruntled Whigs, and pictorial contrasts of the most disloyal kind were drawn between the Tsar (in the absurd role of a model husband) and the Regent. Oxford was more loyal than London and the degree-giving was a magnificent affair (D.C.L. for the Tsar and King of Prussia, L.L.D. for Metternich, Lieven and Blücher). The popular favourite was Blücher and he is the centre of Cruikshank's fantastic *Doctor Blücher*, an evening promenade where Alexander I walks between his sister and Frederick William III. 'The well-dressed crowd (comprising Kings and Princes)', said the *European Magazine*, 'the great number of elegant females, and the greater proportion of academical persons in their sable robes, intermixed with the grotesque appearance of the country folks . . . resembled a carnival'.

---

* English visitors to France were shocked by analogous indelicacies. See Cole's *Paris Journal* (1765), ed. F. G. Stokes (London: Constable, 1931), pp. 278–81. The English were revolted at the universal practice of hawking and spitting, ibid. Pückler-Muskau was astonished at the aversion to this 'crime' 'so pedantically proscribed that you might seek through all London . . . to find . . . a spitting box'.

† Misson de Valbourg (1665) describes the practice: 'if a coachman has a dispute over his fare . . . and the gentleman offers to fight to decide the quarrel, the coachman consents with all his heart', quoted F. Wilson, *Strange Island* (London: Longmans, 1955), p. 53. See above, p. 16.

195 *Promenade Anglaise, C. Vernet/P. L. Débucourt, 1814*

When the grandees had departed and the victory celebrations were over a very different matter created tense excitement. Joanna Southcott, whose career as a prophetess had begun in 1790, had announced in 1813 the miraculous birth of an infant for a certain day in October 1814. Excitement grew as the day approached and passed. A large furnished house was taken for the event; the faithful provided many valuable gifts including a silver cup inscribed 'Hail Messiah Prince of Salem'. Of nine medical men six declared that the (dropsical) symptoms would mean pregnancy in a younger woman – she was sixty-four. The *Sunday Monitor* (the first Sunday paper*) issued bulletins. When the day passed it was announced that she was in a trance. Rowlandson and Cruikshank contributed to the many caricatures; crowded with inscriptions and details, they are unsuited to reproduction but throw light on this curious episode. Uniformly sceptical, the recurrent word is humbug; to the faithful they must have seemed blasphemous. Joanna Southcott was self-deluded. Believed by herself and her followers to be not only divinely inspired but immortal, she died, 27 December 1814, of 'brain disease'.

A year later there was the absorbing spectacle of Napoleon in the *Bellerophon*, anchored off Torbay, surrounded by massed boatloads of sightseers. A series of exhibitions attracted crowds after the building of the Egyptian Hall by William Bullock in 1812. It housed some famous ones till it was demolished in 1905 for the widening of Piccadilly. The first of a long series was the exhibition in 1816 of Napoleon's travelling carriage, taken at Waterloo and sold to Bullock with many accessories, including hat, sword, uniform, and imperial mantle. This was a tremendous attraction, and both Rowlandson and Cruikshank [194] satirized the unseemly behaviour of the visitors and the contents of Bullock's 'Museum'. The coach and the Napoleon relics were a chief attraction at Madame Tussaud's from 1842 till the fire of 1925; one axle survives, carefully preserved.

A sensation that overwhelmed the print shops in 1819 was the velocipede or pedestrian hobby horse, or dandy-hobby, or accelerator. This embryo bicycle was an improved version of the French *Draisine*, patented by Baron Drais in 1813. From the first it was associated with the dandy, as almost any fashion would have been at that time. But that the 'genuine dandy' ever mounted one may be doubted, any more than the Regent or the Duke of York who ride them in caricatures. They were depicted as a threat to the horse. In March the police magistrates forbade them in London streets as a danger to traffic. The rider ran along the road with 'light touches of the feet'. The 'Velocimanipede or Ladies Hobby, a machine to carry One, Two or Three Persons', was advertised. And Robert Cruikshank produced *The Ladies Accelerator* [196], which illustrates the fashions of the day.

In 1824–5 politics seemed forgotten; the Stock Exchange boomed (p. 177) and there was a crop of social sensations.

*'When, lo! the sainted 'Monitor' is born/Whose pious face some sacred texts adorn', George Crabbe, *The Newspaper*, 1785.

One was the affair of the Tenth (p. 197). Another was the appearance of the *Memoirs* of Harriette Wilson, *née* Debouchet, with twenty-eight coloured plates, including portraits, also sold separately at two shillings each. The book was factual (relating to happenings *c.* 1810–15), amusing and frankly blackmailing, 'great nonsense, but very little indecency, indeed none'.[2] Harriette Wilson was in Paris, recently married to a Frenchman on, it was said, the profits of her book. Her publisher issued a list of those to be pilloried in a sequel unless they paid up. The print shops battened on the affair and a highlight was the ridicule of Wellington. 'I asked him if he knew her', Mrs Arbuthnot recorded in her *Journal*, '& he told me he had known her a great number of years ago, so long tho' that he did not think he should remember her again, that he had never seen her since he married tho' he had frequently sent her money when she wrote to beg for it, & that she had offered to keep him out of the book if he would *pay*. This, of course, he refused, & has never given her a farthing since she threatened him.'[3] ('Publish and be damned.')

In *La Coterie Debouché – Intended as a Frontispiece to Harriette Wilson's Memoirs* [197] she is writing the sequel, facing an eager crowd of admirers, some of whom are copied from the portraits in her book.* Wellington's (red) ribbon with the rats illustrates a passage on his frequent evening visits, wearing the ribbon of the Bath, in which she told him he looked exactly like a rat-catcher (rat-catchers wore a broad strap decorated with the skins or corpses of their victims). These visits were allegedly after victories in Spain, but since the Duke was more truthful than the lady, it is probable, as well as more credible, that

they were in fact when he returned from India in 1805 as Sir Arthur Wellesley, K.C.B., and before his marriage in 1806.

Also in 1825 there was a musical sensation, the first appearance in London for a generation of a male soprano, Velluti, the first singer of the age. The contrast with the fashionable adoration for Farinelli and other *castrati* in Hogarth's day was absolute. There were ribald jests – '*non vir sed veluti*'. Again to quote Mrs Arbuthnot, a woman of fashion and great intelligence, 'I went to the Opera last night to hear the Crociato in Egypt, a new Opera by Meyerbeer; the music is very pretty, but the curiosity was Velluti as the principal singer. He is the most disgusting creature I ever saw, high shouldered, sunk in the chest, immensely tall, with long arms and legs and looking more gaunt & unnatural than one can conceive. [He was or had been a handsome man.] Then his voice is like a bag pipe. However, he has great taste and science, which I suppose compensates for all defects, but I do hope we shall have no more such importations from Italy, for it really makes one sick.'[4]

Velluti had the misfortune to coincide with yet another sensation on a lower social level – Seurat, the Living Skeleton.[5] Both were foreigners, who took John Bull's money, that ancient grievance. One, it was said, could be seen in Pall Mall for half-a-crown, the other heard at the Opera for a guinea. In *Foreign Rivals for British Patronage* they fight a duel, each backed by a sandwich-man.

---

* These are Lord Worcester (most prominent here, as in the book), Wellington, the Duke of Devonshire (in the book, but not as a lover), George Lamb, Thomas Raikes (the diarist, known as the Commercial Dandy), the Duke of Argyll, Prince Esterhazy. The man on the extreme right resembles Canning.

Notes to Chapter XXIII

1. E. G. La Rochefoucauld, *A Frenchman in England 1784*, translated S.C. Roberts (Cambridge: C.U.P., 1933).
2. *Correspondence of Charles Arbuthnot*, ed. A. Aspinall, Historical Society of Great Britain, 1941, p. 73 (Mrs Arbuthnot to C A.)
3. *Journal*, ed. F. Bamford and the Duke of Wellington, vol. 1 (London: Macmillan, 1950), p. 378 (19 February 1825).
4. Ibid., vol. 1, p. 400 (26 July 1825).
5. See *Annual Register 1825*, pp. 239*–41*; William Hone's *Every Day Book*, 1825, p. 513.

The LADIES ACCELERATOR.

196 The Ladies Accelerator, R. Cruikshank

197 *La Coterie Debouché – Intended as a Frontispiece to Harriette Wilson's Memoirs*, H. Heath

"nec te tua plurima ×××.
Labentem Pietas, nec Apollinis infula texit"

Drawn by WP — etch. by GCr   Pub June 30 1821 by J Humphrey 27 S¹ James's S¹ London.

Mer de Glace —— *Sea of Ice* —

198 Mer de Glace – Sea of Ice, anon./G. Cruikshank

After the unprecedented check to Continental travel since 1803, there was an unprecedented rush across the Channel in 1814, a frantic scurry back on news of Napoleon's landing, a renewed rush after Waterloo, and thereafter an unceasing flow of tourists. In the Covent Garden panto-mime for 1814–15 Grimaldi, the famous clown, was an English tourist in Paris; in *All the World's in Paris!* he stands in front of Cruikshank's notion of the *Arc de Triomphe*, singing the popular song of the title. 'All the World' includes 'Players, Peers and Auctioneers, . . . Modish airs from Wapping-Stairs . . . And Elegance from Aldgate', and much more. 'All the English in the world are here', Wellesley-Pole wrote from Paris in September 1815, 'and one detests the sight of them. They are heartily quizzed, as we all are, as well as detested.'[1] There were some very conflicting reports on the attitude of the French to their visitors, and doubtless some very conflicting attitudes.

The main topic is not travel at home but travel abroad. The Grand Tourist had shown a lordly indifference to dangers and discomforts; the middle-class tourist is more complaining and less open-handed – an early and classic example was Smollett in 1763–5. In *Inconveniences of a Trip to the Continent*, aquatints by Cruikshank after an amateur's sketches, published in 1821, the old Grand Tour route is followed, more or less. The first scene is the *douane*, with a ruthless *douanier*. Then John Bull at Véry's famous res-taurant in Paris saying, 'D—n your kickshaws'. There are the discomforts and annoyances of a German diligence.

199 To Calais, after F. Marryat

_ To Calais _

Tourists with alpenstocks and guides stagger across the *Mer de Glace* [198]. They climb Vesuvius to encounter a violent explosion, anticipating Byron's lines,

> *Vesuvius shows her blaze, an usual light*
> *For gaping Tourists, from his hackney'd height*.[2]

In Rome, in the Forum, John Bull is annoyed by beggars. And in the *Tribuna* of the Uffizi Gallery in Florence the party display vulgar philistinism. Talleyrand's niece, in 1824, found Switzerland 'flooded with English', 'who go everywhere without looking at anything, make as much noise, and spend too little money, haggle over everything, even the view, and are perfectly intolerable to meet'.[3] The old complaint had been the demoralizing effect of English lavishness.

The first Channel crossing by steam was in 1816: in 1825 steam packets began running from Newhaven and Brighton. In *To Calais* [199] after Marryat in 1824 the small sailing vessel is filled with cockneyfied, would-be dandies, in varying stages of misery, depicted with a sailor's contempt. Those who went to Margate now go to Paris (according to satire). In *Modern Tourists* in 1827 the magic of Paris is urged by a daughter to her father, by one dandy to another,

by one woman to another: 'Lord Madam . . . you can never think of going to Margate – it is so common* . . . Paris is the great resort of pure gentility . . . I always goes to Paris'. British tourists in Paris are fully illustrated in *Doctor Syntax in Paris* with plates by C. Williams, and David Carey's *Life in Paris*, in 1822, illustrated by Cruikshank, an imitation of Egan's *Life in London*. The old notions of frog-eating Frenchmen have disappeared – for the time.

Brighton was established as the most fashionable English pleasure resort, but there were changes. 'You would scarcely know Brighton it is so enlarged since you were here' (1805), Mrs Fitzherbert wrote to Creevey in December 1818, 'and it is at this moment so full there is not a house to be had. I cannot boast of much good company which formerly we abounded with at this season. When I tell you that fifty-two public coaches go from hence to London every day and bring people down for six shillings, you will not be surprised at the sort of company we have; besides which the Royal Palace attracts numbers who are puzzled what to make of the appearance of the building which it is impossible for me, or indeed any one else, to describe.'

---

*The first *O.E.D.* instance of 'common' as 'low class, vulgar, unrefined', is 1866.

200 *Beauties of Brighton, A. Crowquill/G. Cruikshank*

Beauties of BRIGHTON

Pub.d by Tho.s M.c Lean 26 Haymarket Aug. 1.t 1835.

Travelling in England, or a peep from the White horse cellar.

201 *Travelling in England, or a peep from the White horse cellar*, G. Cruikshank

She adds that the Regent, 'never stirs out of his parlour, and no one sees him.'[4]

By 1820 the last phase of the Pavilion's transformation by Nash was almost complete. Its fantastic domes and pinnacles are the background of pictorial lampoons launched against George IV in 1820-1 in a campaign for Queen Caroline that defeated itself by its violence.[5] They are the setting for *Beauties of Brighton* [200], 1826, a promenade of notables by Crowquill etched by Cruikshank, who include Talleyrand (on the extreme right) and the Duke of York, Liston the actor; Nathan Meyer Rothschild walks with his wife; Colonel D'Este (son of the Duke of York by Lady Augusta Murray) gives one arm to his sister, the other to a fat widow, Mrs Coutts, formerly Harriot Mellon the actress, soon to be Duchess of St Albans. The three dandyfied young men arm-in-arm are Crowquill between his brothers, the Forresters. Ennui reigned at the Pavilion, which the King visited for the last time in 1827.

A final Brighton scene in 1832 envisages the coming of

the day-tripper.* In *Probable Effect of the Projected Rail-Road to Brighton* two fashionables turn in horror from a plebeian family exhausted by a day's outing; the father asks morosely 'Wot time was we to be at the Rail-Road again?' She: 'What shocking savages!!' He: 'Oh we must leave this place; it may do for the royal family, but not for a fashionable one.' The dejected trippers are clearly victims of the machine age, not the old low-life characters, and far indeed from the cits who trudged to Islington in Hogarth's day and after.

The railway reached Brighton in 1841, and almost at once most of the London–Brighton coaches stopped. In 1845, Queen Victoria made her last visit to the Pavilion. 'The people are very indiscreet and troublesome here really,' she wrote, 'which makes this place like a prison.'

*The first recorded use (*O.E.D.*) of 'tripper' for excursionist is in 1813; a crowded Margate hoy was accidentally in contact with a ship in quarantine, and in danger of being held up for seven weeks. 'This to the trippers to the seaside for a week would have been a serious affair', *Drakard's Journal*, 5 October 1813, quoted J. Ashton, *Modern Street Ballads*, 1888, p. 80.

And *Punch* published a cartoon, *The New Royal Hunt*, a mob of Brighton sightseers, chasing the Queen and Prince Albert.[6]

But in 1832 the railway was still a portent only – less of one than the steam-carriage. This was the golden age of the stage coach, which had its miseries as well as its splendours. Till superseded by Paddington Station the White Horse Cellar in Piccadilly – Hatchett's Hotel (where the Ritz is now) was the headquarters of traffic for the west, whence Mr Pickwick and his friends departed for Bath after the trial. Dickens's description of the scene is much the same as Cruikshank's protest against 'The Piccadilly Nuisance': *Travelling in England, or a peep from the White horse cellar* [201], 1819, where all is noise and confusion, and passengers are assailed by competitive coach-touts ('cads'), newsboys and street-sellers. There is a companion print, *Travelling in France*, of an old fashioned lurching diligence in a cloud of dust on a country road.

The cleavage between 'Regency' and 'Victorian' England is marked above all by the coming of the railways. This was the sudden extinction of a way of life (though coaches lingered long in outlying parts – East Anglia, Cornwall). Roads and inns deteriorated, coach-proprietors, post-masters, and inn-keepers were ruined: coachmen and ostlers were still more defenceless. Mr Laver quotes the old coachman, Jerry Drag: 'Them as 'ave seen coaches, afore rails came into fashion 'ave seen something worth remembering, them was happy days for Old England, afore reform and rails turned everything upside down and men rode as natur' intended they should on 'pikes with coaches and smart, active cattle, and not by machinery, like bags of cotton or hardware; but coaches is done for ever, and a heavy blow it is. They was the pride of the country, there wasn't anything like them, as I've heard gemmem say from forrin parts, to be found nowhere, nor ever will be again.'[7]

For long distances an *average* speed of eleven miles an hour had been achieved, for short spells at least fourteen. Teams were changed in under a minute, punctuality was exact. The competitive brilliance of rival coaches meant a high level of professional skill, and pride for all concerned.

Another sign of the end of an age was the virtual disappearance after 1830 of the coloured etching in the Gillray manner, which, since 1827, had had a last flare-up in the popularity of prints by William Heath and his imitators. The political bitterness which invaded graphic satire from 1830 impinged on a general movement away from the harshness of the old tradition. This was manifested in the popularity (from 1829) of the decorous *Political Sketches*, lithographs by HB. (John Doyle).* The decade before *Punch* was filled with albums, scrapbooks, annuals and almanacks, pages of humorous etchings, wood-engravings or lithographs responding to the vogue for fantasy, whimsy, puns and the macabre. Outstanding were Thomas Hood's *Comic Annual* (1830–42), and Cruikshank's *Comic Almanack* (1835–53). The monthly *Looking Glass* (1830–6) was also issued as an annual. After six months of etchings by Heath, it consisted of lithographs by Seymour, and did not long survive him. Much of this was humour for the drawing-room or schoolroom. Social satire was lapsing into the illustrated joke. Cockney sportsmen were the chief topic of Seymour's *Humourous Sketches* (1833–6), first published as threepenny lithographs, and reprinted (more cheaply) up to 1888.

Punch (17 July 1841) began a new phase of graphic satire. There was a gulf between illustrated journalism and the individual output of competing print-sellers and artists, which responded to the sensations of the day with the ups and downs of a fever chart. There was no longer scope for the amateur who had provided so many sketches for the professionals. More important, there was a coherent, if wayward, editorial policy. A threepenny weekly which was 'a strange mixture of jocularity and intense seriousness'[8] was a new departure, as Victorian as the old prints had been Georgian. And (though a good deal of outspokenness survived), editorial responsibility was inconsistent with the freedom to attack – to libel – which had been the context of the golden age of English caricature.

*After 1836 the annual output dwindles, rapidly so from 1844; none in 1850, the 917th and last in 1851.

Notes to Chapter XXIV

1. *George Canning and his Friends*, ed. J. Bagot, 1909, vol. II, p. 9.
2. *The Age of Bronze*, 1823.
3. P. Ziegler, *The Duchess of Dino* (London: Collins, 1962), p. 171.
4. *Creevey's Life and Times*, ed. J. Gore (London: John Murray, 1934), p. 115.
5. See M. D. George, *English Political Caricature 1793–1882* (Oxford: O.U.P., 1960), pp. 187–203.
6. C. Musgrave, *Royal Pavilion*, Hill Ltd, 1959, p. 123.
7. James Laver, introduction to *The Regency Road*, N. C. Selway (London: Faber, 1957).
8. C. L. Graves, *Mr Punch's History of Modern England*, vol. I (London: Cassell, 1921), p. 1.

221